普通高等教育土建学科专业"十二五"规划教材
全国高职高专教育土建类专业教学指导委员会规划推荐教材

建筑工程英语

（土建类专业适用）

赵琼梅　胡　莹　主编
吕小青　主审

中国建筑工业出版社

图书在版编目（CIP）数据

建筑工程英语／赵琼梅，胡莹　主编．—北京：中国建筑
工业出版社，2011.7
普通高等教育土建学科专业"十二五"规划教材．全国
高职高专教育土建类专业教学指导委员会规划推荐教材
（土建类专业适用）
ISBN 978-7-112-13415-1

Ⅰ．①建… Ⅱ．①赵… ②胡… Ⅲ．①建筑工程-英语-高等
职业教育-教材 Ⅳ．①H31

中国版本图书馆 CIP 数据核字（2011）第 159212 号

　　本书以《迪拜码头 9AB 地块高层住宅》这一真实项目作为背景，根据工程项目的建设过程，从前期工程、主题结构施工、后期工程到竣工验收四个大部分来进行构架，共分为 14 个单元。每个单元由对话、角色扮演、课文、词汇、练习、翻译技巧等模块组成，并配有漫画插图。编者力图在语言学习与专业学习之间找到一个契合点，当学生完成本课程的学习，具备涉外工程一线施工组织与技术应用管理岗位工作所需的英语阅读、写作、交流能力的同时，也具备一定的工程建设认知能力。本书既考虑了专业能力的宽度与深度，也注重语言词汇从简单到复杂的有序渐进，各单元有机选取真实的涉外工程项目资料作为素材，并穿插原创性的漫画，选材新颖、语言规范、特色鲜明，供高等职业技术院校建筑工程相关专业学生使用，也可供成人教育培训相关专业的学生使用。

责任编辑：朱首明　李　明
责任设计：叶延春
责任校对：赵　颖　刘　钰

普通高等教育土建学科专业"十二五"规划教材
全国高职高专教育土建类专业教学指导委员会规划推荐教材

建筑工程英语

（土建类专业适用）

赵琼梅　胡　莹　主编

吕小青　主审

*

中国建筑工业出版社出版、发行（北京西郊百万庄）
各地新华书店、建筑书店经销
北京永峥排版公司制版
廊坊市海涛印刷有限公司印刷

*

开本：787×1092 毫米　1/16　印张：18　字数：450 千字
2012 年 1 月第一版　2016 年 12 月第六次印刷
定价：**38.00** 元
ISBN 978-7-112-13415-1
（21219）

随着我国建筑行业劳务输出业务不断增长，近年来，高职建筑工程类专业学生出国就业已成增长趋势。与传统的专业英语教学目标定位在外文资料的阅读翻译不同，学生在涉外工程一线施工组织管理岗位工作，其交流、阅读、写作等专业英语应用能力的要求已演变得更加宽泛与灵活。宽泛，体现在贯穿工程项目的全过程要求；灵活，体现在直接面对外籍工程专业人员的交流。高职教育逐渐走上以能力培养为本位的道路，"基于工作过程"已经成为一种有效的高职人才培养教育教学模式。作为语言与专业深度契合在一起的专业英语，给我们的教学提出了同样的要求——专业语言能力是否也可以基于工程项目建设的工作过程，由简单到复杂，贯穿始终来进行培养？为此，笔者在本课程多年教学改革总结的基础上，认为是有效可行的。多年来，我们积累了大量的教学参考资料，尤其是从 2008 年开始，到迪拜就业的几批次学生提供了很多真实的海外工程案例资料，也给我们反馈回来在工程一线工作所要求具备的专业英语能力的宽度与深度，让我们明确了基于工程项目建设过程的编写思路，并以能力培养为基准点进行全面布局。专业教师与英语教师的共同参与，使我们在专业与语言之间找到了一个契合点，那就是：语言的应用贯穿工程建设全过程，语言能力与专业能力相长——学生在培养英语语言能力的同时，也培养工程建设项目工作过程的基本认知能力，或者说，培养工程建设项目的"构造"认知能力。这里的"构造"，不是专业上说的建筑物的构造，而是工程建设过程的全局"构造"。

全书依工程建设过程分为工程简介、施工方案会审、标书与合同、进场、基础工程施工、模板工程、钢筋工程、混凝土工程、安全检查、质量检查、屋面工程、设备工程、装饰工程、竣工说明 14 个单元。每个单元由对话、角色扮演、课文、词汇、练习、翻译技巧等模块组成。内容有机选取了《迪拜码头 9AB 地块高层住宅》这一真实工程项目资料作为素材，既考虑对应专业能力的程度，也注重语言能力从简单到复杂的有序渐进。每个单元根据工程背景设计一幅相应的漫画插图，增强教材界面的活泼性。语言力求规范、流畅，整体特色鲜明、有所创新。

杜国城教授对于本书的酝酿与成书过程的指导，激发了编者创作的灵感，增添了编写此书的信心。建工出版社的编辑与高职土建施工分委员会的领导对编者的帮助，树立了完成全书的恒心，感恩之情潜行于字里行间。

本书由赵琼梅、胡莹担任主编，谭碧云、周艳、唐取文参与编写。谭碧云牵头该门优质课程的建设，刘绮雯设计漫画插图。本书由吕小青主审。鉴于经验与水平局限，疏漏与不妥在所难免，敬请各位读者不吝指正。

编　者
2011 年 7 月

CONTENTS　目录

Part one
Preliminary Works(前期工程)

UNIT *1*

Project Synopsis（工程简介）

DIALOGUE

Mr. Yang, a project manager of China Overseas Construction Engineering Group (COCEG) is now discussing with Mr. Howell, president of World shelter, a local company which specializes in residential buildings, about the possibility of subletting the construction camp.

Howell：What's your first impression of our country？

Yang：It's a beautiful country and it's the centrel of Arabic world. People here are friendly. It seems to me that most of the people here speak quite different English. It's hard to understand them sometimes.

Howell：You will soon get used to it. Only officials, teachers and businessmen speak standard English. Let's get down to business, Mr. Yang. You invite us to bid for a construction camp to accommodate eighty men, and can you put it in more details？

Yang：As you know, the camp will accommodate eighty Chinese overseas workers here. It includes double occupancy staff units（两人房）, four-man occupancy units（四人房）for workers and cooks, a kitchen and dining units, shower bath units, office units, a conference room and a reception unit.

Howell：Do you have any specific requirements？

Yang：I would like to hear your recommendation.

Howell：There is a kind of prefabricated house, which is easy and economical to transport, fast to erect and very convenient to dismantle for either relocation or disposal when the whole project is completed.

Yang：Sounds fine. What's it made of?

Howell：Light concrete slabs.

Yang：Good. Could you please give us a quotation for such a camp on a turn-key basis as soon as possible?

Howell：All right. But who will be responsible for leveling the ground for the camp site?

Yang：We will do that. You will be responsible for the water and power supply. This is a duty-free project. So everything imported for it is duty-free.

Howell：In that case, our quotation will be much lower. When do you want the camp to be completed?

Yang：Within sixty days, starting from our notice to commence the work.

Howell：I hope we can be given the opportunity to work for you and if so, I believe we will surely do a good job.

Yang：I hope so, too.

Notes

1. 会话背景与指南：由于刚刚到达工程施工所在国，承包商（contractor）的主要施工人员还没有到场，机械设备也还没有运至现场（construction site）所以，施工营地（construction camp）的建设常常分包给当地的建筑公司（local construction company）。一般情况下，承包商请业主（employer/client）向其推荐几家比较有信誉的当地公司，然后逐一去了解这些公司的情况。

2. COCEG：中国海外建设工程集团有限公司（简称 COCEG 原 COCE）是经中国政府相关部门批准，并接受中国商务部海外中心管理系列跨国集团公司的业务指导及管理，是中国政府海外发展战略的重要组成部分。COCEG 是集设计、建筑、施工、安装、调试于一体的集团公司，有十多家具有丰富承揽国际工程经验的知名施工企业、设计单位、劳务公司承揽工程项目，而且还将大力发展以建材五金电器为主的国际贸易业务。

3. prefabricated house：装配式房屋，活动房屋 prefabricated house 在口语中常用 prefab来替代。Prefabricated 这个词在工程实施中常常使用，与它搭配的词很多，例如：prefabricated construction（装配式施工），prefabricated pile（预制桩），prefabricated unit（预制构件）。

New Words

sublet ['sʌb'let] vt. 转租；转包给；分包给

accommodate [ə'kɔmədeit] vt. 给方便，帮助，供给... 住宿，容纳

　　e. g. accommodate（sb.）for the night 留（某人）住一夜

economical [iː kə'nɔmikəl] adj. 节俭的，节省的，经济的；经济学的

　　e. g. be economical of one's time 节省时间

dismantle [dis'mæntl] vt. 拆除的设备（装备、家具、防御工事）

e. g. dismantle a car 拆掉汽车上的零件

quotation［kwəuˈteiʃən］n.【商】行情，时价；报价，估价；行市表；估价单，报价单

New Phrases

specialize in 专攻于
residential building 住宅楼
light concrete slabs 轻混凝土板
on a turn-key basis 以交钥匙方式
level the ground 平整场地
duty-free 免税的

Role Play

Making conversations by using the information given below：

Allen is a high school student who is facing the college entrance examination. He wants to be a civil engineer but knows nothing about this course in college. A famous teacher, Professor Green, is trying to explain about civil engineering and encourage him.

TEXT A

A Brief Introduction to the Project
TRIDENT GRAND RESIDENCE
Multi-Storey Residential Building
on Plot No 9AB-Dubai Marina

a. LOCATION

The project occupies plot 9AB（Parcel ID no. 392 – 296）in Dubai Marina, adjacent to the

Royal Lc Meridian Hotel to the North, and JBR to the West. The site runs along D2.

b. THE SITE

The main construction access points will be from the service road at the South West side of the site. The site in its final condition will have vehicular access from the road on the North and West sides. The main pedestrian crossing / walkway will be from the south‑west road. Residential vehicular access will be from the south‑west road, and the retail vehicular access will be from Street D2. The proposed new building is to be constructed within the plot limits.

c. SCOPE OF WORKS

1) The project comprises the construction, completion and maintenance of Residential building, a podium on plot No 9AB, at Dubai Marina and consists of 4 1/2 No., Basement Floors, Ground Floor and two floors from the podium building, and 43 levels of residential tower (including 2 plant floors on the 15th and 39th floors). Total build-up area is approx. 99, 756m^2.

2) The building construction shall also include the provision of all services and the permanent power substation along with all exterior work.

3) The building shall have the following floors:

Basement:

4 1/2 No., basement floors (−5, −4, −2, −1) comprises Water Tanks (B5), car parks, apartment, storage, retail storage, plant/service areas, indoor pool, fitness club and spa, squash courts and other tenant amenities.

Podium:

Ground floor comprises External Landscape Area/Front-of-house (FOH) areas including main residential drop-off and lobby (complete with security desk and office), retail lobbies and F&B outlets, and retail shops.

First floor level comprises retail shops and outdoor terrace seating.

Plenum floor:

Second floor level comprise pool desk with bar area, tennis court and chiller/cooling tower.

Residential Tower:

Second floor level comprises mix of 2 and 3 bedroom apartments.

Third to 14th floors comprise mix of 1, 2 and 3 bedroom apartments.

15th floor level comprises plant areas.

16th to 37th floors comprise mix of 1, 2 and 3 bedroom apartments.

39th floor level comprises plant areas.

40th to 44th floors comprise of 4 bedroom penthouse and duplex apartment with outdoor pool terraces.

Roof level comprises BMU.

Construction of building complete with structure and cladding works all as detailed in relevant drawings and specifications.

MEP services installation for all buildings.

Drainage /Plumbing service to all buildings.

Proposed Civil and MEP work as shown in relevant drawings.

The contractor should submit a detailed construction programme with the tender indicating the construction sequences.

The main contractor will be responsible for the management, supervision and co-ordination of the works.

The contractor should allow for safe access routes into the site through the existing entrances. The contractor will take all reasonable steps to minimize transference of noise, dust and debris.

Notes

1. The Dubai Marina：迪拜码头. 在这座码头完工后，它将取代目前的加州码头成为世界上最大的人造码头，包括 200 多个高层建筑的建筑群，里面有迪拜网络城、媒体城和美国在迪拜的大学。

2. MEP 是 Mechanical, Electrical & Plumbing 的缩写，即机械、电气、管道三个专业的英文缩写，也就是工程行业常说的水电风专业。如 AUTODESK 公司开发的 AUTOCAD MEP，专门为帮助机械、电气和给排水专业人员应对日益严酷的竞争环境而设计。

New Words

pedestrian［peˈdestriən］adj. 步行的；行人的，人行的；n. 行人，步行者，人行道

vehicular［viˈhikjulə（r）］adj. 车辆的

　　e. g. This road is closed to vehicular traffic. 此路不准车辆通过。

maintenance［ˈmeintinəns］n. 维持；保持，维修；保养；维修保养费用

　　e. g. cost of maintenance 维持费

the maintenance of an automobile 汽车保养

podium［ˈpəudiəm］n.（pl. -dia［-die］）【建】裙楼

specificaiton［ˌspesifiˈkeiʃən］n. 详细说明，分类［pl.］清单，明细单；计划书具体要求；［pl.］规范，规格，技术说明

supervision［ˌsjuːpəˈviʒən］n. 监督；管理

　　e. g. The house was built under the careful supervision of an architect.

这房子是在一位建筑师的细心监督下建造的。

co-ordination n. 合作

reasonable［ˈriːznəbl］adj. 合情合理的，有道理的

New Phrases

multi-story residential building　高层住宅楼

vehicular access　车路；车辆通道

Ground Floor　底层，一楼（美 = first floor）

basement floors　地下室层

water tank　水箱，水槽

squash courts　壁球室

tenant amenities　租赁设施，租赁场所
external Landscape Area　外部观景台
Front-of-house　前场
main residential drop-off　主住宅楼落客点
outdoor terrace seating　露天看台
plenum floor　夹层
BNU　楼顶是氨基树脂包板
duplex apartment　复式套间
cladding works　骨架外墙工程；面板工程
be responsible for　对…负责

Role Play

1. Describe a famous building in your country or the one you are familiar with that tourists like to visit. You should say：What kind of feature it is? What is special about it? Why it is popular?

2. Describe the teaching buildings and dormitories in your college.

"What are the advantages and the disadvantages？"

"What is the building design?"

Exercises

I. Answer the following questions .

1. Where is the location of Trident Grand Residence?

2. Would the building construction include the provision of all services and the permanent power substation along with all exterior work？

3. Which floor comprises of 4-bedroom penthouse and duplex apartment with outdoor pool terraces?

4. Who will be responsible for the management, supervision and co-ordination of the works?

II. Complete the sentences with the given words or expression. Change the form where necessary .

1. All that is lacking of good _____ (co-ordinate).

2. The tenderer offer a _____ (reason) quotation.

3. He is _____ (responsibility) of the construction of the whole building.

4. The project comprises the _____ (construct), _____ (complete) and _____ (maintain) of Residential building.

5. Construction of building should comply with technical _____ (specify).

III. Translate the following words or phrases into English.

车辆通道_____　　　　　露天看台_____

底层_____　　　　　复式套间_____

地下室层_____   骨架外墙工程_____

外部观景台_____   房屋保养_____

前场_____   高层住宅楼_____

IV. *Translate the following sentences into Chinese.*

1. The contractor will take all reasonable steps to minimize transference of noise, dust and debris.

_____

2. Ground floor comprises External Landscape Area/Front -of-house （FOH） areas including main residential drop-off and lobby （complete with security desk and office）, retail lobbies and F &B outlets, and retail shops.

_____

_____

V. *Try to Write.*

Direction：*You are required to write a letter of application according to the following information provided. You may refer to the given words and samples.*

假设你是广东建设职业技术学院的一名土木工程专业大三的学生,在 2009 年 9 月 17 日的中国日报上看到珠海市设计院招聘助理设计师的工作,对此很感兴趣,特申请这一职位。

Words for reference：

毕业于……graduate from   专业 major in   申请 apply for

设计院 designing institute   职位 position   助理设计师 designer assistant

专长是…… be skillful at …/ be excellent at …

蓝图 blueprint

Samples：

Dear Sir or Madam,

I'm writing to apply for the position that you advertised on newspaper several days ago. With an excellent achievement, I received my master degree of Civil Engineering in MIT about 2 years ago. I have engaged in some designing work in an institute since I graduated from university. If I have the honor to meet you after this letter, I will bring my blueprints together with me. During working in that institute, I cooperated with my group members so well that we did many good jobs together.

The reason why I want to quit is that I need a brand new working environment to improve my skills and know more friends outside. The payment, I think, is not the key factor for me to choose a job but the prospect.

Hoping to hear from you soon, I am looking forward to the meeting between us.

Yours faithfully,

Peter

VI. *The following is a brief description of a building. Read it carefully and try your best to figure it out by referring to the translation.*

Dubai's "super scraper" makes history in hard times
世界最高建筑 "迪拜塔" 今日落成揭幕

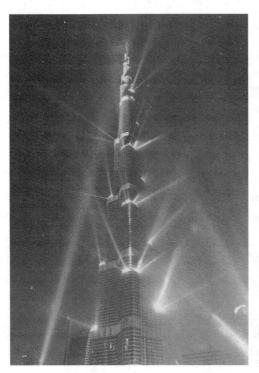 

Started at the height of the economic boom and built by some
12, 000 laborers, the world's tallest building is to open today in Dubai as the glitzy emirate seeks to
rekindle optimism after its financial crisis.

Burj Dubai, whose opening has been delayed twice since construction began in 2004, will mark another milestone for the deeply indebted emirate with a **penchant** for seeking new records.

Dubai, one of seven members of the United Arab Emirates, gained a reputation for excess with the creation of man – made islands shaped like palms and an indoor ski slope in the desert.

With investor confidence in Dubai badly bruised by the emirate's announcement in November that it would seek a debt standstill for one of its largest conglomerates, the Burj Dubai is seen as a positive start to the year after a bleak 2009.

The project has been scrutinized by human rights groups, who have objected to its treatment of laborers, as well as by environmentalists who said the tower would act as a power vacuum, increasing the city's already massive carbon footprint.

But despite the criticism, many say the **edifice**, believed to have cost $ 1. 5 billion to build, is an architectural marvel.

The tower's height has been kept a closely guarded secret until now. Developer Emaar Properties PJSC will reveal the height —known to exceed 800 meters（2，625 feet）—on Tuesday and Dubai's ruler will inaugurate the opening.

Experts believe Dubai's recent financial troubles have not hurt sales of approximately 1，100 residential units in the Burj —meaning tower in Arabic —saying they were nearly all sold.

Dubai's real estate sector crashed at the end of 2008 when the global financial crisis hit the emirate after a six-year economic boom. Thousands of jobs were slashed and projects worth billions of dollars were canceled or delayed.

With analysts suggesting **tax-free** Dubai might sell some of its assets to boost revenues and slash ＄80 billion in debt, many wondered if the tower was on the list for grabs.

Dubai, with few natural resources of its own, expects a budget deficit of 2 percent of GDP this year.

In December, the emirate received a ＄10 billion lifeline from neighboring Abu Dhabi to repay a ＄4.1 billion bond for Nakheel, a property arm of indebted Dubai World, and other obligations.

Words for reference：

rekindle：to revive or renew （重新点燃）

penchant：a strong inclination, taste, or liking for something （强烈的倾向，趣味）

edifice：a building, esp. one of large size or imposing appearance （大厦，大建筑物）

tax-free：not subject to taxation；tax-exempt （免税的，无税的）

世界最高建筑"迪拜塔"今日落成揭幕

世界最高建筑"迪拜塔"于今日落成揭幕，这座高楼于经济鼎盛时期动工，约1.2万名工人参与建造，饱受债务危机之苦的迪拜酋长国希望能借此机会扬眉吐气。

迪拜塔于2004年动工，其揭幕日期两次延后。这座建筑有望打破世界最高建筑纪录，为深陷债务危机的迪拜开创一个新的里程碑。

迪拜是阿联酋七个酋长国之一，拥有人工修建的"棕榈岛"以及位于沙漠中的室内滑雪场，让其名噪一时。

2009年11月，迪拜宣布对其最大的一家集团公司暂停偿债，使投资者信心遭到重创。在这种情况下，迪拜塔的落成被视为黯淡的2009年过后迎接新年的良好开端。

该工程的建造曾受到人权组织的非议，称参与建筑的工人受到不公正待遇；环境保护主义者也曾批评迪拜塔耗能过度，将加剧该城市原本已经很庞大的碳足迹排放。

但尽管争议不断，仍有很多人认为，这座据称耗资15亿美元的摩天大楼是一项建筑奇迹。

直至今日，迪拜塔的"身高"仍是个秘密。开发商艾马尔地产公司将于本周二揭开这一谜底，据称塔高超过800米（2625英尺）。迪拜酋长将主持落成仪式。

专家认为，迪拜最近的债务危机并未影响到迪拜塔的销售，楼内近1100套住宅几乎售罄。在阿拉伯语中，Burj意为"高塔"。

2008年末，在全球经济危机的重创之下，经历了六年经济繁盛期的迪拜的房地产业崩溃。成千上万的工作机会被削减，价值数十亿美元的项目被迫取消或延期。

分析人士称，被称为"免税天堂"的迪拜或许将出售部分资产来增加收入，削减800亿美元的债务，因此很多人怀疑这座高塔是否被列入出售清单。

迪拜酋长国今年的预算赤字预计将占国内生产总值的2%。该国自然资源匮乏。

去年12月，迪拜从其邻国阿布扎比获得100亿美元的资金援助，用于支付 Nakhee 公司所应偿还的41亿美元的到期债券及其他债务。Nakheel 公司是受债务危机困扰的"迪拜世界"旗下的房地产公司。

TEXT B

A Brief Introduction to Civil Engineering

Civil engineering（土木工程）is one of the most diverse branches of engineering. The civil engineer plans, designs（设计）, constructs, and maintains（维护）a large variety of architecture structures and facilities for public, commercial, and industrial use. These structures include residential（住宅的）, office, and factory buildings, highways, railroads, airports, tunnel, bridges, harbors, channels, and pipelines. They also include many other facilities that are a part of the transportation systems（交通系统）of most countries, as well as sewage（污水）and waste disposal systems（废水处理系统）that add to our convenience（方便）and safeguard（保护）our health.

Among its subdivisions are structural engineering（结构工程）, dealing with permanent structures（永久结构）; hydraulic engineering（水利工程）, dealing with the flow of water（水流）and other fluids; and environmental/sanitary engineering（环境或环卫工程）, dealing with water supply（供水）, water purification（水的净化）, and sewer systems（污水处理系统）; as well as urban planning and design（城市规划）.

The term civil engineering originally came into use to distinguish（区别）it from military engineering（军事工程）. Civil engineering dealt with permanent structures（永久性建筑结构）for civilian use（民用）, whereas military engineering dealt with temporary structures for military use（临时性的军用建筑）。

Civil engineering offers a particular challenge because almost every structure or system that is designed and built by civil engineers is unique（独一无二的）. One structure rarely duplicates another exactly. Even when structures seem to be identical（完全相同）, site requirements（选址的要求）or other factors generally result in modification（变更）. Large structures like dams, bridges, or tunnels may differ substantially from previous structures.

Notes

1. …; hydraulic engineering, dealing with the flow of water and other fluids; …
关于水流及其他液体的水利工程

dealing with：处理；关于。在句中充当伴随性状语，后接名词或名词短语。

e. g. Mary brought me a marvelous book, dealing with the political affairs of the Middle

East. 玛丽送给我一本很棒的书，是关于中东政治冲突的。

This book deals with music. 这本书是关于音乐的。

New Words

civil ['sivl] adj. 1. 公民的，平民的；2. 民用的，民事的，民法的

engineering [,endʒi'niəriŋ] n. 工程

architecture ['ɑːkitektʃə] n. 1. 建筑学，建筑术；2. 建筑风格，建筑式样，建筑设计

architect ['ɑːkitekt] n. 建筑师

architectural [,ɑːkitektʃərəl] adj. 建筑学的

building ['bildiŋ] n. 建筑物，房屋

channel ['tʃænəl] n. 沟渠，海峡，通道

construct [kən'strʌkt] vt. 1. 修建，建立，建筑，建造；2. 构成，组成

construction [kən'strʌkʃən] n. 1. 建造，建设；2. 建筑业，建造物，建筑物

craftsman ['kræftsmən] n. 工匠

dam [dæm] n. 大坝

design [di'zain] v. &n. 设计

drainage ['dreinidʒ] n. 排水

facility [fə'siliti] n. 设备，设施

hydraulic 英 [haidrɔːlik] adj. 1. 液力的，液压的，水力学的；2. 水、油等（通过水管等）液压的，水力的

subdivision ['sʌbdivi,ʒən] n. 细［再］分；细分分成的部分

　　e. g. land subdivision 分割土地

environmental [in,vaiərən'mentl] adj. 环境（产生）的；周［包］围的

　　e. g. environmental costs 环境成本

　　　　　environmental waste 环境废物

sanitary ['sænitəri] engineering [,endʒi'niəriŋ] 卫生工程

　　e. g. municipal sanitary engineering 城市卫生工程学

　　　　　public sanitary engineering 公共卫生工程

sewer ['səuə] systems 排水工程

　　e. g. maintenance of sewer system 市政排水系统

originally [ə'ridʒənəli] adj. 起初，原来

distinguish [dis'tiŋgwiʃ] （区别）

military ['militəri] adj. 军人的；军用的；军事的 e. g. a military school 军事学校

permanent ['pəːmənənt] adj. 永久性的，耐久的 e. g. permanent address 永久地址

　　　　　　　　permanent assets【会计】固定资产

civilian [si'viljən] n. 市民，平民，老百姓（与军人相对而言）e. g. civilian use 民用

temporary ['tempərəri] adj. 暂时的，临时的；e. g. temporary workers 临时工

unique [juː'niːk] adj. 唯一的；无与伦比的；独特的 e. g. unique feature 特色

duplicate ['djuːplikeit] vt. 使加倍；使成双 e. g. duplicate expenses 使费用加倍

modification [,mɔdifi'keiʃən] n. 变更，修正；e. g. data modification 数据修改

substantially [səb'stænʃ(ə)li] adv. 主要地；实质上地

 e. g. substantially alters 实质变更

New Phases

civil Engineering 土木工程

civil Engineer 土木工程师

chartered structural engineer 注册结构工程师

chartered civil engineer 注册土木工程师

structural engineering 结构工程

permanent structures 永久结构

hydraulic engineering 水利工程

come into use 开始被使用

 e. g. The new car will come into use next month. 那辆新车将于下月开始使用。

environmental/sanitary engineering 环境或环卫工程

water supply 供水

water purification 水的净化

sewer systems 污水处理系统

urban planning and design 城市规划

military engineering 军事工程

permanent structures 永久性建筑结构

civilian use 民用

Exercises

I. Translate the following words or phrases into English.

土木工程_____   结构工程_____

永久结构_____   水利工程_____

环境或环卫工程_____

供水_____   污水处理系统_____

城市规划_____   军事工程_____

民用_____

II. The following is a brief description of a college. Read it carefully and try your best to figure it out by referring to the translation.

 The college covers an area of 208 acres, with its floor space totaling 139, 322 square meters. It was rewarded as a garden like campus. The campus is mainly divided into several parts; they are the teaching office building area, the faculty dormitory area, the service area, the students dormitory area, the sports area and a plant area. The campus is well provided.

 There is a university elementary school, secondary school, a kindergarten, a post office, a hospital and several shops. The office room where we just held a talk is a temporal office room. The new office building will be set up just facing the gate of the college. The building is under construction and will be finished next year. When you come for a second visit next year, you are sure to see with your own eyes the new office building.

Now we are trying our best to expand our school and further develop our foreign exchange programs. The tall building facing us, which is being built now, will be another teaching building. All the teaching buildings can hold eight thousand students. The tall buildings on our left are student's dormitories. They are flat like. It is very convenient and comfortable. Four students share an apartment. In each apartment there is a closet, a TV set and a desk for study.

校园面积为 208 英亩，建筑面积 139322 平方米，为省级园林单位。校园大致分教学区、教工宿舍区、服务区、学生宿舍区、活动区和植物园。校园设施齐全。

有一所小学、一所附中、一所幼儿园、一所邮电所、几家商店和一所医院。我们刚才会谈的地方是临时的部分办公楼。新的办公楼将建在校园大门的正对面。目前正在施工，预计明年完工。你明年再次来访时，就可看到这座新的办公楼。

目前我们正设法扩大办学规模并进一步开展对外交流。我们前面正在建筑的大楼将是又一栋教学楼。所有的教学楼能容纳近 8000 名学生。我们左边的学生宿舍都是公寓式的，又方便又舒适。每四人一套，里面有壁柜、电视机、自习桌。

TRANSLATION SKILLS

科技英语的特点之一

一、复杂长句多

科技文章要求叙述准确，推理谨严，因此一句话里包含三四个甚至五六个分句的，并非少见。译成汉语时，必须按照汉语习惯破成适当数目的分句，才能条理清楚，避免洋腔洋调。这种复杂长句居科技英语难点之首，要学会运用语法分析方法来加以解剖，以便以短代长，化难为易。

例如：

Factories will not buy machines unless they believe that the machine will produce goods that they are able to sell to consumers at a price that will cover all cost.

这是由一个主句和四个从句组成的复杂长句，只有进行必要的语法分析，才能正确理解和翻译。

现试译如下：

除非相信那些机器造出的产品卖给消费者的价格足够支付所有成本，否则厂家是不会买那些机器的。

节译：只有产品的售价高于成本，厂家才考虑购买机器。

后一句只用了 24 个字，比前句 40 个字节约用字 40%，而对原句的基本内容无损。

可见，只要吃透原文的结构和内涵，翻译时再在汉语上反复推敲提炼，复杂的英语长句，也是容易驾驭的。

二、被动语态多

英语使用被动语态大大多于汉语，如莎士比亚传世名剧《罗密欧与朱丽叶》中的一句就两次用了被动语态：

Juliet was torn between desire to keep Romeo near her and fear for his life, should his presence be detected.

朱丽叶精神上受到折磨，既渴望和罗密欧形影不离，又担心罗密欧万一让人发现，难免有性命之忧。

科技英语更是如此，有三分之一以上用被动语态。

例如：

（a）No work can be done without energy.

译文：没有能量决不能做功。

（b）All business decisions must now be made in the light of the market.

译文：所有企业现在必须根据市场来作出决策。

三、非谓语动词多

英语每个简单句中，只能用一个谓语动词，如果读到几个动作，就必须选出主要动作当谓语，而将其余动作用非谓语动词形式，才能符合英语语法要求。

非谓语动词有三种：动名词、分词（包括现在分词和过去分词）和不定式。

例如：

要成为一个名符其实的内行，需要学到老。

这句中，有"成为"、"需要"和"学"三个表示动作的词，译成英语后为：

To be a true professional requires lifelong learning.

可以看出，选好"需要"（require）作为谓语，其余两个动作："成为"用不定式形式 to be，而"学"用动名词形式 learning，这样才能符合英语语法要求。

四、词性转换多

英语单词有不少是多性词，即既是名词，又可用作动词、形容词、介词或副词，字形无殊，功能各异，含义也各不相同，如不仔细观察，必致谬误。

例如，light

名词：（启发）in（the）light of 由于，根据；

　　　（光）high light（s）强光，精华；

　　　（灯）safety light 安全指示灯

形容词：（轻）light industry 轻工业；

　　　　（明亮）light room 明亮的房间；

　　　　（淡）light blue 淡蓝色；

　　　　（薄）light coating 薄涂层

动词：（点燃）light up the lamp 点灯

副词：（轻快）travel light 轻装旅行；

　　　（容易）light come, light go 来得容易去得快

诸如此类的词性转换，在科技英语中屡见不鲜，几乎每个技术名词都可转换为同义的形容词。

词性转换增加了英语的灵活性和表现力，读者必须从上下文判明用词在句中是何种词性，而且含义如何，才能对全句得到正确无误的理解。

译　文

第一单元　工程简介

对　话

杨先生，中国海外建筑工程集团的项目经理，正在与豪威尔先生讨论施工场地分包事宜。豪威尔先生是世界棚屋公司的总经理，这是当地一家专门从事住宅建设的公司。

豪威尔：你对我们国家的第一印象如何？

杨：这是一个非常美丽的国家，它位于阿拉伯世界的中部。这里的人非常友好。对我来说这里的大多数人讲的英语都很不同，有时很难听懂他们说什么。

豪威尔：你会很快习惯的，这里只有官员、教师和商人讲标准的英语。让我们谈正题吧，杨先生，你邀请我们投标可容纳 80 人的员工生活区工程，你能说得再详细些吗？

杨：正如你所知道的，这个生活区要容纳 80 名中国海外员工。它包括两人房，为工人和厨师提供的四人房，一个厨房，几个就餐厅，淋浴间，办公室，一个会议室和一个接待室。

豪威尔：你有什么特殊的要求吗？

杨：我想听听你的建议。

豪威尔：有一种装配式的房屋，运输容易、花钱少，建造速度快，而且当整个工程完工的时候拆除方便并可进行再次安装使用。

杨：听起来不错。它是什么材料的？

豪威尔：轻混凝土板。

杨：好。请您尽快为这个场地报一个交付使用价格。

豪威尔：好的。但是谁来负责营地场地的平整呢？

杨：这个由我们来做。你们负责水、电的供给。这是一个免税工程，因此所有为此而进口的材料都是免税的。

豪威尔：要是那样的话，我们的报价将会降低很多。你希望生活区地工程什么时候完工？

杨：从我们通知开工起 60 天之内。

豪威尔：我希望我们能够得到这次为你们工作的机会，如果能够有这样的机会，我相信我们一定会把它做好。

杨：我也希望如此。

课文 A　工程简介
TRIDENT GRAND RESIDENCE
迪拜码头 9AB 地块高层住宅

a 位置

本工程位于迪拜码头，占地 9AB（土地块码号 No. 392—296），北面毗邻皇家迈纳宾馆，西部靠近朱美拉海滩步行街，场地沿 D2 街。

b 场地

主要的建设工程通道位于场地西南面的辅助道路。建成后的场地将在北边和西边有车辆通道。主要的人行道与居民车辆通道均在西北方向，零星车辆通道在 D2 街方向，计划中的新建筑必须建造在限定范围之内。

c 工程范围

1）工程包括住宅楼及迪拜码头占地 9AB 矮墙的建造、完工以及维修；包括 4 楼夹层，地下室层，底层和两层基础墙，43 层居民住宅塔楼（包括 15 层和 39 层的两个绿化层）。全部建筑面积约 99756 平方米。

2）建筑物的建造也包括所有服务设施的供应，永久性变电站以及所有的外围工作。

3）建筑物将有以下各层：

地下室

4 楼夹层、地下室层（-5，-4，-2，-1）包含水池（B5）、停车场、公寓、储藏室、零售业仓库、绿化/服务区域、室内游泳池、健身俱乐部和美容院、壁球室和其他租货场所。

podium 裙楼

底层包括外部景观台/前场，包括主建筑楼落客点和大堂（有保安台和办公室），零售厅和餐饮区及零售店。

一层设有零售店及露天看台。

夹层

二层包括带有酒吧的弹子桌区、网球室和冷却塔。

居住塔楼

二层有包含二间和三间卧室的公寓。

三层到十四层由包含一间、二间和三间卧室的公寓组成。

十五层为设备层

十六到三十七层由包含一间、二间和三间卧室的公寓组成。

三十九层为绿化区

四十到四十四层为四室坡顶房屋和带有室外游泳池看台的复式套间。

楼顶是氨基树脂板。

大楼的建造要完成主体结构和骨架外墙工程，所有这些都有详细的相关图纸与说明。

所有建筑物安装 MEP 设备。

所有建筑物设置给排水/管道。

相关图纸上说明的民用的和 MEP 工程。

承包方应随同投标书提交一份说明施工顺序的详细施工进度计划。

主要承包者负责管理、监督以及各项工程的合作事宜。

承包方应留出经由入口的安全通道路线进入施工现场，承包方也应采取合理措施使运输噪声、灰尘和碎片最大限度地减小。

课文 B 土木工程简介

土木工程是最多种多样的工程门类之一。土木工程师对各种各样的民用、商用、工业用途的建筑物及设施进行规划、设计、建造和维护。这些建筑包括住宅、办公楼和工业建筑；公路、铁路、飞机场、隧道、桥梁、港口、沟渠和管线。它们也包括许多其他的交通系统的部分设施，以及带给我们方便的、保护我们健康的污水、废水处理系统。

在它的分支中有研究永久结构的结构工程，关于水流及其他流体的水利工程，有关供水、净水以及污水处理系统的环卫工程以及城市的规划与设计。

土木工程这个术语原本是用来使之与军事工程区别开来。土木工程是指供民用的永久性建筑，而军事工程是指临时性的军用建筑。

土木工程领域是具有特别挑战性的，因为几乎每一个由土木工程师设计并建造的建筑物和建筑群都是独一无二的。很少有一个建筑物与另一个完全相同。甚至当两个建筑物看似完全相同，但由于选址的要求或其他因素一般也会导致变化，像大坝、桥梁或隧道等大型建筑物或许与先前的建筑物截然不同。

UNIT *2*

Construction Method Statement
(施工方案会审)

DIALOGUE

Construction Method Statement

E: After our study of your tender document, I am pleased to inform you that your company is accepted as one of the companies which passed the first stage and is qualified to enter the second stage of the tendering works: negotiation stage.

C: We are very pleased to hear that.

E: Now, let's see the Construction Method Statement. There are so many contents included in it. Let's turn to Chapter 1: **General Description.** As to the site preparation for pile precasting we noticed that your precast concrete piles will be fabricated on site. If the penetration of the piles suddenly becomes abnormal, what are you going to do?

C: We will stop driving and study the driving record, and then make holes to find out the real situation under earth, then decision can be made to increase pile length or to relocate the pile position after consulting the designer.

E: Thanks. Now let's discuss Chapter 2 of the Method Statement: **Construction Schedule.** You should modify these two Key Dates of completion in order to match the start date of the whole project.

C: Although these dates are too tight to reach, we will rearrange our section schedules and submitted the modified one to you.

E：OK. Chapter 3 is the **Organization Chart.**

C：This Organization Chart is a typical one for large industrial plants we have performed.

E：We notice that it looks like a large organization，maybe too large. And I would like to remind you that as long as these key staff is approved to work for the project they should not be removed from the site without our permission.

C：No，they won't. We understand this importance of keeping capable persons for such an important mission.

E：Concerning the Chapter 4：**Labor Chart**，it should show the number of each trade during construction period instead of only the number of workers and also your estimation of total workers for project is not enough. And for chapter 5：**Construction Machine Schedule**，we quite appreciate that you intend to mobilize all necessary construction equipment for the works. But there is still some shortage of equipment to be applied on the site.

C：Thank you for your comments to our submission.

E：We hope that you will submit your revised Method Statement to us on basis of our comments in a week.

C：We will certainly work out a new set of documents and resubmit it to you.

Notes

1. C：contractor 承包商：指在业主接受的投标函中称为承包商的当事人，及其财产所有权的合法继承人。

2. E：engineer/consulting engineer 咨询工程师：系指由雇主任命并在"投标书附录"中指名，为实施合同担任工程师的人员。对于一些公共项目，如果该项目的相关部门没有足够建筑工程人员，或者该项目过于庞大的时候，业主就会通知多个咨询公司他正在寻找该项目的建筑工程师。

New Words

construction ［kən'strʌkʃən］n. 建造，建设；建筑业；施工

inform ［in'fɔːm］vt. 告诉，通知

negotiation ［niɡəuʃiˌeiʃən］n. 协商，谈判，磋商

content ［'kɑntent］n. 1. 所容纳之物，所含之物；2.（书等的）内容，目录 3. 容量，含量

pile ［pail］n. 桩；桩柱

precast ［ˌpriː'kɑːst］adj. 预浇铸的，预制的

fabricate ［'fæbrikeit］vt. 1. 建造；2. 制造，装配，组装

penetration ［ˌpeni'treiʃən］n. 1. 穿透，穿透能力，穿透深度；2. 渗透，侵入

abnormal ［æb'nɔːməl］adj. 反常的，异常的

consult ［kən'sʌlt］vt. & vi. 商议，商量 vt. 请教，咨询

schedule ［'ʃedjuːəl］vt. 排定，安排 n. 时间表，日程安排表

modify ［'mɔdifai］vt. & vi. 修改，更改 vt. 1. 修饰；2. 调整，稍作修改，使更适合

remind［ri'maind］vt. 1. 使想起；2. 提醒

mission［'miʃən］n. 使命，任务，天职

mobilize［'məubilaiz］vt. & vi. 动员起来，调动

shortage［'ʃɔːtidʒ］n. 不足；缺少；缺少量；不足额

comment［'kɔment］n. 1. 评论，意见，解释，批评 vt. & vi. 评论；2. 谈论

submit［səb'mit］vt. 提交，呈递

revise［ri'vaiz］vt. 1. 修订，修改；2. 改变，修改（意见或计划）

New Phrases

tender document　投标文件

be qualified to　具有…的资质

negotiation stage　谈判阶段

construction site　工地

Construction Method Statement（CMS）　施工方案

site preparation　现场准备

general description　概述

precast concrete piles　预制混凝土桩

penetration of the piles　桩的贯入

pile length　桩长

construction schedule　施工进度计划表

key dates of completion　完工关键日期

organization chart　组织机构表

labor chart　劳务配备表

construction machine schedule　施工机械计划表

Role Play

Make a dialogue between the project manager and the representative of the owner on the construction site due to the inferior quality of works and then play the roles.

TEXT A

TRIDENT GRAND RESIDENCE
PLOT 9AB DUBAI MARINA

METHOD STATEMENT
FOR
CONCRETE CURING
（Except for RAFT Foundation）

This Method Statement covers the CURING of slabs, columns, core walls, etc. after the concreting works has been completed except for the raft foundation.

Construction / Work Execution

• For at least seven（7）days, the concrete shall be protected from sunlight, winds, cold, rains or running water right after the compaction has been completed.

• Curing of concrete shall be done using fresh water in accordance with the requirements of the Specification.

HORIZONTAL STRUCTURES（Beams/Slab）

• Immediately after the finishing of concrete has been made, a "POLYTHENE sheet" shall be provided over entire structure.

• Once the concrete final set has been taken place, watering of the structure shall be made for at least seven（7）days.

VERTICAL STRUCTURES（Columns/Walls /Core Wall）

• Formworks shall be striken without disturbing and damaging the structures.

• After striking of formworks, water shall be sprayed thoroughly to the structure and a HESSIAN cloth shall be applied and retained in place for at least seven（7）days.

• The "HESSIAN" cloth shall be kept permanently damp until the required curing time as specified above.

＊＊ A separate Method Statement will be submitted where curing compounds are intended to use and it shall be compatible with waterproofing or other materials that may be applied to the surface of concrete.

Quality Control

• QA/QC Engineer and Site Engineer shall inspect the concrete curing and monitor in a daily basis.

• Any non-conformity observed on site shall be reported directly to the Project Manager.

Notes

1. 混凝土养护有两个目的：一是创造使水泥得以充分水化的条件，加速混凝土硬化；二是防止混凝土成型后因日晒、风吹、干燥、寒冷等自然因素的影响而出现超出正常范围的收缩、裂缝及破坏等现象。混凝土的标准养护条件为温度（20±3）℃，相对湿度保持90%以上，时间28d。在实际工程中一般无法保证标准养护条件，而只能采取措施在经济实用条件下取得尽可能好的养护效果。

2. QA/QC：Quality Assurance /Quality Control 质量保证/质量控制。

New Words

cure［kjuə］vt. 养护

curing［′kjuəriŋ］n. 养护

concrete［′kɔnkri：t］n. 混凝土 vt. 铺以混凝土，以混凝土浇筑 vi. 凝固，固结

slab［slæb］n. 板

column［′kɔləm］n. 柱，圆柱

core wall 隔水墙；岩心墙

raft［rɑ：ft］n. 木筏

execution［ˌeksi′kju：ʃən］n. 实行，执行，实施

compaction［kəm′pækʃən］n. 压实；夯实

specification［ˌspesifi′keiʃən］n. 规范

beam［bi：m］n. 梁，横梁

polythene［′pɔləˌθi：n］n. ＜化＞聚乙烯；聚乙烯化合物

water［′wɔ：tə］vt. 在…浇水［洒水］

hessian［′hesiən］n. 粗麻布；黄麻粗布

permanently［′pəmənəntli］adv. 永久地；长期不变地

damp［dæmp］adj. 潮湿的，不完全干燥的

compound［′kɔmpaund］n. 复合物，化合物，混合物

compatible［kəm′pætəbl］adj. 可以并存的，相容的，协调的

waterproof［′wɔ：təpru：f］adj. 不透水的，防水的 vt. 使防水；使不透水

conformity［kən′fɔ：miti］n. 依照，遵从；符合，一致

New Phrases

core wall 隔水墙；岩心墙

raft foundation 筏式基础；筏式地基；板式基础

in accordance with 与…一致，依照

horizontal structure 水平结构；横向结构

polythene sheet 塑料薄膜

vertical structure 纵向结构；垂直结构

hessian cloth 粗麻布

be compatible with 与…不矛盾，与…一致，与…相容

site engineer 现场工程师

project manager n. 项目管理人［经理］

Role Play

Try to describe the following pictures according to the words and phrases given below.

Figare1　Supervisor /Engineer /Reinforcement
Inspection/Alternative rebar

Figare2　Rebar fixing/ Inspect reinforcement
work /tension force

Exercises

I. Answer the following questions.

1. What does this Method Statement covers? Does it include the concreting works of the raft foundation?

2. How long should the concrete be protected from sunlight, winds, cold, rains or running water right after the compaction has been completed?

3. What shall be provided in entire structure immediately after the finishing of beam?

4. What shall be applied and retained in place for at least seven（7）days after striking formworks of columns?

5. Who shall inspect the concrete curing and monitor in a daily basis?

II. Complete the sentences with the given words or expression. Change the form where necessary.

1. All the work should _____ （submit）to the client before Tuesday.

2. The project manager should _____ （inspection）the construction site often.

3. The concrete shall be protected after the _____ （compact）has been completed.

4. What you have provided should be in _____ （accord）with facts.

5. Site engineer should report any _____ （conform）to the Project Manager.

III. Translate the following words or phrases into English.

投标文件_____ 谈判阶段_____

工地 _____ 施工方案 _____

现场准备_____ 桩长 _____

水平结构_____ 垂直结构_____

现场工程师_____ 项目经理_____

IV. Translate the following phrases into Chinese.

precast concrete piles _____

penetration of the piles _____

construction schedule _____

organization chart _____

labor chart _____

construction machine schedule _____

core wall _____

raft foundation _____

polythene sheet _____

hessian cloth _____

V. Translate the following sentences into chinese.

1. This Method Statement covers the CURING of slabs, columns, core walls, etc. after the concreting works has been completed except for the raft foundation.

2. For at least seven (7) days, the concrete shall be protected from sunlight, winds, cold, rains or running water right after the compaction has been completed.

3. Once the concrete final set has been taken place, watering of the structure shall be made for at least seven (7) days.

4. After striking of formworks, water shall be spray thoroughly to the structure and a HESSIAN cloth shall be applied and retained in place for at least seven (7) days.

VI. *The following is a brief description of Construction Organization Management Structure. Read it carefully and try your best to fill in the blanks by referring to the Chinese.*

Construction Organization Management Structure

Since the construction is complicated, with _____, hard crafts and arts, we should have high quality, _____ and safety to fulfill the expected _____.

According to the scientific ISO9001 management system of our company, we will assign the intelligent and capable leading staff to ensure the construction running smoothly.

Mr. _____ will be appointed as _____.

Mr. _____ will be appointed as _____.

Mr. _____ will be appointed as _____.

Project Manager：_____, the universal agent of Part B.

Site Work Leader：_____, in charge of the control and plan of the construction.

Technical Leader：_____, in charge all of the technical affairs at the site.

1. Construction Department：

Chief：_____ Supervisor：_____

2. Technology Department：

Chief：_____ Designer：_____ Clerk：_____

3. Quality & Safety Department：

Chief：_____ Quality inspector：_____ Safety inspector：_____

4. Material Department ：

Chief：_____ Buyer：_____ Mechanic：_____

5. Financial Department：

Chief：_____ Accountant：_____ Cashier：_____

6. General Affairs Department：

Chief：_____ Member：_____

7. Chiefs of Construction Teams：

Ceiling team：_____; cement team：_____;

Hardware team：_____; Glass team：_____;

Furniture team：_____; electrical engineering team：_____.

Construction Achievement：

施工组织管理机构

本工程设计装饰施工工艺难度大、构造复杂、质量要求高，施工工期紧，为了优质、高效、安全地完成这一工程的施工任务，实现预期的管理目标。根据公司具有科学性的ISO9001管理体系，我们将选派精明能干的领导负责这项工程，确保工程的顺利进行。

项目经理：（填人名）代表乙方的全权代理人。

现场负责人：（填人名）负责现场工程全面调度、统筹。

技术负责人：（填人名）负责现场工程所有技术问题。

1. 施工组：

组长：（填人名）

施工员：（填人名）施工员：（填人名）施工员：（填人名）

2. 技术组：

组长：（填人名）设计员：（填人名）资料员：（填人名）

3. 质安组：

组长：（填人名）质检员：（填人名）安全员：（填人名）

4. 材料组：

组长：（填人名）采管员：（填人名）机械员：（填人名）

5. 财务组：

组长：（填人名）会计：（填人名）出纳：（填人名）

6. 后勤组：

组长：（填人名）成员：（填人名）

7. 各施工队队长：

天花板施工队：（填人名）水泥施工队：（填人名）

五金施工队：（填人名）玻璃施工队：（填人名）

家具施工队：（填人名）电气施工队：（填人名）

工程业绩：

VII. The following is a construction method statement of a design works. Read it carefully, and answer the questions before the passage. Then try your best to figure it out by referring to the translation.

Questions

1. Which company intends to design, carry out, co-ordinate and complete the Works?

2. What should the Project Director be responsible for?

3. Who will produce design outlines, preliminary design data and sketches?

4. What will be submitted to the Client for review and approval?

CONSTRUCTION METHOD STATEMENT

1.0 PURPOSE & SCOPE

This document describes how Interior Contract Int'l Ltd. (ICIL) intends to design, carry out, coordinate and complete the Works and to fulfill all its contractual obligations and the achievement of milestones.

2.0 ORGANIZATION-RESPONSIBILITIES

The Project Director is responsible for overall management of the project. This includes determining quality management policy and addressing quality problems across the project. He shall have overall responsibility for the Design work undertaken by Interior Contract Int'l Ltd. in connection with this project.

The Senior Project Manger is responsible to assist the Project Director to provide design development, integration, prepare detailed design, shop drawings and in charge of other submittals as required. The Senior Project Manager shall interpret the design concepts, and coordinate with the main contractor and other trades of works.

The Project Manager is to dedicate his full time to the project and he is responsible for the overall management of the project under the leadership of the Project Director.

The Logistic & Procurement Officer is responsible to the Corporate Project Management for the overall operation of the procurement function, to ensure material and labour that meets with the requirements of the project as effected on site at the planned programme time.

The Quality Assurance Engineer is responsible for overall operation and effectiveness of the Quality Management System.

3.0 METHOD

The Corporate Project Management shall review all management and operation activities that are relevant to the execution of this Project. He shall ensure that the Management System is conceived, prepared, documented, implemented and maintained to meet the objectives of the Contract.

The planning activity shall include but not limited to:

Defining the organization and allocate responsibilities to ensure the Project requirements are met.

Defining the structure of the management system documentation and the relationship among the documents.

Defining the scope of all documents (plans, manuals, procedures and method statements).

Reviewing Interior Contract Int'l Ltd. requirements for controls, special processes, equipment resources and skills and ensure these are identified and suitable for provisions made.

Ensuring there is compatibility between design, installation process, inspection and testing.

Ensuring the inspecting and testing activities are appropriate to the scope of work within this project, and that suitable equipment is available.

Ensuring that sufficient time is made available in the construction programme for the development of any special techniques.

Establishing suitable inspection and verification activities at appropriate stages of the construction programme and establishment of appropriate standards.

The identification of all quality records.

4.0 SUBMISSION

The following items will be submitted to the Client for review and approval:

Drawings Submission

Samples Submission

Procurement & Delivery Programme

Construction Programme

Progress Report / Daily Report (Include Progress Photo)

Monthly Labour Analysis / Plant Analysis / Material Analysis

Safety Report

Testing Results（if applicable）

Notes

1. Interior Contract Int'l Ltd.（ICIL）京匯国际工程有限公司

int'l: international

int'l tansfers　转乘国际航班

Int'l Check-in　国际航班乘机手续

New words for reference

coordinate [kəu'ɔːdineit] vt. 使协调；使调和 vi. 协调，协同

milestone ['mailˌstəun] n. 里程碑

address [ə'dres] vt. 设法解决；满足（需求）；处理，对付；讨论，论述

responsibility [riˌspɔnsə'biliti] n. 1. 责任；2. 责任感，可信赖性；3. 职责，所负责任的事；4. 义务；负担

assist [ə'sist] vt. & vi. 帮助，协助，援助；促进

integration [ˌinti'greiʃən] n. 结合；整合；一体化

submittal [səb'mitl] n. 提交 [供]，服从，屈服

interpret [in'təːprit] vt. 解释；说明

procurement [prə'kjuəment] n.（尤指为政府或机构）采购，购买

assurance [ə'ʃuərəns] n. 1. 保证，担保，确信；2. 把握，信心；3.（人寿）保险

execution [ˌeksi'kjuːʃən] n. 实行，执行，实施

conceive [kən'siːv] vt. & vi. 想出（主意、计划等）；，构想，设想

client ['klaiənt] n. 业主

submit [səb'mit] vt. 提交 e. g. submit a case to the court 向法院提出诉讼

amend [ə'mend] vt. 改正，改良，改善；正式地修正（议案等）；校正；变更

　e. g.　amend the Constitution 修改宪法；

implement ['implimənt] vt. 实现，使生效，执行

compatibility [kəmˌpæti'biliti] n. 适合，适应（性）；一致（性），协调（性）

　e. g.　Mechanisms of monitoring and mutual compatibility are to be highlighted. 需要强调的是监督机制和政策的相互协调性。

inspection [in'spekʃən] n. 检查；检验；检阅；验收

　e. g.　Inspection Certificate of Weight 重量检验证书

verification [ˌverifi'keiʃən] n. 证实 [明，据]；验证，核对；

　e. g.　verification of machines 机器的核准 [检定]

submission [səb'miʃən] n. 提交，呈递

New phrases for reference

contractual obligation　合同义务

project director　项目总监

quality management policy　质量管理方案

in connection with　关于…；与…有关；有联系

　　e. g. His name was mentioned in connection with the invention.
他的名字连同这项发明一起被提及。

Project Manager　项目经理

Senior Project Manager　高级项目经理

shop drawings　施工图

in charge of　负责，主管

　　e. g. He is in charge of recreation.　他负责娱乐活动。

be dedicated to…　致力于…

be responsible for …　对…负责

logistic & procurement office　后勤物资采购室

Quality Assurance Engineer　质保工程师

Corporate Project Management　公司项目管理

be relevant to　与…有关

　　e. g. These facts are relevant to the case　这些事实和此案有关

Procurement & Delivery Programme　采购与运输计划

Construction Programme　建筑计划

Progress Report ／ Daily Report　进度报告/ 日报告

Safety Report　安全报告

Testing Results　检验

施 工 方 案

1.0　目的与范围

　　本文件阐述京汇国际工程有限公司如何对工程进行设计、执行、协调以及完工并且履行其所有的合同义务，取得里程碑性的成就。

2.0　组织机构——责任

　　项目总监负责工程全面的管理，这里包括确定质量管理方案并且说明整个工程的质量问题。他还应当对由京汇国际工程公司承担的与此工程相关的设计工作负全责。

　　高级项目经理负责协助项目总监提供设计的进展、设计方案的统一，准备详细的设计方案、施工图并在需要时负责提交其他相关文件。高级项目经理还要讲明设计理念，并且与承包方及工程的其他方面进行协调。

　　项目经理要把所有时间投入到其项目上，在项目总监的指导下负责该项目的全面工作。

　　后勤物资采购部在采购整体工作上向公司项目管理部门负责，确保材料和工人都能在项目的计划时间到达现场，满足施工现场的需求。

质量工程师负责质量管理体系的全面运行与实施效果。

3.0 施工步骤

公司项目管理部门将对与本项目相关的所有管理和操作环节进行审查，要确保所有的管理制度有计划、有准备、有文件且被执行，以达到合同的目标要求。

计划中的施工还应包括：

划分组织并分配职责，以确保项目合乎要求。

制定管理体系文件的框架及明确各文件之间的关联。

制定职责范围内的所有文件（如计划，手册，程序和方法，报表等）。

按照公司内部合同对于监督、特殊工艺、设备资源和技能的要求，确保有相应的明确规定。

确保设计、安装过程、检测的兼容性。

确保检测在本项目的范围内，并有相应的可用设备。

确保在施工方案中为特殊技术的发展留有足够的余地。

施工方案的各阶段建有相应的审核和检查，并建立相应的标准。

所有质量记录都有标识。

4.0 提交

以下项目要提交业主进行审查批准：

图纸

样本

采购与运输计划

施工进度计划

进度报告/ 日报告（包括进展图片）

月劳动分析/ 设备 分析/ 材料分析

安全报告

检验报告（如果可行）

TEXT B

EVELEIGH HERITAGE WALK
CONSTRUCTION METHOD STATEMENT

1 SCOPE OF METHOD STATEMENT

This method statement relates to the construction of foundations and superstructures for a pedestrian overbridge across the rail corridor at the western end of the Redfern Station platforms.

The scope of work comprises the construction of the footbridge and associated pedestrian ramps and stairs on North Eveleigh Plaza and the Australian Technology Park, on the north and south sides of the corridor respectively.

2 GENERAL APPROACH TO CONSTRUCTION

The construction staging of the project will involve activities on the sites of the North Eveleigh Plaza and the Australian Technology Park, with sporadic works during night possessions and specific weekend possessions of some of the tracks of the rail corridor. In parallel with the site construction activities, prefabrication of the bridge and ramp structures will proceed off-site.

The work will culminate with the erection of the pedestrian bridge over the rail corridor, to be carried out during a special weekend possession of most of the tracks in the rail corridor, followed by completion of the bridge internal finishes and completion of construction of the access ramps on the North Eveleigh Plaza and the Australian Technology Park sites.

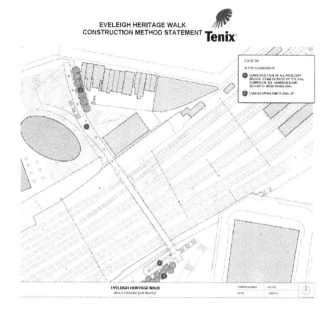

Notes: The table shows the last stage of construction works:

Stage 3B

After possession

①Construction of all ancillary（辅助的）bridge items outside of the rail corridor; Handrails（扶手）and security mesh paneling（安全防护网）.

②Landscaping and clean up.

3　RESOURSES

The following resources will be needed for construction of the bridge over the rail corridor:

Materials

- Reinforced and prestressed concrete, precast and cast-in-situ.
- Structural steel.
- Stainless steel wire mesh.
- Pipes, conduits, electrical cables, telephones, CCTV.

Equipment

- Earth moving equipment for site preparation (eg. D7, D8 dozers, graders, excavators).
- Pile boring rigs.
- Excavators and spoil removal trucks.
- Scaffolding and formwork.
- Concrete construction plant (mixers, pumps).

- Plate compactors, vibratory roller compactors.
- Cranes for erection of falsework, structural steel and precast concrete.
- Flood lights for night work during track possessions.
- New Jersey barriers for demarcation of danger and safe zones.
- Bridge launching equipment, including high-tensile bars and hydraulic jacks.
- Hydraulic jacks for the final lowering of the bridge to its permanent bearings.

Human Resources

Special staff qualified as PO4 (Rail Corporation) will be needed to supervise all operations near the live railway tracks.

4 POTENTIAL CONSTRUCTION IMPACTS

The potential construction impacts resulting from construction of the bridge include:

- Runoff.
- Noise.
- Dust Emissions.

Notes

1. Eveleigh: 伊夫利, 位于澳大利亚悉尼市的郊区

2. Redfern Station: 澳大利亚悉尼郊区的红坊火车站, 红坊 (Redfern) 住有大量的澳大利亚原住民。

3. North Eveleigh Plaza 北伊夫利公园

4. Australian Technology Park 澳大利亚科技园

5. CCTV: Closed Circuit Television 闭路电视, 工业电视

New Words

superstructure ['sjuːpəˌstrʌktʃə] n. 上层建筑;【建】上部结构; 上层构造

pedestrian [peˈdestriən] adj. 步行的; 行人的, 人行的

overbridge ['əuvəbridʒ] n. (跨越铁路或公路的) 天桥; 旱桥

　e. g. pedestrian overbridge 人行天桥

　railroad overbridge 铁路跨线桥 (铁路线在上)

footbridge ['futbridʒ] 行人天桥

sporadic [spəˈrædik] adj. 不定时发生的; 偶发性的; 零星的

possession [pəˈzeʃən] n. 拥有; 占有; [pl.] 所有物; 财产, 财富; 所有权

　e. g. get possession of 拿到, 占有, 占领

　personal possessions 个人财产

prefabricaiton n. 预先制造;【化】预加工

culminate ['kʌlmineit] vi. 达到极点, 达到最高潮;【天】到子午线, 到中天 [最高度]; 告终, 完结 (in)

　e. g. The tower culminates in a 40 – foot spire.

这塔的顶端是一个 40 英尺高的塔尖。

习惯用语：culminate in …以…而终结，以…而达到顶峰，（结果）竟成

ancillary ［æn'siləri］adj. 辅助的，附属的（to）

precast ［'pri：'kɑ：st］vt.，adj.【建】预制（的）；预浇铸（的）

　　e. g. a precast bridge 预制构件桥

dozer ［'dəuzə］n 推土机

grader ［'greidə］n. 平地［土，路］机，推土［筑路］机

excavator ［'ekskəveitə］n. 开凿者；发掘者；挖掘机；挖土机；挖沟机；电铲

scaffold ［'skæfəld］n.【建】脚手架，鹰架；交手（临时搭的）展览台；看台

formwork ［'fɔ：mwə：k］n. 模板，样板；量规；模板成形

crane ［krein］n. 吊车，起重机，升降架，升降设备

falsework ［'fɔ：lswɜ：k］n. 脚手架，工作架，临时支架

demarcation ［di：mɑ：'keiʃən］n.（＝demarkation）边界，分界，设界限

New Phrases

pedestrian ramp　人行道斜坡（坡道）

in parallel with　与…平行

　　e. g. The trees stand in parallel with the road.　这些树与公路平行。

Reinforced and prestressed concrete　预应力钢筋混凝土

cast-in-situ　现浇；就地浇筑；原地铸造

　　e. g. cast-in-situ concrete unit　现浇混凝土组件 cast-in-place pile　灌注桩；现浇桩

structural steel　结构钢

Stainless steel wire mesh　不锈钢金属网

electrical cables　电缆线

boring rig　钻车，钻探架，钻探设备

concrete mixer　水泥搅拌车，混凝土搅拌车

Plate compactors　平板夯实机

vibratory roller compactors　振动压路机

flood light　泛光灯

high-tensile bar　高强度钢条

hydraulic jack【化】液压千斤顶；水力千斤顶

Exercises

I. Translate the following words or phrases into English.

土木工程_____　　　　　　　结构工程_____

永久结构_____　　　　　　　水利工程_____

环境或环卫工程_____

供水_____　　　　　　　　　污水处理系统_____

城市规划_____　　　　　　　军事工程_____

民用_____

II. The following is a brief description of construction. Read it carefully and try your best to figure it out by referring to the Chinese.

Construction

Construction is the translation of a design. It is as important and complicated（复杂的）as the design in order that the structure should performed as it was intended and the work is finished within the required time at the lowest cost（以最低的造价）.

The designer must be in close contact with（保持密切的接触）everything that is done during the construction work so that any change in the site conditions（工地条件）, materials and work being done can be evaluated（判断）and, if necessary, corrected or improved.

The constructors（施工人员）should have the same knowledge of the working-plan（施工计划）as the designer（设计者）. They must also know the details（细节）of the design and must understand any unusual aspect of the design. Both the designer and constructors must always work in harmony（协调一致地）.

More workers are employed during the peak period（施工高峰期）. The employees should be given training（培训）for working skills（工作技能）and knowledge about quality and safety（安全）as early as possible. It will improve the working efficiency（工作效率）a lot.

The construction work can be divided into a number of stages：

1. evaluation of plans, specifications, basic demands and features of the site；
2. plan and speed of the job；
3. making the site ready；
4. building the structure；
5. cleaning up.

The first stage of evaluation consists of a careful study of demands of design and of the site itself. Too often this is not done until the third and fourth stage are under way, which is far too late.

The second stage is most important if the job is to be done economically. The equipments, labor and materials for cach stage in the construction must be provided at time. The third stage is to make the warehouse, concrete mixers, offices and housing for the workman ready.

Of course, this work is often just the beginning; the arrangements are changed several times during the progress of the work.

The major part of the time and money is spent on the building stage.

With the development of science and technology, construction methods（施工方法）have changed in all areas. For example, intellectual building blocks（智能楼宇）are being constructed in a lot of cities. Many daily functions will become automated（自动化）and computer - controlled（由计算机控制）. Thus there will be a demand for more skilled workmen, primarily those having technical background.

New words for reference

complicated ['kɔmplikeitid] adj. 结构复杂的

intend［in′tend］vt. 1. 意欲，打算，计划，想要；2. 打算使，想让…做

evaluate［i′væljueit］vt. 评价，估计，估价

detail［′diːteil］n. 细目，细节 vi. &vt 详细列举；详细说明；详述

constructor［kən′strʌktə］n. 施工员

economically［ˌiːkə′nɔmikəli］adv. 节约地，节俭地；节省地；经济地

safety［′seifti］n. 1. 安全，平安；2. 安全性

efficiency［i′fiʃənsi］n. 1. 效率，效能，功效；2. 实力，效益

evaluation［iˌvælju′eiʃən］n. 估价，评价；估算

warehouse［′wɛəhaus］n. 仓库

automate［′ɔːtəˌmeit］vt. & vi. 1.（使）自动化 adj. ；2. 自动化的

residential［ˌrezi′denʃəl］adj. 1. 住宅的，适于作住宅的；2. 与居住有关的

New phrases for reference

be in contact with　和…接触，有联系

working-plan　施业计划

in harmony　和睦相处

peak period　高峰期

quality and safety　质量与安全

plan and speed of the job　工作的计划与进度

cleaning up　清场

consist of　由…组成

be under way　在进行当中

access road　进场道路

concrete mixer　水泥搅拌车，混凝土搅拌车

施　工

　　施工就是把设计方案变为现实。施工和设计同样是一个非常重要、非常复杂的工程问题，以便使建筑物能起到预期的作用，同时能在要求的时间内以最低的造价完成工程任务。

　　设计者必须在施工时与要做的每一件事保持密切的接触，以便在工地条件、材料和已在做的工作发生任何变化时能够加以判断，必要时可修改设计，做出调整。

　　同样，施工人员应该和设计者一样了解施工计划，施工人员必须熟悉设计细节，必须了解任何例外的设计情况。设计和施工人员必须自始至终，协调一致地工作。

　　在施工高峰会招聘许多工人，必须提前对这些雇工进行工作技能和质量安全方面的培训，那会大大提高工作效率。

　　施工工作可分为几个阶段：

　　1. 设计、规范、基本要求和现场特点等的评价；

　　2. 工程计划和进度；

　　3. 现场准备；

　　4. 修建结构物；

5. 清场。

第一阶段的评价包括详细研究设计要求和现场本身的要求，往往出现这种情况：第三阶段和第四阶段的工作已在进行，而第一阶段的工作还没有做出评价，这实在是为时太晚了。

如果要求工程能经济地完成的话，第二阶段是至关重要的。施工过程中每个阶段所需的设备、劳力和材料都必须按时供应。

第三阶段包括修建进场道路和准备好仓库、混凝土搅拌机、工作人员的办公室和住房。

当然这些工作往往只不过是刚开始，在工程进展的期间内，这些安排常常还要改变好几次，大部分时间和资金都花在施工阶段上。

随着科学技术的发展，施工方法在各个领域都将发生变化。比如，智能楼宇正在多个城市兴建。许多日常工作特别是住宅楼的施工都将自动化，并由计算机控制。因此，将需要更多的专门人才，主要是受过技术培训的人才。

III. *Read the following passage carefully and make the multiple choices.*
The organization chart of a project

The organization chart provided by this contractor of DA Long power station is a typical organization for large plants.

There are around 200 people composing the project management. The top management has 3 people only. They are project manager（项目经理）, deputy project management（项目副经理）and chief engineer（总工）.

Under project management there are five departments：works, technical, procurement, administration and quality department.

Works department（工程部）is the largest one and responsible for all construction sections（工段）and terms, whose manager is also the deputy project manager（项目副经理）.

Procurement department（物资部）is in charge of material and construction equipment supply and warehouse（仓库）.

Quality department（质保部）is a special agency（机构）controlled by both project management and the headquarter（总部）of the company. The quality works will be supervised（监管）by the superior（上级）of the site management, and it is rather independent（独立）of quality department to make decisions without any interference（干涉）from the site management people.

Administration department（行政部）is in charge of（掌管）all matters related to finance and public relationship.

Technical department（技术部）is in charge of all matters about drawings and designing of temporary facilities and deals with the subcontract（分包）matters.

1. How many people are involved in the top management?
A. around 200　　　　B. about 200　　　　C. 3　　　　D. 5

2. How many departments are under project management?
A. 5　　　　B. 3　　　　C. 6　　　　D. None.

3. Which department is rather independent?

A. Works department   B. Procurement department

C. Quality department   D. Technical department

4. Which department is in charge of the warehouse?

A. administration department   B. technical department

C. procurement department   D. works department

5. Who will supervise quality department?

A. CEO of the company   B. the project manager

C. both the project manager and the chief engineer

D. both the project manager and the headquarter of the company

TRANSLATION SKILLS

科技英语特点之二

科技文章文体的特点是：清晰、准确、精练、严密。那么，科技文章的语言结构特色在翻译过程中如何处理，这是进行英汉科技翻译时需要探讨的问题。现分述如下：

一、大量使用名词化结构

《当代英语语法》（A Grammar of Contemporary）在论述科技英语时提出，大量使用名词化结构（Nominalization）是科技英语的特点之一。因为科技文体要求行文简洁、表达客观、内容确切、信息量大、强调存在的事实，而非某一行为。例如：

1. Archimeds first discovered the principle of displacement of water by solid bodies.

阿基米德最先发展固体排水的原理。

句中 of displacement of water by solid bodies 系名词化结构，一方面简化了同位语从句，另一方面强调 displacement 这一事实。

2. The rotation of the earth on its own axis causes the change from day to night.

地球绕轴自转，引起昼夜的变化。

名词化结构 the rotation of the earth on its own axis 使复合句简化成简单句，而且使表达的概念更加确切严密。

3. If you use firebricks round the walls of the boiler, the heat loss. can be considerably reduced.

炉壁采用耐火砖可大大降低热耗。

科技英语所表述的是客观规律，<u>因之要尽量避免使用第一、二人称；此外，要使主要的信息置于句首</u>。

4. Television is the transmission and reception of images of moving objects by radio waves.

电视通过无线电波发射和接受活动物体的图像。

名词化结构 the transmission and reception of images of moving objects by radio waves 强调

客观事实，而谓语动词则着重其发射和接受的能力。

二、非限定动词

如前所述，科技文章要求行文简练，结构紧凑，为此，往往使用分词短语代替定语从句或状语从句；使用分词独立结构代替状语从句或并列分句；使用不定式短语代替各种从句；介词十动名词短语代替定语从句或状语从句。这样可缩短句子，又比较醒目。试比较下列各组句子。

1. A direct current is a current flowing always in the same direction.

直流电是一种总是沿同一方向流动的电流。

2. Radiating from the earth, heat causes air currents to rise.

热量由地球辐射出来时，使得气流上升。

3. Materials to be used for structural purposes are chosen so as to behave elastically in the environmental conditions.

结构材料的选择应使其在外界条件中保持其弹性。

4. There are different ways of changing energy from one form into another.

将能量从一种形式转变成另一种形式有各种不同的方法。

三、后置定语

大量使用后置定语也是科技文章的特点之一。常见的结构有以下五种：

1. 介词短语

The forces due to friction are called frictional forces.

由于摩擦而产生的力称之为摩擦力。

A call for paper is now being issued .

征集论文的通知现正陆续发出。

2. 形容词及形容词短语。

In this factory the only fuel available is coal.

该厂唯一可用的燃料是煤。

In radiation, thermal energy is transformed into radiant energy, similar in nature to light.

能在辐射时，转换成性质与光相似的辐射能。

3. 副词

The air outside pressed the side in .

外面的空气将桶壁压得凹进去了。

The force upward equals the force downward so that the balloon stays at the level.

向上的力与向下的力相等，所以气球就保持在这一高度。

4. 单个分词，但仍保持较强的动词意义。

The results obtained must be cheeked .

获得的结果必须加以校核。

The heat produced is equal to the electrical energy wasted.

产生的热量等于浪费了的电能。

5. 定语从句

During construction, problems often arise which require design changes.

在施工过程中，常会出现需要改变设计的问题。

The molecules exert forces upon each other, which depend upon the distance between them.

分子相互间都存在着力的作用，该力的大小取决于它们之间的距离。

Very wonderful changes in matter take place before our eyes every day to which we pay little attention.

（定语从句 to which we pay little attention 修饰的是 changes，这是一种分隔定语从句。）

我们几乎没有注意的很奇异的物质变化每天都在眼前发生。

四、常用句型

科技文章中经常使用若干特定的句型，从而形成科技文体区别于其他文体的标志。例如 It…that…结构句型；被动态结构句型；结构句型，分词短语结构句型，省略句结构句型等。举例如下：

It is evident that a well lubricated bearing turns more easily than a dry one.

显然，润滑好的轴承，比不润滑的轴承容易转动。

It seems that these two branches of science are mutually dependent and interacting .

看来这两个科学分支是相互依存，相互作用的。

It has been proved that induced voltage causes a current to flow in opposition to the force producing it.

已经证明，感应电压使电流的方向与产生电流的磁场力方向相反。

It was not until the 19th century that heat was considered as a form of energy.

直到十九世纪人们才认识到热是能量的一种形式。

Computers may be classified as analog and digital.

计算机可分为模拟计算机和数字计算机两种。

The switching time of the new-type transistor is shortened three times .

新型晶体管的开关时间缩短了三分之二。（或……缩短为三分之一。）

This steel alloy is believed to be the best available here .

人们认为这种合金钢是这里能提供的最好的合金钢。

Electromagnetic waves travel at the same speed as light .

电磁波传送的速度和光速相同。

Microcomputers are very small in size , as is shown in Fig. 5.

如图 5 所示，微型计算机体积很小。

In water sound travels nearly five times as fast as in air .

声音在水中的传播速度几乎是在空气中传播速度的五倍。

Compared with hydrogen, oxygen is nearly 16 times as heavy .

氧与氢比较，重量大约是它的十六倍。

The resistance being very high , the current in the circuit was low.

由于电阻很大，电路中通过的电流就小。

Ice keeps the same temperature while melting .

冰在溶化时，其温度保持不变。

An object, once in motion, will keep on moving because of its inertia.

物体一旦运动，就会因惯性而持续运动。

五、复合词与缩略词

大量使用复合词与缩略词是科技文章的特点之一，复合词从过去的双词组合发展到多词组合；缩略词趋向于任意构词，例如某一篇论文的作者可以就仅在该文中使用的术语组成缩略词，这给翻译工作带来一定的困难。例如：

    full-enclosed 全封闭的（双词合成形容词）

    feed-back 反馈（双词合成名词）

    work-harden 加工硬化（双词合成词）

    criss-cross 交叉着（双词合成副词）

    on-and-off-the-road 路面越野两用的（多词合成形容词）

    anti-armoured-fighting-vehicle-missile 反装甲车导弹（多词合成名词）

    radiophotography 无线电传真（无连字符复合词）

    colorimeter 色度计（无连字符复合词）

    maths（mathematics）数学（裁减式缩略词）

    lab（laboratory）实验室

    ft（foot/feet）英尺

    cpd（compound）化合物

    FM（frequency modulation）调频（用首字母组成的缩略词）

    P. S. I.（pounds per square inch）磅/英寸

    SCR（silicon controlled rectifier）可控硅整流器

    TELESAT（telecommunications satellite）通信卫星（混成法构成的缩略词）

    根据上述的科技文章的特点，在翻译过程中就要注意各种不同的翻译技巧与方法。例如被动态的译法、长句的处理方法、倍数的译法等等。

译　文

第二单元　施工方案会审

对　话

施工方案会审

咨询工程师：在对你们的投标文件进行研究之后，我很高兴地通知贵公司有资格进入工程投标第二个阶段，即谈判阶段。

承　包　商：我们很高兴听到这个消息。

咨询工程师：现在，让我们看看施工方案会审。在方案里包含内容很多，让我们先翻到第一章：概述。对于桩预制的现场准备方面，我们注意到你们要在现场制作预制混凝土桩。如果桩在穿透时发生异常情况，你们会怎么做呢？

承　包　商：我们会停止打桩并研究打桩记录，然后用钻孔来弄清楚地基的真实情况，与设计师研究后再做决定增加桩的长度或重新确定桩的位置。

咨询工程师：谢谢，让我们讨论一下施工方案会审的第二章：施工进度计划表。你应该修改这两个主要竣工日期，使之与整个工程的开工日期相匹配。

承　包　商：虽然这些时间太紧很难完成，但我们会重新安排我们的阶段进度计划表，再将修改后的计划表交给你们。

咨询工程师：好吧。来看看第三章组织机构表。

承　包　商：这是一个典型的组织机构表，是为我们曾经施工的大型工业项目而制定的。

咨询工程师：我们看到它看起来像一个庞大的机构，或许太大了。我想要提醒你，只要这些主要工作人员获准为这个项目工作，那么没有我们的允许他们就不能擅自调离。

承　包　商：是的，他们不会。我们明白有能力的人员对于这样一个重要的任务是非常重要的。

咨询工程师：对于第四章劳务配备表，它应该说明在施工阶段每一项工作的人数而不仅仅只是工人数。并且你们对于这个项目所需要的工人数估计不足。对于第五章施工机械计划表，我们赞赏你们为工程调用所有必要的机械设备，但是现场需要用的机械设备仍有不足。

承　包　商：谢谢你对我们投标所提的意见。

咨询工程师：我们希望你们能够在一周之内根据我们的意见修改施工方案并提交会审。

承　包　商：我们一定会制定一套新方案提交给你们。

课　文　A
迪拜码头9AB区 特瑞德特大型居民楼
混凝土养护施工方案
（筏式基础除外）

该施工方案涵盖了混凝土浇筑完工后，除筏式基础之外的楼板、柱、岩心墙等的养护工程。

施工/工程的执行

● 混凝土自压实后，至少在七（7）天内，应免受日晒、风吹、寒冷、雨水或流水等自然因素的影响。

● 混凝土的养护应按规范的要求使用淡水。

水平结构（梁/板）

● 混凝土初凝后应立即以塑料薄膜覆盖整个结构物。

● 混凝土终凝后应洒水进行自然养护，洒水应持续至少7天。

垂直结构（柱/幕墙/岩心墙）

● 模板工程不得影响和破坏结构物。

● 模板工程结束后，结构物表面应洒水、彻底湿润并以粗麻布覆盖至少7天以上。

● 麻布应保持湿润直至上文规定的混凝土养护的时间。

＊＊如使用混凝土养护剂，其应与混凝土表面使用的防水剂或的其他材料相容；并且应另外再上交一份施工方案。

质量控制

● 质量工程师及现场工程师应监督混凝土的养护过程、并每日进行监测。

● 若发现现场有任何不符合规范的操作，应直接向项目经理汇报。

课　文　B
伊夫利 海瑞特人行道施工方案会审

1. 方案会审范围

本方案会审有关红坊火车站站台西端横跨铁轨步行天桥的基础和上部结构的工程建

设。工程范围包括行人天桥工程以及在北伊夫利公园和澳大利亚科技园方向建设与之相连的人行道斜坡和台阶，它们分别位于铁路线的北端和南端。

2. 施工方法概述

工程施工阶段包括在北伊夫特公园和澳大利亚科技园施工现场的项目，在夜间及特定周末有临时施工。现场施工中，桥体和坡体的预制工作在场外完成。跨轨道人行天桥的架设，要在一个专门的周末施工，天桥内部工程以及在北伊夫利公园和澳大利亚科技园现场入口斜坡工程完工，意味着整个工程完工。

备注：图形表明施工的最后一个阶段。

第三阶段。

进场后。

①铁轨外桥体辅助设施的施工，包括扶手安全防护网。

②园林美化及清场。

3. 物资

跨轨道天桥施工需要以下物资：

材料

- 预应力钢筋混凝土，预制和现浇
- 钢材
- 不锈钢金属网
- 管线，导线，电缆线，电话，闭路电视

设备

- 现场准备的运土设备（如 D7、D8 推土机，平土机，挖掘机）
- 钻探设备
- 挖掘机和运土卡车
- 脚手架和模板
- 水泥搅拌车（搅拌机，泵）
- 压路机，振动压路机
- 用于架设脚手架，结构钢件及预制混凝土构件的起重机
- 用于夜间工作的泛光灯
- 危险区域和安全区域的新泽西护栏
- 隔离架设桥梁的滑曳设备，包括高强度钢条的液压千斤顶
- 用于将桥体安装就位于其永久性支座上的液压千斤顶

人力资源

- 需要专门的有资格认证的 P04（铁道公司）人员来监督在铁路线旁所有工作的实施

4. 潜在的施工影响

在建桥过程中可能会带来的施工影响包括：

- 溢水，漏水
- 噪声
- 灰尘的扩散

UNIT *3*

Tender Document and Contracts
（标书与合同）

DIALOGUE

C：Good afternoon! Nice to meet you!

E：Good afternoon! Nice to meet you too. Welcome to our company for tendering of the multi-storey residential building. Here is the tender document for the civil works.

C：There are so many volumes.

E：Yes. Volume 1 is the Contract Conditions, Volume 2 is the Bill of Quantities, Volume3 is Scope of Works, Volume 4 and Volume 5 are Technical Specifications.

C：Are Contract Conditions worked out on the basis of FIDIC Conditions (Conditions of contract for Works of Civil Engineering construction standardized by Federation Internaitonale Des Ingenieurs-Conseils)?

E：Yes, as you know the FIDIC Conditions are fair to both contractor and client, we hope that you will agree with these conditions.

C：Is the contract price a lump sum or a rate basis one?

E：The initial contract price will be calculated out by multiplying rates and quantities presented in the Bill but the final price will be adjusted in accordance with the quantities actually completed by the contractor.

C：Volume 6 is Quality assurance.

E：Yes，the requirement of quality system is similar to ISO 9002 which your company has passed the examination and Volume 7 is drawings. All these drawings are stamped by for "Tender Use". In case you win the tender for the project，you will be issued the drawings stamped by "for Construction Use".

C：That's just what we want to obtain.

E：Now you must see to it that all attachments are to be fulfilled and submitted according to the requirement：

　　1）Letter of Agreement

　　2）Construction Method Statement

　　3）Quality and Safety Programs

　　4）Bill of Quantities

C：OK. Thank you for your explanation.

Notes

1. C：contractor 承包商 E：engineer 咨询工程师

2. Federation Internaitonale Des Ingenieurs – Conseils：国际咨询工程师联合会

3. FIDIC Conditions：即国际咨询工程师联合会编写的《土木工程施工合同条款》，常简称为 FIDIC 条款。它以科学的制度设计和极强的可操作性有效保障工程质量和降低成本而著名，是目前国际上标准、权威的工程管理制度之一，从实际效果上看，它也是铲除工程腐败的重要机制之一。

4. Is the contract price a lump sum or a rate basis one? 合同价格是包干价合同还是单价合同？

New Words

tender [ˈtendə] n. 投标，清偿，偿付

storey [ˈstɔːri] n. 楼层

residential [ˌreziˈdenʃəl] adj. 1. 住宅的，适于作住宅的；2. 与居住有关的

volume [ˈvɔljuːm] n. 1. 卷，册，书卷；2. 体积；容积，容量

specification [ˌspesifiˈkeiʃən] n. 规范

　　e. g. technical specification 技术规范

contractor [ˈkɔnˌtræktə] n. （建筑、监造中的）承包人；承包单位，承包商

subcontractor [ˌsʌbkənˈtræktə] n. 转包商，次承包者，分包商

client [ˈklaiənt] n. 业主

multiply [ˈmʌltiplai] vt. &vi. 乘

adjust [əˈdʒʌst] vt. & vi. （改变…以）适应；调整；校正

assurance［ə′ʃuərəns］n. 保证，担保，确信

stamp［stæmp］vt. 1. 在…上盖章；盖上…的戳记；8. 在…上压印图案（或标记等）

issue［′isju：］vt. 1. 发表，发布；2. 分配，发给

obtain［əb′tein］vt. 获得，得到

attachment［ə′tætʃmənt］n. 1. 附着，附属；2. 附属物，附件

fulfill［ful′fil］vt. 1. 履行（诺言等），完成（任务等），实现；2. 执行（命令等），服从

New Phrases

multi-storey residential building　高层居民楼

tender document　标书

Contract Conditions　合同条款

Bill of Quantities　工程量清单

Scope of Works　工程范围

Technical Specifications.　技术规范

a lump sum　一次性总付款，包干价

a rate basis contract　单价合同

in accordance with［inə′kɔ：dənswið］与…相符

e. g.　in accordance with convention or custom. 与惯例或者风俗一致。

Quality Assurance（QA）　质保手册

be similar to　与…相似

Tender Use　投标专用

win the tender　中标

for Construction Use　施工专用

Letter of Agreement　协议书

Quality and Safety Programs　质量和安全措施

Role Play

Suppose you are the person in charge of a dwelling building. Write a Tender Document in your group, consulting the materials in this unit. Then read the Tender Document to your partner.

TEXT A

AGREEMENT

Agreement

This Agreement made：the 7ᵗʰ day of July 2007.

Between **TRIDENT INTERNATIONAL HOLDING.**, P. O. Box 54426.

Dubai, United Arab Emirates（hereafter called "the employer"）

of the one part and **CSHK Dubai Contracting LTC.** ,
P. O. Box 31496. , Dubai, United Arab Emirates (hereafter called "the contractor") of the other part.

Whereas the employer is desirous the certain works should be executed by the Contractor, viz **Construction of multi-storey Residential Building on Plot 9AB-Dubai Marina, Dubai, UAE** and has accepted a Tender by the Contractor for the execution and completion of such works and the remedying of any defects therein.

Now this agreement witnessed as follows:

1. In this Agreement words and expressions shall have the same meanings as are respectively assigned to them in the Conditions of Contract hereinafter referred to.

2. The following documents shall be deemed to form and read and construed as part of this agreement, viz:

    a. The letter of intent

    b. The said Tender

    c. The Conditions of Contract

    d. The specification

    e. The drawing; and

    f. The Bill of Quantities

3. The consideration of the payments to be made by the Employer to the Contractor hereby covenants with the Employer to execute and complete the works and remedy any defects therein in conformity in all respects with the provisions of the contract.

4. The employer hereby covenants to pay the contractor in consideration of the execution and completion of the works and the remedying of defects therein in the Contract Price or such other sum as may become payable under the provision of the Contract at the times and in the manner prescribed by the contract.

In Witness whereof the authorized representative of the parties have hereunto set their respective hands the day and year first above written

Signed by: _____

Name: _____

Duly authorized to sign this agreement for and on behalf of the **Employer.** In the presence of:

Name: _____

Signature: _____

Address: _____

Occupation: _____

Signed by: _____

Name: _____

Duly authorized to sign this agreement for and on behalf of the **Contractor.** In the presence of:

Name：_____

Signature：_____

Address：_____

Occupation：_____

Notes

1. viz abbreviation【略语】videlicet：adv. That is to say 就是说；namely 即
2. United Arab Emirates 阿拉伯联合酋长国（＝UAE）
3. Dubai 迪拜（阿拉伯联合酋长国的酋长国之一）

New Words

agreement［ə'gri：mənt］n. 协定，协议，契约

employer［im'plɔiə］n. 业主

construction［kən'strʌkʃən］施工

desirous［di'zaiərəs］adj. 渴望…的；想得到…的；希望…的

execute［'eksikju：t］vt. 履行，执行，贯彻，实行，实施；完成

execution［ˌeksi'kju：ʃən］n. 实行，执行，实施

tender［'tendə］n. &vt. 投标

remedy［'remidi］n. 处理方法；改进措施；补偿 vt. 改正；纠正；改进

defect［di'fekt］n. 缺点，过失，瑕疵，缺陷，毛病

therein［ðeər'in］adv. 1. 在那里，在那方面，在那时，在其中 2.（用于强调某事是由某种
情况引起的）那就是，此即，缘此

witness［'witnis］n. 1. 目击者；证人 vt. 亲眼看见，目击 2. 作证，证明

deem［di：m］vt. 认为，相信 vi. 想

construe［kən'stru：］vt. 1. 理解；领会 2. 翻译；作句法分析

covenant［'kʌvənənt］n.（有法律约束的）协议，盟约，公约；承诺，合同
vi. 立约，立誓

　　covenant with 与… 立约

remedy［'remidi］n. 1. 药品，治疗法 2. 补救办法，纠正办法 3. 处理方法；
改进措施；vt. 改正；纠正；改进

representative［ˌrepri'zentətiv］n. 代表

signature［'signitʃə］n. 1. 签名，签字 2. 署名；签署

occupation［ˌɔkju'peiʃən］n. 工作；职业

New Phrases

conditions of contract　合同条件

refer to…　提及；涉及，谈到，提到；关系到

in conformity　与…相符合

on behalf of　代表…
letter of intent　意向书
contract price　合同价格

Role Play

Suppose you will make a contract to build a students'dormitory. Discuss with your partner and tell the students your main consideration. Write a Contract Project Agreement in the form of the sample and read it to all students.

Exercises

I. Answer the following questions.

1. Who is the employer? Who is the contractor?

2. What is the project?

3. Which documents shall be deemed to form and read and construed as part of this agreement?

II. Complete the sentences with the given words or expression. Change the form where necessary.

1. He is _____ (authorize) to sign the agreement on behalf of the company.

2. She is the _____ (represent) of the client.

3. You must read the technical _____ (specify) carefully otherwise you won't be able to understand the details.

4. The employer will arrange to visit the _____ (construct) site.

5. The quality of civil works should be in _____ (accord) with the international standards.

III. Translate the following words or phrases into English.

高层居民楼_____

标书_____

合同条款_____

工程量清单_____

工程范围_____

技术规范_____

质保手册_____

协议书_____

施工方案_____

质量和安全措施_____

意向书_____

合同价格_____

IV. *Translate the following sentences into chinese.*

1. FIDIC Conditions are fair to both contractor and client.

_____

2. The initial contract price will be calculated out by multiplying rates and quantities presented in the Bill but the final price will be adjusted in accordance with the quantities actually completed by the contractor.

_____

_____

_____

V. *Fill in the blanks according to the situation given.*

招 标 书

日期：

一、中华人民共和国从世界银行申请获得贷款，用于支付 CNCM 项目的费用。部分贷款将用于支付工程各种合同。所有依世界银行指导原则具有资格的投标者，都可参加投标。

二、中国 ABC 公司邀请具有资格的投标者提供密封的标书，提供完成合同工程所需的劳力、材料、设备和服务。

三、具有资格的投标者可从以下地址获得更多的信息，或参看招标文件：

ABC 公司

（地址）中华人民共和国安徽省合肥市屯西路 262 号

四、每一位具有资格的投标者在交纳 2000 元人民币，并提交书面申请后，均可从上述地址获得招标文件。

五、每一份标书都要附一份投标保证书，且应不迟于 2001 年 7 月 25 日提交给 ABC 公司。

六、所有标书将在 2001 年 7 月 30 日当着投标者代表的面开标。

七、如果具有资格的国外投标者希望与一位中国国内的承包人组建合资公司，需在投标截止日期前 30 天提出要求。业主有权决定是否同意选定的国内承包人。

八、标前会议将在 2001 年 7 月 27 日于合肥市假日大酒店召开。

INVITATION TO TENDER

Date：

1. The _____ has applied for a _____ from the World Bank towards the cost of CNCM Project. It is intended that part of the proceeds of this loan and credit will be applied to eligible（符合条件的）payment under various _____. Tendering is open to all _____ from eligible source countries as defined under the "Guidelines for procurement" of the World Bank.

2. ABC Company now invites sealed tenders from pre-qualified tenderers for provision（供应）of the necessary _____, _____, _____ and _____ for the construction and completion of the project.

3. Prequalified tenderers may obtain _____ from, and inspect the tender documents at the office of: ABC company.

4. A complete set of tender documents may be _____ by any pre-qualified tenderer for the cost of RMB _____ on the submission of a written application to the above.

5. All tenders must be accompanied by a Tender Security in an acceptable form and must be delivered to ABC Company at the above-mentioned address (refer to Item 3) on or before _____ .

6. Tenders will be opened in the presence of those tenderers'_____ _____ who choose to attend at July 30, 2001.

7. If a prequalified foreign tenderer wishes to form _____ with a _____ , such a request will be considered if received within _____ days before the closing date for submission of tenders. The selected local contractor shall be subject to approval by the _____ .

8. The Pre-Tender Meeting will be held on July 27, 2001 at the following address: _____ .

(reference: People's Republic of China, loan, contracts, tenderers, labor, materials, equipment, services, further information, obtained, 2000, July 25, 2001, representatives, joint venture, domestic contractor, 30, employer, Holiday Inn, Hefei City)

VI. The followings are samples of a letter of agreement. , a letter of tender and a letter of acceptance. Read them carefully and try your best to figure them by referring to the Chinese.

Sample 1
Letter of Agreement (协议书)

1. This Agreement made the _____ day of _____ 2000 between _____ of _____ (hereinafter called "the Employer") of the one part, and _____ of _____ (hereinafter called "the Contractor") of the other part.

2. The Employer and the Contractor agree as follows:
   (a) The Letter of Acceptance dated _____
   (b) The Letter of Tender dated _____
   (c) The Addenda nos _____
   (d) The Conditions of Contract
   (e) The Specification
   (f) The Drawings, and
   (g) The completed Schedules

3. In Witness whereof the parties hereto have caused this Agreement to be executed the day and year first before written in accordance with their respective laws.

协 议 书

1. 本协议书于 200 ____年____月____日由_____的_____（以下简称"雇主"）为一方，和 _____的_____（以下简称"承包商"）为另一方协商签订。

2. 雇主和承包商达成协议

如下：

(a)（日期）的中标函

(b)（日期）的投标函

(c) 补充文件第 号（填编号）

(d) 合同条件

(e) 规范

(f) 图纸，以及

(g) 已填写的资料表

3. 此协议书由双方根据各自法律签字之日起实施，特立此据。

Sample 2
Letter of Tender（投标函）

NAME OF CONTRACT：

To：_____

We have examined the Conditions of Contract, Specification, Drawings, Bill of Quantities, the other Schedules, the attached Appendix and Addenda Nos <u>（填文件号）</u> for the execution（实施）of the above-named Works. We offer to execute（实施）and complete the Works and remedy（修补）any defects（缺陷）therein in conformity with（与……一致）this Tender which includes all these documents, for the sum of（in currencies of payment）<u>（用支付货币填写）</u> or such other sum as may be determined in accordance with（与……一致）the Conditions of Contract.

We accept your suggestions for the appointment of the DAB（Dispute Adjudication Board 争端裁决委员会），as set out in Schedule.

We agree to abide（遵守）by this Tender until <u>（日期）</u> and it shall remain binding upon US and may be accepted at any time before that date. We acknowledge（承认）that the Appendix forms part of this Letter of Tender.

If this offer is accepted, we will provide the specified Performance Security, commence（开始）the Works as soon as is reasonably practicable after the Commencement Date（开工日期），and complete the Works in accordance with the above-named documents within the Time for Completion（竣工时间）.

Unless and until a formal Agreement is prepared and executed this Letter of Tender, together with your written acceptance thereof, shall constitute a binding contract between US.

We understand that you are not bound to accept the lowest or any tender you may receive.

Signature _____ in the capacity of _____

duly authorized to sign tenders for and on behalf of _____

Address：_____

_____

_____

Date：_____

投 标 函

合同名称：

致：

    我方已研究了为实施上述工程的合同条件、规范、图纸、工程量表、其他资料表、所附的附录及第_____号（填文件编号）补充文件。我方愿以的总额（用支付货币填写），或按照合同条件可能确定的此项其他总额的报价，按照本投标书，包括所有这些文件，实施和完成工程并修补其中任何缺陷。

    我方接受贵方在资料表中列出的关于任命争端裁决委员会（以下简称 DAB）的建议。我方同意遵守本投标书直至_____，在该日期前，本投标书对我方一直具有约束力，随时可接受中标。我方承认所附附录为本投标函的一部分。

    如果我方中标，我方将提供规定的履约担保，将在开工日期后，尽早开工，并在竣工时间内，按照上述文件完成所述工程。

    除非并直到制定并实施正式协议书，本投标函以及你方书面中标通知，应构成你我双方间有约束力的合同。

    我方理解贵方没有必须接受最低标或任何投标的义务。

签字_____职务_____

正式授权签署投标书代表_____

地址：_____

日期：_____

Sample 3
A Letter of Acceptance（中标通知书）

The Nanjing No. 1 Construction Company, May13th, 2006, 7520, 000

2011, SHENGHUA office building, April, 15th, 2006, Jianye Zhang

Form of Letter of Acceptance

Contract NO. 1 _____

［date］：2 _____

To：3 _____ ［name and address of the successful bidder］

Dear Sirs,

This is to notify you that the works of your 4 _____ ［bid dated］for

construction of 5 _____ ［name of project］for the contract price

of 6 _____ Yuan（RMB）is hereby accepted by our agency. You are asked to be ready for signing the contract. Yours faithfully

7 ＿＿＿＿＿＿＿＿＿＿ ［signature，name，and title of signatory authorized to sign on behalf of the employer］.

Date：may，13th，2006

Key to the blanks：

1. 2011

2. May 13th，2006

3. The Nanjing No. 1 Construction Company

4. April 15th，2006

5. SHENGHUA office building

6. 7520，000

7. Jianye Zhang

中标通知书格式

合同号：2011

日期：2006、5、13

致：南京第一建筑公司［中标人名称和地址］

先生们：贵单位于 2006 年 4 月 15 日为建设盛华办公楼［工程名称］以人民币 752，000 元所提交的投标书已被我方接受。请做好签署合同的准备。谨致。

张建业［被授权代表业主签署本通知书的人签字并加盖公章］

2006 年 5 月 13 日

TEXT B

Instructions to Tenderers

SUBMISSION OF TENDERS

Tenders should be submitted in duplicate and will be accepted only on the form of Tender provided which shall be completed in full.

The tender shall be signed by a principal duly authorized to represent and bind the tenderer.

The amount of tender and the rates and prices inserted in the Bills if Quantities shall be fully inclusive，without limitation，of all liabilities and obligations to be borne by the contractor in accordance with the Contract.

The amount of tender and all rates and prices shall be in UAE Dirhams.

A lump sum firm price shall be submitted.

The duplicated Forms of Tender together with all appendices shall be completed in

full and submitted with the following：

a) The Tender Bond together with a duplicate copy in the style set out by the Specimen Form of Tender Bond annexed to these instructions and valid for the period stated in the Form of Tender.

b）All the additional information required by the Appendices to the From of Tender for the purpose of adjusted tenders e. g. the name of any sub-contractors to whom it is intended to sub-let part of the Works.

c）Fully price out duplicate copies of the Bills of Quantities.

d）The return of all Tender Documents provided by the employer for the purpose of tendering.

The tender and any accompanying documents shall be enclosed in a sealed envelop, whose cover shall not have any mark indicating the name of the sender, but which shall be marked in Arabic and English as:

Tender for: Main Building Contract

                  Multi-storey Residential Building on Plot 9AB, Dubai Marina

                  Dubai

                  United Arab Emirates

Shall be addressed to: Trident International Holdings

                  P. O. Box 5446

                  Dubai

                  United Arab Emirates

The tender shall be delivered not later than the time and date stated in the letter of invitation to tender.

The award of a contract following a favorable assessment of this tender shall not imply approval of any sub-contractor, supplier or proposed manufacturer so named by the tenderer in his submission.

The tenderer shall enclose with his tender a letter with his company's letterhead, giving full particular as follows:

a）the full name and address of the tenderer.

b）the full name and business address of the owner or the chief executive of the tenderer's company.

c）the full name and address of the tenderer's sponsor, agent or representative in Dubai if the tender is not a local Dubai Company.

TEDNER OPENING

Tenders will be opened by the Employer together with representative from the consultants.

Tenderers will not be invited to the Tender opening unless by prior arrangement with the employer.

TENDER DOCUMENTS

The tender document provided for the purpose of tendering are:

a）instructions

b）the form of tender, together with all appendices

c）the Conditions of Contract

d）the drawings listed in the Project Specification

e）the Project Specification

f）the Bill of quantities

ACCEPTANCE OR REJECTIOM OF TENDERS

The employer does not bind itself to accept the lowest or any tender and will not assign any reason for the rejection of any tender.

The employer will not be responsible for paying any expenses or losses, which may be incurred by any tenderer in the preparation of this tender.

COMPLETION OF DOCUMENT

The completion of all tender documentation shall be in Blank ink.

CONFIDENTIALITY

All documents issued and information given to the tenderer shall be treated as confidential.

Notes

UAE Dirhams 阿拉伯联合酋长国货币迪拉姆

New Words

tenderer ['tendərə] n. 投标人

duplicate ['djuːplikit] n. 复制品，抄件；adj. 完全一样的，复制的，成双的，成对的；vt. 其他读音：[djuːplikeit]. 复制，复印，使成双，使成对

authorize ['ɔːθəraiz] vt. 授权，批准；委托

insert [in'səːt] vt. 插入，嵌入

inclusive [in'kluːsiv] adj. 包括…的，包括一切的

liability [ˌlaiə'biliti] n. 责任，义务；倾向

obligation [ˌɔbli'geiʃən] n. 义务；责任；职责

appendices [ə'pendiˌsiːz] n. 附录，附属品

specimen ['spesimən] n. 1. 范例，典范，实例；2. 样品，标本

annexed ['æneksid] adj. 附加的，附属的

valid ['vælid] adj. 1. 有效的；2. 有法律效力的；3. 系统认可的；4. 奏效的，生效的

accompany [ə'kʌmpəni] vt. 1. 陪伴，陪同；2. 伴随…同时发生

enclose [in'kləuz] vt. 把…装入信封，附入

seal [siːl] vt. 1. 盖章于，盖戳，在…上加盖检验封印；2. 密封

assessment [ə'sesmənt] n. 评估，评定，评价

sponsor ['spɔnsə] vt. 赞助，资助 n. 助者，赞助商，资助者

representative [ˌrepri'zentətiv] n. 1. 代表；2. 代理人

consultant [kən'sʌltənt] n. 顾问

prior [praiə] adj. 1. 优先的，在前的，较早的；2. 占先的，较重要的；3. 在前面的

rejection [ri'dʒekʃən] n. 拒绝；退回

bind [baind] vt. & vi. （使）结合，（使）联合在一起

expense [iks'pens] n. 1. 消耗，花费；2. 花费的钱，费用，开支，花费

confidential. [ˌkɔnfiˈdenʃəl] adj. 秘密的，机密的

New Phrases

a lump sum firm price　包干价合同价格
form of Tender　标书格式
for the purpose of…　为了…的目标
not later than…　不得迟于…
the award of a contract　授标
approve of…　赞成，赞同
a letter of invitation to tender　招标函
chief executive　总经理
tender opening　开标

Exercises

Read the following English material and try to translate it into Chinese.
Contract

The content in the contract needed to be fulfilled and submitted by the contractors：

1）Letter of agreement
2）Construction method statement
3）Quality and safety programs
4）Bill of quantities

Letter of agreement is the promise of the Contractor to the Employer. It mentions the total initial contract price, the commence date, the completion date and the maintenance period. It must be signed by the legal representative of the contractor or his authorized person.

For construction Method Statement, several attachments should be accomplished by contractors, which include Construction Method Description, Construction Schedules, Site Organization Chart, Key Person's Information, Workmen Schedules, Construction Equipment Schedule, Layout for Production Area and Living Area, Charts of Electricity and Water Requirement, List of Main Supplier and Subcontractors, List of Repair Parts, and so on.

Part 3 is Quality Program and Safety Program and Part 4 is the bill of quantities, which is rather complicated. When calculating the contract value, each rate should include direct cost (e. g. material cost, labor cost, machine cost) and indirect cost (e. g. staff salary, office fees, camp cost, transportation of workers, overheads, profit, taxes, bank guarantees, insurance).

Contrary to only considering the tender price, the employer or engineer will accept the very contractor in accordance with their comprehensive analysis and judgment to tender documents of contractors.

TRANSLATION SKILLS

从词汇、句法、篇章看工程英语翻译

工程英语作为英语的一种文体，正日渐成为工程科技人员与国外同行进行信息交流的重要手段。与文学等其他文体不同，工程英语所阐述的内容主要是过程、规律、规则和概念等事实，其表达形式简练而重点突出，句式严谨，逻辑性强。因此，工程英语的翻译应与该专业的自身特点相结合，与中国最新颁布的设计规范相结合，力求准确、专业、严谨、流畅。针对工程英语翻译中词汇、句法和篇章等方面的特点进行分析，探讨工程英语的翻译方法和技巧。

一、工程英语的语言特点

1. 词汇特点

工程英语的词汇与城市规划、建筑结构、材料、设备、施工以及管理等密切相关，基础英语很少涉及这些专业化的词汇。因此，常用词汇专业化的现象非常普遍。同时，工程英语词义内涵比较广泛，词的用法灵活，一词多义、一词多用等现象较多。加上大量复合词、缩略词以及各种构词法所创造的新词，使得工程英语的词汇错综复杂且歧义颇多。

例如：stress 在基础英语中常翻译为"重压、强调"，而在工程英语中常以"应力"出现；boring 不是"令人厌烦的"，而是"钻孔"；weather 不仅是"天气"，还是"风化、侵蚀"；moment 不是"片刻"，而是"力矩"。

2. 句法特征

工程英语大都是一些说明性质的论文，注重事实和逻辑推导，严谨精确，毫不含糊，因而大量使用冗长而复杂的句子，从句带短语，从句套从句，相互依附，相互制约，错综复杂，盘根错节。所以在句子分析上存在很多修饰成分。例如，分词短语、定语从句、宾语从句、表语从句等。表述中多使用被动语态，避开人的感情因素，使对现象的表述、对规律的论证、对事理的分析和对事物的相互关系的推理更显客观。

3. 文体形式

工程英语的文体结构严谨，逻辑严密，文体形式常见的有科技论文、文摘、实验报告、工业标准、专题评述、专利说明书等，体裁以说明文为主。

二、工程英语的翻译

英语和汉语属两种完全不同的语系，无论在词汇，还是在语法结构上都存在巨大差异。因此，工程英语翻译者要在忠实原文的前提下，摆脱原文形式的束缚，使自己的译文通顺流畅，更符合译文的语言规范。在翻译过程中，一方面要求译文与原文的信息具有等价性，保证信息的等价转化；另一方面还要求译文具有较强的传递性，保证目的语的读者能够完整而准确地获得原作信息。工程英语翻译中几种常用翻译技巧和方法总结如下：

1. 词汇翻译力求"信、准"

英语译成汉语时，首先需要解决的问题是单词词义的选择，力求"信、准"，同时要合乎专业规范术语要求，为翻译句子"达、顺"打基础。因此，译者必须具备相当的工程专业基础知识。

2. 同义词和近义词的翻译

在工程英语翻译中，翻译者常遇到同义词或近义词的选词问题。例如"淤泥"一词，对应的英文词，有的词典用 silt（牛津英汉双解词典），有的书上用 muck，还有的用 ooze、sludge 等。事实上，这些词都不十分恰当，因为"淤泥"一词严格来说在英文中没有对等的词，在中文中它代表一种特殊土，"淤"代表一种成因，"土"代表组成物质，在英汉互译时我们应根据具体描述来确定选词，而不能简单直译，必要时可以加注。又如 foundation、base、basis 都可译成基础，通过查阅工程词典，可知道 base 有"底垫层、打底层"等含义，而 foundation 则侧重"地基"。再结合工程内容来选词，因此路面施工中的"基层"要译为 base course；而"桩基"应译为 pile foundation。Basis 表示"根据、基础"主要用于比喻意义中。

3. 缩略词的翻译

在工程英语翻译中经常会遇到许多缩略词，要弄清这些缩略词所代表的含义，工程翻译人员不但要熟悉工程的背景情况，而且要了解这些缩略词的缩略方式。一般来说，有以下几种缩略方式：

（1）列出固定词组中每一个词的首字母，例如：RIP 和 EDM 分别是由 Road Improvement Program（道路改造工程）和 Electronic Distance Measuring（电子距离测量）缩略而成的。

（2）半缩略词。一般是采用词组中的前两个词的首字母加后面的词构成的：例如：A-D line 是由 Advance-Decline line（升降线）缩略成的。

（3）缩略某词的一部分，如词的开首部分或结尾部分。例如：auteq 和 atht 分别是由 automatic equipment（自动设备）和 atomic heat（原子热容量）缩略而成的。

（4）外来缩略词的使用。如：vs，i. e，lb，e. g。等。它们分别是拉丁 versus（与相对），idest（即），Libra（磅）和 exempli gratia（例如）的缩略词。

4. 句法翻译争取"达、顺"。

工程英语的句子大多主次分明、指代清楚、关联严密，这要求在翻译时，按照句式特点和句子的本身的内在逻辑关系灵活组织译文。

5. 篇章翻译做到"畅、雅"

工程英语作为一种信息文体，着重说明事物的特点性能、阐明观念原理，强调准确性、严密性和逻辑性，因而在语篇形式上特别强调逻辑衔接。这种衔接一般体现在连接词的使用上。例如：

To obtain a QSRR model, the compounds must be represented by molecular descriptors and retain as much structure information as possible. Here quantum chemical descriptors were used because they could be easily obtained using quantum chemistry program and also had specific chemical meaning.

这段话使用了多种连接手段，如表示并列的"and"，表示递进的"also"，表示因果关系的"because"。这些连接词不仅使语篇衔接连贯，还有助于使作者的复杂思维显得清晰流畅、层次分明。还有一些段落在翻译时，如果按照原有的结构形式难以达到条理分明、干脆利落的表达效果，此时可采用化整为零的方法，先归纳，然后逐一说明。

对于篇章的翻译，由于工程英语要求客观公正，避免随意性，因此，语气特征以陈述句为主，文体特征客观朴素，几乎不使用隐喻、夸张、拟人、反语等修辞手法。工程英语翻译不是简单地传达原文意思，而应在理解和忠实原文的基础上，摆脱原文的束缚，不拘泥于词与词、字与字、句与句，按意思和逻辑关系，综合运用翻译技巧和方法进行翻译。

译　文

第三单元　标书与合同

对　话

承　包　商：下午好！见到你很高兴！

咨询工程师：下午好！见到你也很高兴！欢迎参加我们公司的高层居民楼投标会。这是民用建筑投标书。

承　包　商：有这么多章节。

咨询工程师：是的，第1章是合同条款，第2章是工程量清单，第3章是工程范围，第4章和第5章是技术规范。

承　包　商：合同条款是依据FIDIC条款（国际咨询工程师联合会编写的《土木工程施工合同条款》）拟定的吗？

咨询工程师：是的，正如你所了解的一样，FIDIC条款对承包商和业主双方都是公平的。我们希望你们会同意这些条款。

承　包　商：合同价格是包干价合同还是单价合同？

咨询工程师：起初的合同价格由清单上的定额乘以数量得出。但是最终的价格要根据承包商实际完成的数量做些调整。

承　包　商：第6章是质保手册。

咨询工程师：质量体系的要求与你们已通过检查的ISO 9002类似。第7章是图纸。所有这些绘图都要加盖"投标专用"章。一旦你们项目投标成功，您将得到加盖"施工专用"章的图纸。

承　包　商：正如我们所想。

咨询工程师：根据要求，你们必须完成和提交投标书的所有内容：

1）协议书

2）施工方案

3）质量和安全措施

4）工程量清单

承　包　商：好的。谢谢你给我们的解释。

课文 A　协议书

本协议书于2007年7月7日由特瑞得特国际控股公司阿拉伯联合酋长国迪拜54426邮箱（以下简称"业主"）为一方，与CSHK迪拜承包有限公司阿拉伯联合酋长国迪拜

31496 邮箱（以下简称"承包人"）为另一方签定。鉴于业主欲由承包人承建本项工程，即位于阿拉伯联合酋长国迪拜，占地 9AB 的高层住宅楼建造工程，并已接受承包人提出的承担该项工程之施工、竣工并修补其任何缺陷的投标书，兹为以下事项达成本协议：

1. 本协议书中的措辞和用语应具有与下文提及的合同条件中分别赋予它们的相同的含义。

2. 下列文件应被认为是组成本协议书的一部分，并应作为其一部分进行阅读和理解：

    a. 意向书

    b. 上述投标书

    c. 合同条件

    d. 规范

    e. 图纸；以及

    f. 工程量清单

3. 考虑到下文中提及的业主准备付给承包人各项款额，承包人特此立约向业主保证在各方面均遵守合同的规定进行施工及竣工并修补任何缺陷。

4. 业主特此立约保证在合同规定的各项期限内以合同规定的方式向承包人支付合同价格或合同规定的其他应支付款项，以作为本工程施工、竣工及修补其任何缺陷的报酬。

特此立据。上述日期由双方授权代表在此签署订立

业主签名＿＿＿＿＿＿＿＿＿＿

姓名＿＿＿＿＿＿＿＿＿

经授权代表业主并为业主签署本协议。

本合同在以下证人在场时签订：

姓名

签名

地址

职业

承包方签名

姓名

经授权代表承包人并为承包人签署本协议

或由以下证人在场签订：

姓名

签名

地址

职业

课文 B 标书说明

标书的递交

递交的标书应一式两份且必须将所提供的标书表格逐项填全。

标书应由经授权代表投标方并对投标方有约束力的公司负责人签字。

承包方应依照合同负担包含所有数额在内的账单所列投标金额及全部费用，并承担所有责任和义务。

投标金额和全部费用应以阿拉伯联合酋长国货币迪拉姆表示。

递交的合同价格应为包干价。

标书应一式两份连同所有附件应在全部填完后连同以下文件一起递交：

a）投标保函和一份标书合同表格样本的复印件，附加说明且按标书表格格式予以有效阐述。

b）标书附件所需的全部附加材料，为调整标书之用，比如有意承担工程转包项目的分包商的名字。

c）全额算出的工程量清单一式两份。

d）返还由业主提供的为投标之用的所有投标文件。

标书及其附带文件需装入信封并密封，信封上不应有任何说明发信人名字的标记，但上面应用阿拉伯语或英语写明：

投标工程：阿拉伯联合酋长国 迪拜

占地 9AB 的高层住宅楼

主楼合同

应 寄 往：阿拉伯联合酋长国 迪拜

特瑞得特国际控股公司

54462 邮箱

标书寄送时间应不晚于招标函后注明的日期和时间。

对于获得好评的投标书进行授标。但授标并不意味着对该投标商在其投标书中提及的分包商、供应商及生产厂商的认可。

标书内应附上用公司专用信笺书写的文件，具体内容如下：

a）投标方的全称和地址。

b）投标方公司老板或董事长的全名及业务地址。

c）如果投标方不是迪拜当地公司，则要有投标方在迪拜担保人，代理人或代表的全名和地址。

开标

业主连同咨询公司代表一块进行开标活动。

投标方除非业主事先安排否则将不予邀请参加开标仪式。

标书文件

为投标之用的标书文件有：

a）说明

b）标书表格，以及所有附件

c）合同条件

d）工程规范中所列图纸

e）工程规范

f）工程量清单

接受与拒绝标书

业主不保证接受的是最低报价，不承诺接受某一标书且没有义务说明拒绝标书的理由。业主不负担任何投标人为标书的准备而产生的费用及损失。

文件的完成

所有标书文件都应用黑墨水完成。

保密性

所有投标方提交的文件及资料都将视为机密。

UNIT 4

Access to the Site（进场）

DIALOGUE

Laying out the Site

（To start the execution of the works, the contractor needs to take possession of the site from the owner and plan the layout of the whole site for approval by the owner. Today, Mr. Bian, project manager from the Contractor, and Mr. Cheng, chief engineer, are talking to the owner's Representative, Mr. Sukhnandan about the plan to lay out the whole site.)

Sukh：The other day, you told me that you were going to build up two camps on the site. Could you elaborate on your plan?

Bian：According to our construction plan, our first camp, which we call "Camp A", will be located at the junction of the two access roads leading to the construction site. It will mainly be used for storage of construction materials and spare parts. A parking lot and a repair shop will be set up within this area.

Sukh：What will be the size of this camp?

Bian：It will cover an area of about 4000 square meters.

Sukh：That's acceptable. This piece of land belongs to the government. We'll get it approved soon. What about the other camp?

Bian: The other camp, which we call "Camp B", is mainly for the accommodation of the Chinese professionals and the offices, which belongs to main camp.

Sukh: Where will it be located?

Bian: On the right-hand side of the access road, about a mile from Camp A. it will occupy approximately the same area. Now, I would like Mr. Cheng to describe our plan to arrange the other temporary facilities on the site.

Cheng: Based on our investigations, we have found a piece of land with a gentle slope, where we want to locate the batching plant and the crushing system because it is very close to the construction site and easy to be flattened.

Sukh: That's good. Will you submit to us all the layout of the temporary works together with a letter of application? We'll try to get them approved soon, if possible.

Bian: The sooner, the better.

Sukh: I will do my best. All I can promise is that you will have a reply within a week, whether positive or negative.

Bian: That's what the Contract says!

Notes

1. 由于能否及时占有现场直接关系到承包商是否能顺利地实施工程，承包商在施工准备阶段（construction preparation stage）的最重要的任务之一就是督促业主将现场按时移交（hand over the site on time）。一旦业主没按时移交现场，承包商要在规定的时间内，向业主发出有关工期及费用的索赔意向通知（notification of his intention to claim），以弥补自己的损失。

2. 合理的现场布置有助于承包商高效率地进行工作。生活营地（man camp），材料储存场（storage area），混凝土搅拌厂（batching plant），以及施工设备停放场（parking lot）的安排要以便利施工为标准。但现场的布置一般要征得业主的同意。由于环境保护等方面的原因，有时现场的设置还要经主管部门（appropriate department）审批。承包商要尽力说服业主同意自己安排并寻求主管部门的批准。为此，承包商可向业主作出一些有关的承诺。

New Words

execution [ˌeksiˈkjuːʃən] n. 实行，实施；执［履］行，完成

　　e.g. carry/put into execution 实行，实施，完成

approval [əˈpruːvəl] n. 核定；批准；赞成；认可；通过，证明

　　e.g. give one's approval to 批准

representative [ˌrepriˈzentətiv] n. 代表，代理人

　　e.g. sales representative 销售代表

elaborate [iˈlæbərət] -rated, -rating 详细阐述

　　e.g. The chairman just wanted the facts; You don't need to elaborate on them.

"主席只想了解事实，你不必作详细说明。"

accommodation ［ə'kɔmə'deiʃən］ n. 膳宿，预订铺位，适应性调节，调和，

　　e. g. How about the accommodation? 住宿情况怎么样?

temporary ［'tempərəri］ adj. 暂时的，临时的；一时的

　　e. g. temporary workers 临时工

facility ［fə'siliti］ n. ［常用复］便利，设备，器材，工具，装置

approve ［ə'pruː v］ vt. 赞成，赞许；批准，审定，通过，验收

　　e. g. The teacher looked at John's work and approved it.

老师看了约翰的作业表示赞许。

Congress approved the budget. 国会批准了国家预算。

His behavior under fire approved him a man of courage.

他在战火中的表现证明他是一个勇敢的人。

New Phrases

lay out v. 摆开，展示，布置，安排，投资

　　e. g. Lay out a town, garden　设计城市、布置花园

take possession of　占有，拥有

chief engineer　主任工程师，总工程师，总技师

access road　入口通道

a parking lot　施工设备停放场

man camp　生活营地

batching plant　混凝土搅拌厂

crushing system　破碎机

Role Play

What preparation should be made by the contractor when undertaking projects overseas? Based on the dialogue and make a discuss with your partner.

TEXT A

Site Establishment（1）

SITE ESTABLISHMENT

The Employer, through the Engineer shall hand over the work site to the Contractor according to the Drawings. The work site means all land and other locations which the Employer passes to the Contractor to construct the works mentioned in the Contract.

The Contractor is responsible for all the setting out of line and levels of the Works and shall employ adequate qualified staff to carry this out.

The Contractor shall provide sites for the plant and workshops necessary for the construction of the Works and shall pay any rents, easements and license fees levied in connection therewith. Dubai Municipality's formal approval to the site for the Contractor's plant and workshop must be received prior to occupying the proposed site.

Site offices for the Engineer and the Contractor shall be erected on a site provided by the Employer as shown in the Drawings. No Contractor's plant and workshops will be permitted within this compound. It is the Contractor's responsibility to obtain all necessary No Objection Certificate (NOC) for the occupation of the sites.

The Contractor shall construct suitable entry and exit roads to and within the compound and provide a covered parking area as specified in Appendix C. The contractor shall take all necessary precautions to avoid storm water flooding within the compound accesses.

The Engineer's office shall be erected and fully equipped to the satisfaction of the Engineer.

Within six weeks after the completion of the Whole of the Works and in accordance with the provisions of Clause 2.1 the whole area of the compound shall be reinstated to its original condition and all rubbish and refuse removed.

The Contractor's proposed access routes to and within the site shall be provided and maintained as agreed with the Engineer. The Engineer may at any time withdraw his approval for the use of any route and may order such widening, strengthening or repair work as he considers necessary.

The Contractor shall employ watchmen for the security of the site establishment.

The Contractor shall employ watchmen and maintain temporary fence erected by others throughout the contract period.

Notes

No Objection Certificate 常缩略为 N. O. C. 无异议证书；用于工程项目的施工或其他的许可证或授权书等。

New Words

workshop ['wə：kʃəp] n. 工场，车间，工厂

easement ['i：zmənt] n. 在他人土地上的通行权，地役权

levy ['levi] vt. 征收（捐税，罚款等）；

  e. g levy a fine [tax] on sb. 向某人征收罚金 [税款]

erect [i'rekt] vt. 使竖立，使直立，树立，建立

permit [pə (：)'mit] vt. (permitted; permitting) 允许，许可，准许，容许

  e. g. The facts permit no other explanation.

    事实不容许有其他的解释。

    Circumstances do not permit me to help you.

    情况不许可我帮助你。

compound ['kɔmpaund] n. 围场，围地（场内有建筑物）

precaution [pri'kɔ：ʃən] n. 预防，警惕，谨慎，小心；预防措施 [方法]

e. g. noise precaution 噪声预防

safety precaution 安全预防措施

fire precaution 防火办法

reinstate［'ri：in'steit］vt. 使恢复原状［原位］；使恢复（权利等）；使复职

withdraw［wið'drɔ：］vt.（‐drew［'dru：］；withdrawn［‐'drɔ：n］）取回；收回；领回；撤回；缩回；移开；拉开；取消；撤消；撤退

e. g. withdraw one's hand from the hot stove 把手从热火炉旁缩回

withdraw money from the bank 从银行取款

withdraw troops from a place 从某地撤军

New Phrases

hand over 移交，交出

e. g. Hand this money over to him. 把这钱转交给他

Hand over power to an elected government 把权力移交给经选举产生的政府

setting out 放样；定线；划定地界

Dubai Municipality 迪拜市政府

prior to prep. 在…之前

e. g. It happened prior to my arrival 这发生在我到达之前。

in accordance with adv. 与…一致，依照

in accordance with convention or custom. 与惯例或者风俗一致。

Role Play

What is the responsibility of contractor when prepaing for the site? Based on the text and your experience, make a discuss with your partner.

Exercises

I. Answer the following questions.

1. Who shall hand over the work site to the Contractor according to the Drawings?

2. What should the contractor be responsible for when establishing a site?

3. What must be received prior to occupying the proposed site?

4. Whose responsibility to obtain all necessary No Objection Certificate（NOC）for the occupation of the sites?

5. When should the whole area of the compound be reinstated to its original condition and all rubbish and refuse removed?

II. Complete the sentences with the given words or expression. Change the form where necessary.

1. Contractors shall pay any rents, easements and license fees ＿＿＿＿＿＿（levy）.

2. Whether _____ (permit), we can go camping.

3. Dubai Municipality's formal _____ (approve) to the site for the Contractor's plan and workshop must be received prior to occupying the proposed site.

4. The Contractor shall construct _____ (suit) entry and exit roads to and within the compound.

5. The Contractor shall employ watchmen for the _____ (secure) of the site establishment.

III. Translate the following words or phrases into English.

1. 无异议证书_____

2. 噪声预防_____

3. 迪拜市政府_____

4. 销售代表_____

5. 临时工_____

6. 设计城市_____

7. 总技师_____

8. 入口通道_____

9. 施工设备停放场_____

10. 生活营地_____

11. 混凝土搅拌厂_____

12. 破碎机_____

IV. Translate the following sentences into Chinese.

1. The Contractor shall provide sites for the plant and workshops necessary for the construction of the Works and shall pay any rents, easements and license fees levied in connection therewith Dubai Municipality's formal approval to the site for the Contractor's plan and workshop which must be received prior to occupying the proposed site.

_____

_____

_____

2. The Engineer may at any time withdraw his approval for the use of any route and may order such widening, strengthening or repair work as he considers necessary.

_____

V. Try to translate the sample into Chinese.

Sample

Apartment for Rent

FINCE-WARDEN, lrg 2br bsmt, new reno bright, lndry, eat-in kit, w-o balc, close to TTC/shops. No smoke/pets, +, 1st/last. 222-2222 - leave mess.

Notes

1. FINCH-WARDEN：这间房是位于或邻近 Finch 和 Warden 街交界处。

2. lrg 2br bsmt：lrg = large，2br = two bedrooms，bsmt = It is in a basement（below ground）. 这是地下的两房套间。（注意，两房是指两个睡房，洗手间，厨房，厅肯定是有的，所以不写出来）。

3. new reno bright reno = renovation，最近才装修过，很光亮。

4. lndry，eat-in kit，w-o balc lndry = laundry，指有洗衣机干衣机，eat-in kitchen 指厨房大，可在厨房里放饭桌吃饭。w-o balc = walk out to a balcony，指有扇门打开可通阳台。

5. close to TTC/shops 靠近公共交通（Transit Commission），购物商场。

6. No smoke/pets 不接受吸烟或养宠物的租客。

7. ＋，租金包括水电煤气。

8. 1st/last 首尾两个月的租金必须先交作为定金。

9. 222-2222 - leave mess 打电话 222-2222 留言联系房东。

● 招租广告常用缩略词 1

A/C Air conditioning 空调

appl appliance（refrigerator，stove，dish washer，cloth washer，dryer）家用电器

bachelor 一个只有一间房（同时作为睡房和起居室）的套间，里面另有洗手间浴室。

BR/BDRM 睡房	Basement/BSMT 地库/地下层
cable 有线电视	furn = furnished 带家具
hrdwd = hardwood 硬木地板	p/w 每周
p/m 每月	p. p. 每人
m/f 男/女	n/s or ns 不吸烟者
Excl 除外	Incl 包括
Furn 含家具	Unfurn 不含家具
dep. and ref. 押金和推荐信	Ch 中央暖气
Gch 煤气和中央暖气	Ech 电式中央暖气
w/m or w/mach 洗衣机	K&b 厨房与卫生间
nr. BR 靠近铁路	Dg 双层窗户
o. n. o. 最低价	

studio = bachelor 一个只有一间房（同时作为睡房和起居室）的套间，里面另有洗手间、浴室。

U/G = underground parking 地下停车场

util = utilities 水电煤气

Please translate the following into Chinese.

Exercise 1

3 Bedroom plus two rooms that can become 2 extra bedrooms. 2 bathrooms and 3 toilets, lounge and family area very well designed. Central vacuum system and double garage. Handy to Botany and Meadowlands Shopping Malls and school.

Tel. 269955

Mob. 025498950 Sam Kim

Reference：*Exercise 1* 　该房有三个卧室外加两个可改为两个额外卧室的房间，两个浴室，三个洗手间，设计合理的起居室与家居空间，且配有中央空调系统和两个车位的车库。从该房去 Botany/Meadowlands 购物中心和学校都很方便。联系电话：269955，手机025498950 联系人 Sam Kim。

Exercise 2

Apartment for Rent Quiet（near community park），12 Renmin Rd，10th fl，95 sq ms，2 bed，1　bath，1　living，with parking space price：5000 yuan/month（utilities not included）. Call 5124　3698，Ms. Li.

Reference：*Exercise 2*　房屋出租/安静(靠近社区公园)，人民路 12 号 10 楼,95 平方米,两室一厅一卫,带车位,房租每月 5000 元(不含水电),请致电 5124-3698 找李女士。

TEXT B

Site Establishment（2）

OFFICE AND FACILITIES FOR THE CONTRACTOR

The Contractor shall make provision for installation, maintenance and removal at the completion of the works, of his offices, sheds, and shelters. He shall provide and maintain on site at his own cost sanitary facilities, first aid and fire fighting equipment, drinking water facilities, electricity and telephone for the duration of the contract.

The Contractor shall be responsible for the security of the site and the safety of public and adjoining property and shall be liable for any claims arising from loss or damage suffered. He shall employ watchmen for this purpose.

All temporary accommodation shall be maintained in an efficient condition during the period of the contract and shall be available for inspection by the Government Medical Officer of Health.

The Contractor must comply immediately with any instruction given by the Medical Officer for cleaning, disinfestations and maintenance of any building to a hygienic and sanitary condition The Contractor shall confine his apparatus, the storage of materials and the operations of his workmen to the limits indicated by law, ordinances, and permits of direction of the Engineer. The Contractor shall erect temporary fences as required by the engineer. The site boundary lines shall be subject to the approval of the Engineer.

The Contractor shall provide and maintain water, electricity and power supply required for the works including that required by the subcontractors. Pay all charges and bear all costs for the necessary temporary installation including pipe work, pumps, water wagons, water tankers, storage tankers, generating equipment, etc. and get all these facilities removed upon completion of the works and see to it that all the works are done in a smooth and good manner.

The Contractor shall provide facilities, for the workers including those of nominated/domestic subcontractors consisting shaded area, canteen, rest areas, adequate toilet facilities and drinking water complying with D. M. requirements and to the Engineer's prior approval.

CONSTRUCTION PLANT AND WORKSHOP FOR THE CONTRACTOR

The Contractor shall make provision of the installation, maintenance up to the completion of the works and removal of fully equipped workshops and stores. The Contractor shall also provide all necessary construction plant, equipment and tools necessary for the proper execution of the works. All plant and equipment required for the contract is subject to the approval of the Engineer.

Notes

1. D. M. Dubai Marine 迪拜码头

New Words

installation［ˌinstəˈleiʃən］n. 安装，装配，设置

maintenance［ˈmeintinəns］n. 维持，维修；保养；维修保养费用

    e. g. the maintenance of an automobile 汽车保养

removal［riˈmu：vəl］n. 移［调］动，迁移

    e. g. removal van 搬运卡车（特别是供搬家用）

The factory announced its removal to another town.

这家工厂宣布迁往另一座城市。

completion［kəmˈpli：ʃ（ə）n］n 完成，实现

    e. g. bring［be brought］to completion 使完成

The teacher retired at the completion of the school year.

那位老师执教满任后便退休了。

maintain［menˈtein］vt. 保持；维持；供养；扶养；维修，保养（机器、道路等）；坚持，维护；主张，拥护

    e. g. maintain a highway 保养公路

        maintain one's family 养家

sanitary［ˈsæniˌteri：］adj. 1. 清洁的，卫生的，保健的；2. 环境卫生的，公共卫生的

duration［djuəˈreiʃən］n. 持续；持久；持续时间；延续性；期限［间］；存在时间

    e. g. the duration of flight 续航时间

adjoin［əˈdʒɔin］vt. & vi. 邻近，毗连

property［ˈprɔpəti］n. 1. 财产，资产，所有物；2. 房地产，不动产

claim［kleim］n. （根据保险政策、赔偿法等）要求的付款；索款、索赔

disinfestations［ˌdisinˌfesˈteiʃən］n. 灭（昆）虫法

hygienic［haiˈdʒi：nik］adj. 1. 卫生的，保健的；2. 清洁的；3. 卫生学的

confine［kənˈfain］vt. 限制；局限于

apparatus［ˌæpəˈreitəs］n. （pl. -es）（通常指有专门用途的成套）仪表，器械，仪器，装置，设备

tanker ［'tæŋkə］n. 运送大量液体或气体的轮船［卡车］；油轮；罐车；油槽车

nominated ［'nɔmineitid］adj. 被提名的；被任命的

New Phrases

sanitary facilities　卫生设施

on site　现场

first aid　急救

fire fighting equipment　消防设施

drinking water facilities　饮用水设施

adjoining property　邻产

be liable for..　对…应负责任的

　　e. g. He is found by the judge to be liable for the accident.

　　法官判处他对事故承担法律责任。

Government Medical Officer of Health. 政府医疗卫生官员

comply with　依从，服从，遵从

　　e. g. We should comply with the rules. 我们应该遵守规定。

water tanker　运水车

storage tank　贮存罐

generating equipment　发电机

toilet facilities　盥洗设施

drinking water　饮用水

Exercises

I. Read the sample carefully and simulate to write a short composition.

RESIDENTIAL LEASE（租赁协议）

1. PARTIES AND PREMIES：

This lease agreement is made on Jan. 10, 2005, between Mrs. Jones herein referred to as Landlord and Mr. Wei herein referred to as Tenant. （该租赁协议是由琼斯夫人（业主）与韦先生（承租人）于 2005 年 1 月 10 日在此签订）

Landlord rents to Tenant and Tenant rents from landlord for use as a residence, a furnished apartment, located at the 10# Building of the No. 6 Street in the City of Philadelphia, State of Pennsylvania.

2. TERM（期限）：

The initial term of this lease is six months to commence on Feb. 10, 2005 and to end on Aug. 10, 2005 on the following terms and conditions.

3. RENT：

Tenant agrees to pay as rent for the demised premises 800 Dollars（$ 800）per month, payable by check or cash（现金或支票均可）, without demand, in advance on the 1st day of each month. Rent will be considered late if not received by Landlord before the 6th of the month, unless a written agreement is in effect with an alternative payment plan. Late payments affect Tenant credit references（迟缴租金会影响承租方的信誉）.

4. SECURITY DEPOSIT（保证押金）:

On execution of this agreement, Tenant deposits with Landlord the additional sum of 800 Dollars（＄800）, receipt of which is acknowledged by Landlord, as security for the full and faithful performance by Tenant of this agreement, all of which shall be refundable within 14 days from the date of surrendering the premises, provided Landlord may retain all or a portion of the security deposit for the following:

    a. Non-payment of rent;

    b. Damage to property of the Landlord, unless the damage is the result of normal wear and tear or the result of actions or events beyond the control of Tenant.
（对业主房屋造成损坏，不包括因为正常使用造成的折旧/损耗，或因承租方不可抗拒的原因造成的损害。）

    c. Non-payment of all utility charges for which Tenant is responsible and which may constitute a lien on the property, or other utility charges which Tenant was required to pay directly to Landlord;

    d. Fail to bring the apartment back to a level of cleanliness equal to when the Tenant occupied the dwelling unit.

5. UTILITIES:

The responsibility for payment to entities providing utilities and other services to the premise during the lease shall be as follow:

    Heating: …

    Electric: …

    Water/ Sewer: …

    Trash: …

    Other（Specify）: …

6. EVICTION:

Any failures by the Tenant to pay rent or other charges promptly when due shall constitute a default（构成违约）herein under and permit Landlord at its option to terminate this tenancy upon 14 days' written notice to Tenant. Failure to comply with any other material term or condition herein shall also constitute a default and permit Landlord at its option to termination（s）, all leasehold rights of Tenant under this agreement shall be forfeited and Tenant shall surrender possession.

New Words for reference

herein［ˈhiəˈin］adv. 在此处，如此，鉴于

tenant［ˈtenənt］n. 房客

Philadelphia 费城（美国宾西法尼亚州东南部港市）

commence［kə'mens］vt. & vi.〈正〉开始，开始发生；着手

premise［'premis］n.［复数］［合同、契约用语］上述各点；上述事项；上述房产［复数］房屋；房屋连地基；生产经营场所 n.［pl.］房产

execution［ˌeksi'kjuːʃən］n. 实行，执行，实施

deposit［di'pɔzit］n. 订金；押金，保证金

acknowledge［ək'nɔlidʒ］vt. 1. 承认；2. 告知已收到

utility［ju'tiliti］n. 公用事业

lien［liːn］n.〈法〉留置权，扣押权

default［di'fɔːlt］n. 违约

forfeit［'fɔːfit］vt.（因犯错）丧失，被没收

Now try to write a rent lease under the direction as follow

Supposing that you are a landlord of an apartment in the Room 501 of 3# Building in the No. 5 Residential Area of Happy Street, Zhongshan Road, Zhuhai. Miss Zhang wants to rent it for 1 year since Feb. 1st, 2005 to Feb. 1st, 2006. It has been made an agreement about 500 Yuan per month as charter money either on credit card or in cash.

II. *Translate the following advertisement into Chinese.*

INTERNATIONAL SHOPPING CENTER

TIANJIN OFFICE FOR LEASE

The newly‑decorated small offices are ready for lease, suitable for foreigners. The useful areas are 28 sqm to 82 sqm.

Located at the golden section of the city of Tianjin, convenient for transportation, very closed to all kinds of government branches, lots of meeting-halls which reach the international standard inside, good facilities, plenty of parking spaces. The lowest management expenses. Compared with the same kind of office building in Tianjin. It's an ideal choice for foreign business representatives. Please contact: Miss Shen/ Mr. Wang At Tel: 3358-2856

TRANSLATION SKILLS

专业英语翻译基础知识

一、专业英语翻译的标准

科学技术的飞速发展是专业英语得以自成一体的客观条件。到 20 世纪 90 年代初期，全世界发表的科技文献，包括期刊论文、会议文献、科技报告等，其中有 65% 是用英语发表的，所以，作为楼宇智能化专业的学生应掌握一些专业英语翻译理论和翻译方法。

所谓翻译就是把一种语言文字所表达的意义用另一种语言文字表达出来的语言转换过程，是通过译者在不同语言之间进行的一种语言交流活动。这一交流与转换过程，要

求译者能够准确地表达译文所要表达的全部信息。

好的翻译作品能把原文的内容、思想、观点、立场等充分地在译文中体现出来，要想真正地做好翻译，除了懂英语，还必须不断提高语言文字水平以及文化、专业只是水平，并在实践中不断地磨练。

专业英语的基本特点是：概念新、文字简练、陈述句型多、被动语态多、动词的非谓语形式出现的频率高、简略表达多、复杂长句多、复合句多、每句包含的信息量大。而一篇高质量的专业英语的译文应是原文语言、本民族语言、科技知识三者高度统一的产物。因此，要做好英语专业的翻译工作，必须认识到专业文献的特殊性。专业英语的翻译标准有别于文学翻译。

就专业英语的特点和用途而言，其翻译标准应该是：准确规范、通顺易懂、简洁明晰。

（一）准确规范

所谓准确，就是忠实地、不折不扣地传达原文的全部信息内容。要做到这一点，译者必须充分的理解原文所表述的内容，其中包括对原文词汇、语法、逻辑关系和专业内容的理解。专业翻译的任何错误，甚至是不准确都会给科学研究、学术交流等带来不良影响或巨大损失，甚至是灾难。

（二）通俗易懂

所谓通俗易懂，即指译文的语言符合译文语法结构及表达习惯，容易为读者所理解和接受。也就是说，译文语言需要明白晓畅、文理通顺、结构合理、逻辑关系清除，没有死译、硬译、语言晦涩难懂的现象。

（三）简洁明晰

简洁明晰是专业英语的又一特点。同样，在翻译过程中，译文的简洁明晰也是专业英语翻译的最基本要求之一：就是译文要简短精炼、一目了然，要尽量避免烦琐、冗余和不必要的重复。

在专业英语翻译中，译文的通顺必须以准确为基础和前提。倘若准确但不通顺，则准确的意义尽失；倘若通顺而又不准确，则背离了翻译的基本原则及标准。在做到准确和通顺的基础上，如能做到简洁，则应是专业英语翻译的理想境界。

二、专业英语的基本翻译步骤

专业英语翻译的过程主要是理解和表达的过程，大致可认为理解、表达、校核三个阶段。其中理解是前提，主要是通读全文，零落全文大意、明辨语法、弄清关系、结合上下文推敲词意；表达是关键，初译时以忠实为主；校核时应忠实逻辑，定稿要润色文字。

（一）理解过程

1. 要加深对原文的理解，首先要通读原文，领略全文的大意。只有这样，才能便于选择词义，便于行文造句。

2. 同时,明辨语法形式,弄清句子成分之间的关系,也是正确理解原文的重要方面。

例：Those projects capable of providing advanced manufacture technique and production technology, manufacturing new products all needed urgently by the city of shanghai to promote the development and utilization of new energy. 从字面上看这是一个很长的句子，但实际它是一个以形容词短语作后置定语的一个名词性短语。在形容词的定语中，capable of 后面接了两个现在分词 probiding 和 manufacturing，这两个分词又分别带着自己的宾语 dvanced manufacture technique and production technology 和 new products，而 products 又由一个省略形式的从句修饰。只有弄清句子的这些语法关系，才能翻译出忠实、通顺的译文：这些项目提供先进的制造工艺和生产技术，并制造出促进上海市新能源的开发利用所急需的新产品。

由此可见，翻译科技文章时，应正确理解原文，仔细推敲句子结构，才能翻译出符合原文意义的译文。

（二）表达过程

在深刻理解原文的基础之上，只有准确地表达原文，才能翻译出准确、通顺的译文。因此，准确选词、恰当造句、历久简练是翻译工作者应该做到的工作。

1. 准确选词

由于英语和汉语的语言习惯不尽相同，在考虑词汇时应符合汉语的语言习惯，合理搭配词的顺序。如："the result indicate……"如果将其翻译成"结果指示……"就会给人不太顺畅、词汇搭配不太恰当的感觉，而将它翻译成"结果表明……"就比较好。

2. 恰当造句

翻译基本上是以句子为单位的，翻译时，首先必须要有一个忠实原文、通顺明确的句子。

例：The truck was engaged to low gear and driven in a zigzag course at a terrifying speed. 汽车挂上低速挡以惊人的速度高速行驶在弯路上。

这个句子翻译得没有什么问题，而且比较通畅。但译者对 at a terrifying speed 的理解上出现了错误。汽车离合器在低速挡上离合怎能高速行驶呢？译文应修改成"汽车挂上低速挡，以令人恐惧的速度在弯路上行驶"。

3. 力求简练

简练就是要使译文尽可能简短、精炼、不重复、啰嗦。在翻译科技英语中，在保证准确的前提下，应注意文字的修辞，力求简洁明快是十分必要的。

例：Each product must be produced to rigid quality standard.

可译成：每件产品均需达到严格的质量标准。如果译成：每件产品都要生产得满足严格的质量标准，就显得有些啰嗦生硬。

（三）校核过程

在翻译的过程中不出错误的人是几乎没有的。翻译完后的校对工作非常重要。校对过程就是检查译文的错漏之处，检查译文的前后关系，保持专业英语的逻辑性。

译　文

第四单元　进场

对　话

布置现场

（为保证工程的进行，承包方需要从业主那里得知现场情况并在业主的同意下对整个现场的布置进行规划。今天，布埃恩先生，承包方的项目经理和程先生，总工程师正在与业主方代表，斯科南丹先生讨论整个现场的布置计划。）

斯　科：几天前，你告诉我你们要在现场建两个区，你能详细说说你们的计划吗？

布埃恩：根据我们的施工计划，我们的第一个区，我们称之为 A 区将建在通往施工现场两个入口通道的连接处。它主要用于存放建筑材料和零件。在这个地方还将建一个停车场和一个修理厂。

斯　科：这个区有多大？

布埃恩：它占地面积大约 4000 平方米。

斯　科：这个可以接受。这块地属于政府所有，我们将尽快报批。另一个区呢？

布埃恩：另一个区，我们称之为 B 区，主要用于中国技术人员住宿和办公室，这属于生活区。

斯　科：它要建在什么地方？

布埃恩：在入口通道的右边，离 A 区约一英里远。占地面积与 A 区大约相同。现在，我想请程先生说明一下现场其他临时设施的安排计划。

　　程：根据我们的调查，我们发现有一块坡缓的地，我们想在那儿设混凝土搅拌场和破碎机，因为它离施工现场很近而且容易推平。

斯　科：好的。你把所有临时设施的布置连同申请书一起交给我们好吗？如果可能的话，我们将努力尽快获准。

布埃恩：越快越好。

斯　科：我会尽力的。我所能承诺的就是不论能否批准你们都会在一周之内得到答复。

布埃恩：那也是合同上所说的！

课　文　A

现场设施 1

业主通过咨询工程师根据图纸把施工场地交给承包商。施工场地指业主交给承包商按照合同要求进行施工的所有土地和其他设置。

承包商负责工程所有界限的划定和工程阶段的确定，并雇佣适当的有资格的人员来进行此项工作。

承包商要为工程建设所需的必要厂房提供场地并且要付所有的租金，地役费以及与迪拜市政府对承包商计划用场地和厂房正式批准有关所征收的许可费。这些费用必须在进驻场地之前交纳。

咨询工程师和承包商的办公室要按向业主提供的图纸在施工现场搭建。这个围墙内不允许承包商建工厂和车间。承包商有责任去取得场地使用所需要的无异议证书。

在围墙内外承包者要建适当的出入口，还要按附件 C 指定建一个遮盖式停车场。承包人员要采取一切必要的防范措施防止暴雨在围墙入口处积水。

要建咨询工程师办公室，所有设置要达到咨询工程师的满意。

在整个工程完工后 6 周之内，根据合同条款 2．1 整个围地范围内的垃圾要运走，使其恢复原样。

场地内外承包者计划的通道路线要根据咨询工程师的意见提供并保留，咨询工程师可以随时撤回其对某条路线使用的批准并可以在其认为必要时，发出对道路进行加宽、加固和修理的指令。

承包者要雇佣安全员负责现场建设的安全。

在施工期间要建临时性围栏与场外间隔。

课 文 B

现场设施2

承包方的办公及设施

　　承包方要保证办公室，仓库，住所的安装、维护，并要在工程完工之时进行拆除。在合同期间，他还要在合同期内为现场提供卫生、急救和消防设施，饮水设施以及用电和通话设施。

　　承包方要对现场的安全负责，确保人身安全及邻产安全。同时需对事故所造成的损失及投诉负责。为了保证安全需雇佣安全员。

　　在合同期间所有的临时住所都应条件齐全，随时可以接受政府医疗卫生官员的检查。为清洁环境卫生，承包方应根据政府医疗卫生人员的要求，对周围环境进行清理、灭虫并对建筑物的清洁进行维护。

　　承包方应按法律、法令指定以及咨询工程师的许可将其设备、存放的材料以及工人的工作范围加以限定。承包方应按咨询工程师的要求搭建临时围墙。现场边界线的划定需由咨询工程师批准。

　　承包方应提供并保持工程所需，包括分包方所需的水和电，负担所有费用并且承担所有必要的临时设施的费用，包括管线、泵、运水车、贮存罐，发电机等等，在工程完工后运走，并且保证整个工程运行良好，顺利进行。

　　承包方还要为工人，包括国内分包方的工人提供生活设施，包括乘凉区，餐厅、休息处，足够的盥洗设施以及饮用水，上述均要符合迪拜码头要求，并得到咨询工程师许可。

承包方的工厂和车间

　　承包方应安装、维护设备齐全的工地和工棚直至工程结束进行拆除。承包方要为工程正常进行提供必要的工棚、设备和工具。所有合同所需的工棚和设备均要由咨询工程师批准。

Part two
Construction of Main Frame
(主体结构施工)

UNIT *5*

Construction of Underground Works
（基础工程施工）

DIALOGUE

E：It is very clear that the quality of underground works is critical for the whole works. We can't expect a stable superstructure without a solid foundation.

C：That's true. It's our duty to comply with the specification.

E：Did you train the workers according to the procedure?

C：Yes, we did. Before starting the works we had a trial operation in an empty area. After making sure that each group of workers was able to do the job smoothly, we started the work. You will be satisfied if you see the result of the soil consolidation.

E：Really? It is mentioned in your Method Description that you would use the Vacuum Prestressing for the main building area after the wick drains were inserted in the ground.

C：Yes, it is. Here we are. This big settlement of the area is achieved within eight months by the vacuum method.

E：Well, the soil consolidation is a very successful operation. Now I would like to see the operation of driving precast concrete piles. What preparation did you make before driving the precast piles?

C: First, the site should be even and solid enough to move piling machines. The second thing is that the axial lines and the piles position should be rechecked. The third thing is that the barriers such as stones or old concrete blocks should be removed before driving piles.

E: How many piling tests have you made?

C: Eight piling tests have been made.

E: What is the vertical tolerance for the piling?

C: According to the specification, the vertical error cannot be over 0.5% of the pile length after the driving operation.

E: What test will you make after the piles have been driven to the position?

C: We will carry out the strength variation test to make sure that the piles are driven properly.

Notes

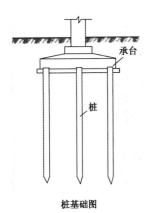

桩基础图

桩基础

由基桩和连接于桩顶的承台共同组成。若桩身全部埋于土中，承台底面与土体接触，则称为低承台桩基；若桩身上部露出地面而承台底位于地面以上，则称为高承台桩基。建筑桩基通常为低承台桩基础。高层建筑中，桩基础应用广泛。

New Words

critical ['kritikəl] adj. 紧要的，关键性的

superstructure ['sju：pəˌstrʌktʃə] n. 【建】上部结构；上层构造，

foundation [faun'deiʃən] n. 地基，地脚；底座

   e. g. a stone foundation 石基

settlement ['setlmənt] n. 沉降

   e. g. differential settlement 不均匀沉降

consolidation [kənˌsɔliˌdeiʃən] n. 巩固，加强，强化

precast ['priː'kɑ：st] vt. adj. 【建】预制（的）；预浇铸（的）

   e. g. a precast bridge 预制构件桥

precast piles 预制桩

axial ['æksiəl, –sjəl] adj. 轴的，轴向的，轴流式的

   e. g. axial force 轴向力

       axial load 轴压；轴向载重

       axial strain 轴向应变

       axial stress 轴向应力

       axial tensile strength 轴向抗拉强度

New Phrases

underground works 　地下工程
a trial operation 　试验施工
soil consolidation 　土壤固结
Method Description 　施工方案
Vacuum Prestressing 　真空预压
precast concrete pile 　预制混凝土桩
piling machine 　打桩机
concrete block 　混凝土块
vertical tolerance 　垂直度误差
strength variation test 　应力变化测试

Role Play

Discuss with your partner how to drive the precast concrete piles and its preparation works.

TEXT A

PILING

BORED CAST-IN-PLACE PILES
PERMANET CASING

Permanent casing shall be required for those piles where instability may occur due to inadequate lateral support from the ground or the effect of ground water. Permanent casing will be free of distortions or any encrustations which might prevent the proper formation of piles immediately prior to being lowered down the borehole.

DRILLING FLUID

a）SUPPLY

Bentonite, as supplied to the Site and prior to mixing, shall be in accordance with specification DECP 4 of the Oil Company Materials Association.

b）MIXING

Bentonite shall be mixed thoroughly with clean fresh water to make a suspension which will maintain the stability of the pile excavation for the period necessary to place concrete and complete construction. The temperature of the water used in mixing the bentonite suspension, and of the suspension when supplied to the borehole, shall not be lower than 5℃. Where saline or chemically contaminated groundwater occurs, special precautions shall be taken to modify the bentonite suspension or hydrate the bentonite in fresh water in advance so as to render it suitable in all respects for the construction of piles.

c）TESTS

The frequency of testing drilling fluid and the method and procedure of sampling shall be proposed by the Contractor prior to the commencement of the work.

DIAMETER OF PILES

The diameter of a pile shall not be less than the diameter stated in the Contractor's design as passed to the Engineer for his comments.

BORING

a）TEMPORARY CASING

Temporary casing of approved quality, or an approved alternative method, shall be used to maintain the stability of pile excavations which might otherwise collapse.

Temporary casings shall be free from significant distortion. They shall be of uniform cross-section throughout each continuous length. During concreting they shall be free from internal projections and encrusted concrete which might prevent the proper formation of piles.

b）STABILITY OF PILES EXCAVATION USING DRILLING FLUID

Where the use of drilling fluid is approved for maintaining the stability of a boring, the level of the fluid in the excavation shall be maintained so that the fluid pressure always exceeds the pressure exerted by the soils and external groundwater, and an adequate temporary casing shall be used in conjunction with the method to ensure stability of the strata near ground level until concrete has been placed. The fluid level shall be maintained at a level not less than 1m above the level of the external groundwater.

c）PUMPING FROM BOREHOLES

Pumping from a borehole shall not be permitted unless a casing has been placed into a stable stratum which prevents the flow of water from other strata in significant quantities into the boring, or unless it can be shown that pumping will not have a detrimental effect on the surrounding soil or property.

d）ENLARGED PILE BASES

An enlarged base mechanically formed shall not be smaller than the dimensions specified and shall be concentric with the pile shaft within a tolerance of 10% of the shaft diameter. The sloping surface of the frustum forming the enlargement shall make an angle to the horizontal of not less than 55°.

e）CLEANLINESS OF PILE BASES

On completion of boring, loose, disturbed or remolded soil and rock fragments shall be removed from the base of the pile.

f）INSPECTION

Each pile boring shall be inspected prior to the placing of concrete in it. The pile base will be onto fresh and undisturbed ground, from debris of fragments.

（Extracted from structural specification of multi-story residential building on plot 9AB, Dubai Marina, P. 1~13.）

Notes

1. British Standard Code of Practice for foundations, BS 8004. 英国基础规范 BS 8004.

2．Bored cast-in-place piles：钻孔灌注桩

灌注桩是指在工程现场通过机械钻孔、钢管挤土或人力挖掘等手段在地基土中形成桩孔，并在其内放置钢筋笼、灌注混凝土而做成的桩，依照成孔方法不同，灌注桩又可分为沉管灌注桩、钻孔灌注桩和挖孔灌注桩等几类。

钻孔灌注桩在高层、超高层的建筑物和重型构筑物中被广泛应用。按成桩工艺，钻孔灌注桩可以分为：干作业法钻孔灌注桩；泥浆护壁法钻孔灌注桩；套管护壁法钻孔灌注桩。钻孔灌注桩的施工，因其所选护壁形成的不同，有泥浆护壁法和全套管施工法两种。

泥浆护壁施工法：冲击钻孔，冲抓钻孔和回转钻削成孔等均可采用泥浆护壁施工法。该施工法的过程是：平整场地→泥浆制备→埋设护筒→铺设工作平台→安装钻机并定位→钻进成孔→清孔并检查成孔质量→下放钢筋笼→灌注水下混凝土→拔出护筒→检查质量。施工顺序（如图所示）：

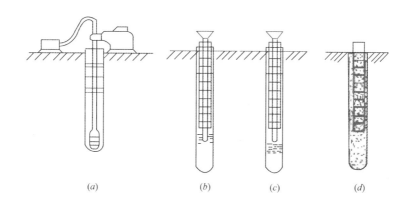

泥浆护壁钻孔灌注桩施工顺序图
（a）钻孔；（b）下钢筋笼及导管；（c）灌注混凝土；（d）成型

New Words

instability［′instə′biliti：］n. 不稳定，不稳固

inadequate［in′ædikwit］adj. 不充足的，不适当的

lateral［′lætərəl］adj. 侧面的，从旁边的，至侧面的

distortion［di′stɔ：ʃən］n. 扭曲；变形；失真，歪曲

encrustation［inˌkrʌs′teiʃən］n. 结壳，用覆盖物，镶嵌，硬壳

borehole［′bɔ：houl］n. 钻孔

fluid［′flu：id］n. 浆体、泥浆体

supply［sə′plai］n. 供给，供应，补给

Bentonite［′bentəˌnait］n.〈美〉斑脱土（火山灰分解成的一种黏土）

suspension［sə′spenʃən］n. 悬浮液

excavation［ˌekskə′veiʃən］n. 发掘；挖掘；开凿

saline［′seiˌli：n］adj. 1. 含盐的，咸的；2. 盐的 n. 1. 盐湖，盐泉；2. 盐溶液

contaminate〔kən'tæmineit〕vt. 把…弄脏，污染

precaution〔pri'kɔːʃən〕n. 预防措施；预防；防备

hydrate〔'haiˌdreit〕vt. & vi. （使）水合

commencement〔kə'mensmənt〕n. 开始，开端

diameter〔dai'æmitə〕n. 直径

bore〔bɔː〕vt. & vi. 挖，掘，钻，开凿（洞、井、隧道等）

dimension〔di'menʃən〕n. 1. 尺寸，度量；2. 方面，部分

concentric〔kən'sentrik〕adj. 同一中心的，同轴的

tolerance〔'tɔlərəns〕n. 1. 宽容，容忍，忍受；2. 偏差，公差，容限

fragment〔'frægmənt〕n. 碎片；片段

New Phrases

bored cast-in-place piles   钻孔灌注桩

permanent casing   永久性套筒

temporary casing   临时护筒

drilling fluid   钻探泥浆

Role Play

Tell your partner the construction sequence of driving bored cast-in-place piles and special consideration involved in the process.

Exercises

I. Answer the following questions.

1. Why should permanent casing be required for those piles where instability may occur?

2. What are the requirements when placing permanent casing?

3. What will maintain the stability of the pile excavation for the period necessary to place concrete and complete construction?

4. What are the requirements when placing temporary casing?

5. When shall pumping from a borehole be permitted?

II. Complete the sentences with the given words or expression. Change the form where necessary.

1. The client is satisfied with the result of the soil _____ (consolidate).

2. When designing the foundation, we should consider the _____ (settle) of the whole building.

3. The permanent casing should be free from _____ (distort).

4. Temporary casing of approved quality, or an approved alternative method, shall be used to maintain the _____ (stable) of pile excavations which might otherwise collapse.

5. The _____ （commence） date of this project is set.

III. Translate the following words or phrases into Chinese.

1. Where saline or chemically contaminated groundwater occurs, special precautions shall be taken to modify the bentonite suspension or prehydrate the bentonite in fresh water so as to render it suitable in all respects for the construction of piles.

_____

_____

2. Where the used of drilling fluid is approved for maintaining the stability of a boring, the level of the fluid in the excavation shall be maintained so that the fluid pressure always exceeds the pressure exerted by the soils and external groundwater, and an adequate temporary casing shall be used in conjunction with the method to ensure stability of the strata near ground level until concrete has been placed.

_____

_____

_____

3. On completion of boring, loose, disturbed or remolded soil and rock fragments shall be removed from the base of the pile.

_____

_____

IV. Translate the following words or phrases into Chinese.

1. superstructure _____
2. trial operation _____
3. precast concrete piles _____
4. strength variation test _____
5. Board cast-in-place piles _____
6. Permanent casing _____
7. Temporary casing _____
8. drilling fluid _____

V. The following is a brief description of foundation. Read it carefully and try your best to figure it out by referring to the Chinese.

Foundation

Foundation is a part of a structure. It is usually placed below the surface of the ground, and transmits the load to the underlying soil or rock. All soils compress when they are loaded and cause supported structure to settle. The important requirements in the design of foundations are that the total settlement of the structure shall be limited to a tolerably small amount and that differential settlement of various parts of the structure shall be eliminated as nearly as possible.

Foundation designer must consider the effects of construction on buildings nearby, and effects on the environments of such factors as pile driving vibrations, pumping and discharge of ground water, the disposal of waste materials and the operation of heavy mechanical equipment.

Foundation must be durable to resist attack by aggressive substances in the sea and river, in soil and rock and in ground water. They must also be designed to resist or to suit movement from external causes such as seasonal moisture changes in the soil, landslide, earthquake and mining subsidence.

Generally speaking, the strength of soil increases with depth. But it can happen that it becomes weaker with depth. Therefore, in choosing the foundation pressure and level for this will give you an idea of the settlements. There are several causes of settlement apart from the forces due to load. They are the frost action, chemical change in the soil, underground erosion by following water, reduction of the underground water, the construction tunnels nearby or vibrating machinery such as vehicles.

基础通常是设置在地面以下，并将荷载传递给下面土壤或岩石的结构部分。所有土壤在受荷载作用时都受到压缩，并引起所支撑的建筑物沉降。在基础设计中有两个重要要求：（1）结构总体的沉降要限制到尽量小的程度；（2）要尽可能消除结构各部分的不均匀沉降。

设计基础时，必须考虑施工对附近建筑物的影响，以及诸如打桩振动、抽出和排泄地下水、处理废料和操作重型机械设备等因素对周围环境的影响。基础必须是耐久的，以抵抗大海和河流中、土壤和岩石中以及地下水中侵蚀物质的腐蚀。设计基础时，必须考虑到抵抗或适应由于外界原因，诸如土壤中季节性的湿度变化、山崩、地震和坑井塌陷引起的位移。

一般说来，土的强度都随其深度而增加。但是强度随深度减少的情况也可能发生。因此在选择基础压力和这类土的层位时，土力学的知识就很重要，因为这将使人们对可能发生的沉降有所了解。造成沉降的原因除了承受荷载以外，还有别的原因，包括冻结作用、土的化学变化、流水的地下侵蚀作用、地下水位的降低、附近的隧道施工或车辆一类的机械振动。

TEXT B

Foundation

Every large civil engineering job starts with a social mechanics survey in its early stages. The first visit on foot will show whether the site might be suitable to construction, in other words, whether money should be spent on sending soil-sampling equipment out to it.

The soil samples, the laboratory results obtained from the triaxial tests and sheer tests will show at what depth the soil is likely to be strong enough to take the required load.

What are foundations? They are bases usually made of concrete. Foundations are placed on the ground so as to spread a vertical load on it.

A foundation may be built in one of many different materials. It may be of steel joists encased in concrete, of reinforced concrete or of plain concrete without reinforcement. Structures built on strong rocks generally need no foundation, since rock is usually as strong as concrete and goes much deeper.

One of the commonest foundation is that of a concrete column. It is generally designed for the same maximum load as the column, and usually is an independent pad foundation.

The pads in one row become so large that they nearly touch; it is convenient to join them into a continuous foundation which will be cheaper to dig and to concrete than the same foundation built separately as pads.

The soil under a high building often settles. The key to the design of the foundation is to keep the total settlement of the building within reasonable limits. If one column settles much more than its neighbor, the building will certainly crack and may look as if it were breaking into pieces. Obviously, every structure designer wishes to avoid the impression.

The design of a high building on compressible soil is difficult and therefore very interesting. A concrete foundation design will apply a higher bearing pressure to the smaller foundation and a lower one to the larger foundation. The exact calculation of these different bearing pressures is very difficult.

The two essential requirements in the design of foundations are that the total settlement of the structure shall be limited to a tolerably small amount and that differential settlement of the various parts of the structure shall be eliminated as nearly as possible .

To limit settlement as indicated, it is necessary（1）to transmit the load of the structure to a solid soil stratum and（2）to spread the load over a sufficiently large area of that stratum to minimize bearing pressure.

New Words

mechanics［miˈkæniks］n. 力学；机械学

triaxial［traiˈæksiəl］adj. 三轴的，三维的，空间的

sample［ˈsɑːmpl］n. 样品，标本，样本；vt. 抽样调查；抽样检验；取样；采样

sheer［ʃiə］adj. 1. 陡峭的；垂直的；2. 极薄的，轻的，透明的

vertical［ˈvəːtikəl］adj. 垂直的，竖的

reinforce［ˌriːinˈfɔːs］vt. 加固；使更结实

column［ˈkɔləm］n. 柱，圆柱

pad［pæd］vt. 给…装衬垫，加垫子；n. 垫，护垫

convenient［kənˈviːnjənt］adj. 方便的，便利的，合适的

continuous［kənˈtinjuəs］adj. 连续的，没有中断的

concrete［ˈkɔnkriːt］n. 混凝土；vt. 铺以混凝土，以混凝土浇筑

separately［ˈsepəritli］adv. 分离地；个别地，分别地，单独地

crack［kræk］vt. & vi.. （使…）开裂，破裂

compressible［kəmˈpresəbl］adj. 可压缩的，可压榨的

calculation［ˌkælkjəˈleiʃən］n. 1. 计算，计算（的结果）；2. 推断；预测，估计

differential［ˌdifəˈrenʃəl］adj. 不同的，有分别的；基于差别的；区别性的

eliminate［iˈlimineit］vt. 1. 消除；2. 排除；3. 淘汰

transmit［trænzˈmit］vt. 传播；播送；传递

stratum ［'stretəm］ n. 1. 岩层；2. 地层；3. 社会阶层
sufficiently ［sə'fiʃəntli］ adv. 足够地，充分地
minimize ［'minimaiz］ vt. 把…减至最低数量［程度］

New Phrases

a soil mechanics survey　土力学勘察
soil - sampling equipment　取土样的设备
soil sample　土样
sheer test　剪力试验
a vertical load　垂直荷载
the triaxial test　三轴试验
reinforced concrete　钢筋混凝土
plain concrete without reinforcement　不加钢筋的素混凝
independent foundation　柱下独立基础
continuous foundation　连续基础
compressible soil　软土
the total settlement　总沉陷量
differential settlement　不均匀沉降
bearing pressure　支撑压力

Exercises

I. Translate the following Chinese items into English.
1. 地下工程＿＿＿＿＿＿＿＿＿＿
2. 打桩机＿＿＿＿＿＿＿＿＿＿
3. 连续基础＿＿＿＿＿＿＿＿＿＿
4. 软土＿＿＿＿＿＿＿＿＿＿
5. 剪力实验＿＿＿＿＿＿＿＿＿＿
6. 独立垫式基础＿＿＿＿＿＿＿＿＿＿

II. Translate the following English items into Chinese.
1. vertical tolerance ＿＿＿＿＿＿＿＿＿＿
2. triaxial tests ＿＿＿＿＿＿＿＿＿＿
3. a soil mechanics survey ＿＿＿＿＿＿＿＿＿＿
4. soil sample ＿＿＿＿＿＿＿＿＿＿
5. different settlement ＿＿＿＿＿＿＿＿＿＿
6. soil stratum ＿＿＿＿＿＿＿＿＿＿
7. steel joists ＿＿＿＿＿＿＿＿＿＿

8. plain concrete without reinforcement _____

III. *Translate the following sentences into Chinese.*

1. The key to the design of the foundation is to keep the total settlement of the building within reasonable limits and if one column settles much more than its neighbor, the building will certainly crack and may look as if it were breaking into pieces.

_____

_____

2. As to compressible soil, a correct foundation design will apply a higher pressure to the smaller foundation and a lower one to the larger foundation.

_____

3. One of the two essential requirements in the design of foundation is that differential settlement of the various parts of the structure shall be eliminated as nearly as possible.

_____

TRANSLATION SKILLS

专业英语翻译的一般方法

要把一种语言文字所表达的意义用另一种语言文字表达出来，除了有较高的语言文字水平以及文化、专业知识外，还必须掌握一些常见的翻译方法。

一、直译和意译

直译就是基本保持原文表达形式及内容，不做大的改动，同时要求语言通顺易懂，表述清楚明白。直译所强调的是"形似"，主张将原文内容按照原文的形式（包括词序、语序、语气、结构、修辞方法等）用译语表述出来。

例1：Physics studies force, motion, heat, light, sound, electricity, magnetism, radiation, and atomic structure.

物理学研究力、运动、热、光、声、电、磁、辐射和原子结构。

例2：The outcome of a test is not always predictable.

实验结果并不总是可以预料的。

意译：意译是将原文所表达的内容以一种释义性的方式用译语将其意义表达出来。意译强调"神似"，也就是不拘泥于原文在词序、语序、语气、语法结构等方面的形式，用译语的习惯表达方式将原文的本意（真实含义）翻译出来。

例1：The law of reflection holds good for all surfaces.

反射定律对一切表面都适用。

例2：We can get more current from cells connected in parallel.

电池并联时提供的电流更大。

在翻译实践中，直译与意译不是两种完全孤立的翻译方法，译者不应该完全拘泥于其中的某一种，必须学会将直译和意译有机地结合起来。要以完整、准确、通顺地表达出原文的意义为翻译的最终目的。

二、合译和分译

翻译英语句子时，我们可以把原文句子的结构保留下来，并在译文中体现出来。但不少情况下，我们则必须对原句子结构作较大的改变，合译法和分译法就是改变原文句子结构的两种常用方法。

合译：合译就是把原文两个或两个以上的简单句或复合句，在译文中用一个单句来表达。

例1：There are some metals which possess the power to conduct electricity and ability to be magnetized.

某些金属具有导电和被磁化的能力。

分译：分译就是把原文的一个简单句中的一个词、词组或短语译成汉语的一个句子，这样，原文的一个简单句就被译成了汉语的两个或两个以上的句子。

例2：With the same number of protons，all nuclei of a giver element may have different numbers of neutrons.

虽然某个元素的所有原子和都含有相同数目的质子，但他们含有的中子数可以不同。

汉语习惯于用短语来表达，而英语适用长句较多，由于英汉两种语言句型结构的这种差异，在科技英语翻译过程中，要把原文句子中复杂的逻辑关系表述清楚，经常采用分译法。

三、增译和省译

英语与汉语在表达上有着很大的差异。在汉译的过程中，如果按原文一对一的翻译，译文则很难符合汉语的表达习惯，会显得生搬硬套、牵强附会。在翻译过程中，译者应遵循汉语的习惯表达方式，在忠实原文的基础上，适当地进行增译或省译。

增译：所谓增译，就是在译文中增加英语原文省略、或原文中无其词而有其义的词语，使译文既能准确地表达原文的含义，又更符合汉语的表达习惯和修辞需要。

例1：The amount of cell respiration depends upon the degree of the organism.

细胞呼吸量的大小由生物体活动的程度来决定。（增译了形容词"大小"）

例2：High technology is providing visually and hearing impaired people with in creased self - sufficiency.

高科技设备在不断增强视力和听力损伤者的自理能力。（增译了名词"设备"，副词"不断"）

省译：严格来说，翻译时不允许对原文的内容有任何删略，但由于英汉两种语言表达方式的不同，英语句子中有些词语如果硬是要译成汉语，反而会使译文晦涩难懂。为使译文通顺、准确地表达出原文的思想内容，有时需将一些词语省略不译。

例1：For the purpose of our discussion, let us neglect the friction.

为了便于讨论，我们将摩擦力忽略不计。（省译了名词 purpose）

例2：Little information is given about the origin of life.

关于生命起源方面的资料极少。（省译了谓语动词 is given）

例3：The coupling bolts should go into place when tapped lightly with a hammer.

用榔头轻轻的敲打，结合螺栓便能进入固定的位置。（省译了连词 When）

从以上例句中不难看出，不但介词、连词、冠词等虚词可以增译或省译，动词、名词等实义词有时也可增译或省译。但是，无论是增译或是省译，都必须以完整、准确地表达原文，以符合译语的表达习惯为原则，来进行适当的增译或省译，切不可随意使用。

四、顺译和倒译

顺译：就是按照原文相同或相似的语序进行翻译。顺译可以是完全顺译，也可以是基本顺译。基本顺译是指为了表达准确和通顺而进行个别语序的调整。

例1：The nylon nut must not protrude above the metal surface.

尼龙螺母不应高出金属表面。

例2：Space programs demand tremendous quantities of liquid gydrogen and oxygen as rocket fuel.

航天计划需要大量的液氢和液氧作为火箭燃料。

倒译：有时完全按照原文的词序来翻译是很困难的，为了使译文更加通顺，更符合汉语的表达习惯，须采用完全不同于原文词语顺序的方法来翻译，我们称之为倒译。

例1：The converse effect is the cooling of a gas when it expands.

气体在膨胀时对其冷却的一种逆效应。

例2：Too large a current must not be used.

不得使用过大的电流。

在翻译实践中，顺译和倒译的使用不可能是完全孤立的，很多情况下，不可能完全顺译，也不可能完全倒译，译者需要根据具体情况将两种方法有机地结合起来灵活使用。

以上我们所介绍的各种翻译方法必须灵活应用，无论是采用哪一种方法，其目的都是为了能准确、通顺地用译文表达原文的思想内容。事实上，在翻译实践中，我们不会也不可能完全孤立地使用某一种方法。译者需要将各种译法融汇贯通，有机地结合使用，以使译文达到理想的翻译标准：准确规范、通顺易懂、简洁明晰。

译　文

第五单元　基础工程施工

对　话

咨询工程师：我们都清楚地下工程的质量对于整个工程来说是至关重要的。没有一个坚固的地基就不会有一个稳固的上部结构。

承　包　方：你说的对。照章施工是我们的责任。

咨询工程师：你们根据程序对工人进行培训了吗？

承　包　方：是的。在工程开始之前我们在一块空场地进行了实验施工。在确保每组工人都能顺利完成工作之后我们才开工。如果你看到土壤固结的效果你一定会满意的。

咨询工程师：真的吗？在施工方案中你提到将排水带嵌入地面后主楼区域要采用真空预压方法。

承　包　方：是，我们是这样做的。用真空方法，这一大片面积的沉降八个月之内即可完成。

咨询工程师：好，土壤固结这项操作的确很成功。现在我想看看打预制混凝土桩的操作。

在预制桩打桩前你们做了哪些准备工作?

承 包 方:首先,施工现场必须平整且坚固以便开动打桩机。第二是重新核准定位轴
线和桩的位置。第三是在打桩前要去除现场的障碍物如石头和混凝土块。

咨询工程师:你们做了几次打桩测试?

承 包 方:做了八次。

咨询工程师:桩的垂直误差是多少?

承 包 方:根据规范,垂直误差不能超过打桩前桩长度的0.5%。

咨询工程师:在桩打入指定位置后你们将做什么测试?

承 包 方:我们将做应力变化测试,测定桩打的是否合适。

课文 A 桩基成孔

钻孔灌注桩

永久性套管

在那些由于来自地面的侧支撑不足或地表水的影响会导致不稳固的地方需要采用永
久性的套管。永久套管不会变形,且不会形成影响桩体灌柱的硬壳。

液体

a)原料供给

在搅拌前供应到现场的斑脱岩要与石油公司材料协会中DECD 4的规范说明一致。

b)搅拌

斑脱岩应用干净新鲜的水充分搅拌后使其悬浮,这将保持桩挖掘孔在添放混凝土和
整个工程期间必要的稳定性。搅拌斑脱岩悬浮物的水温以及灌注到钻孔的悬浮物的温度
不应低于5℃。在有含盐分水或受化学污染地下水的地方要采取特殊措施来调整斑脱岩
悬浮物或用清水预先水化斑脱岩使其溶解且适合于所有桩基础的建造。

c)检测

在开工前,对于钻探泥浆的测试次数,采样的方法和程序应当由承包商提出。

桩的直径

桩的直径应不小于由承包方递交且已由咨询工程师同意的设计中所说明的直径大小。

钻孔

a)临时套管

符合规定质量要求的临时套管或者其他可行的方法用于维护孔壁的稳定性,以免其
倒塌。

临时套管应没有明显的变形。它们每个连续长度套管的截面是一致的,在灌注混凝
土过程中它们不应有内部凸出的地方以及影响桩正确形成的混凝土硬块。

b)灌注钻孔泥浆中桩孔挖掘处要保持稳固

在灌注钻孔泥浆的地方必须要保持钻孔处的稳固,开凿的桩孔里面的液体应保持一
定的高度以便使其液压总是高于土壤和外部地表水所施加的压力。临时性的套管连同使
地层稳固的方法一并使用直到混凝土填充完毕。液面应保持在不低于外部地表水面以上
一米的位置。

c)清孔

只有套筒被放置在能够阻止水流从其他地层大量流入孔内的稳定土层内,或者确定
清孔不会影响周围土的性质的情况下才能进行清孔。

d) 扩孔

使用机械扩大的桩基不应小于规定的尺寸，并且与桩身一致，轴径的偏差控制在10%以内。桩身的斜坡面角度应不大于5°。

e) 清孔

钻孔完成后，松散的，有影响的或翻动了的土和石块都应从桩基处清理出去。

f) 检查

在灌入混凝土之前，必对每个钻口进行检查。桩基将被放置在清除钻渣后的新的原状土层上。

（摘自迪拜码头9AB高层住宅楼结构规范）

课文 B 地 基

每一项大型土木工程施工在初期阶段都从土力学勘察开始，通过第一次踏勘将会查明场地是否适合建筑，换句话说，是否值得投资把取土样的设备送到那里去。

取出的土样和三轴试验、剪力试验将表明，土在什么深度有可能具备足够的强度以承受必要的荷载。

什么是基础呢？它们通常是用混凝土做的基座。它们置于土地上，以便通过它把垂直荷载分布到土基上去。

基础可在许多不同材料中任选一种来修建。它可以用钢梁封入混凝土，用钢筋混凝土或不加钢筋的素混凝土。建造在坚固岩石上的结构时，由于岩石一般像混凝土一样坚固，而且厚度还要大得多，一般就不需要基础。

一种最常用的基础是混凝土柱，它通常是按与柱子相同的最大荷载设计的，一般是独立的垫式基础（柱下独立基础）。

如遇到一排这样的垫式基础其柱身大得几乎可以相互碰着时，最好把它们连结成为连续基础，这种基础的开挖和浇筑混凝土比单独建筑的同等的垫式基础一般都要便宜。

高层建筑物下面的土壤常常下沉，基础设计的关键是把建筑物的总沉陷量限制在合理范围内，如果一个柱子比邻近的柱子沉陷太多，则建筑物必将开裂，看上去就好像要倒塌的样子，显然每个结构设计者都希望避免出现这种情况。

在软土上设计高层建筑物是困难的，因而也富有吸引力。合理的基础设计应考虑到基础面较小时将承受较高的压应力，基础面较大时则承受较低的压应力。精确计算这些不同的承载压力的确是特别困难的。

设计者要达到两个基本要求：一是建筑物的总沉降要限制到尽可能小的程度，二是要尽可能消除各部分结构不均匀沉降。

为了限制上述沉降，必须做到：（1）把建筑物的荷载传递到有足够强度的土层；（2）把荷载分布在该土层足够大的面积上，以减少压应力。

UNIT *6*

Form Works（模板工程）

DIALOGUE

Inspection of Formwork

E: As you know without formwork the concrete will not be cast into its required shape. Let's have a look at the erection of the formwork in the site. This piece of formwork for the wall is quite large, and how can you fix it firmly?

C: We call this kind of formwork large prefabricated formwork. Firstly it should be erected on hard ground with enough locating area and good drainage. Secondly it should be supported by anchor shoring and frames in accordance with its erection drawings.

E: What method are you using to avoid the concrete from flowing out from the joints of formwork?

C: We use a foam material and a plastic paste tap to seal the joints. It is quite effective.

E: I think the bolts here for fixing the large prefabricated formworks between two faces of the concrete wall have not complied with the design drawings. It should be dia. 25mm bolt but your workers are fixing with dia. 12mm bolts. Would you find out what the reason for replacing it is? I am waiting for your answer within 10 minutes.

C: (5 minutes later) I am very sorry to tell you that there is a big mistake in it. I was told that it was short of supply of the dia. 25 mm and then the replacement was made for avoiding of time waste. Now I have ordered the foreman to remove all dia. 12mm for this section of wall formwork and to fix dia. 25mm bolts instead.

E：It is far from enough just to make the replacement. It is mentioned in the contract conditions that anything in the drawings can not be modified without approval from the engineer. In my opinion the foreman who made the order to change should be fired in order to warn everybody in the site. At least he should be punished and then to make an announcement to all on the site that this mistake is very serious and make sure it will not happen again on this site.

C：We will take effective action to make it clear to all site people that this mistake is a very serious quality problem and some strong measures will be taken to avoid problems of this kind happening again.

Notes

1. Without formwork the concrete will not be cast into its required shape.
   没有模板，混凝土就不能浇筑成形。
2. dia.：diameter 直径

New Words

formwork ［'fɔ：mwə：k］ n. 模板，样板；模板成形；模板工程
cast ［kæst］ vt. & vi. 浇筑（过去式 & 过去分词：cast）
concrete ［'kɔnkri：t］ n. 凝结物，混凝土
erection ［i'rekʃən］ n. （垂直，设备）安装，装配；架起
prefabricate ［pri：'fæbri͵keit］ vt. 预制 n. 预制
erect ［i'rekt］ vt. 使直立；竖起
drainage ［'dreinidʒ］ n. 排水（法）；排水装置
  e. g. the drainage of the swamps 沼泽地的排水
  drainage and irrigation work 排灌工程
anchor ［'æŋkə］ n. 1. 锚；2. 给人安全感的物（或人）vt. 抛锚
  vt. & vi. （把…）系住，（使）固定
shoring ［'ʃɔ：riŋ］ n. 利用支柱的支撑，支柱
joint ［dʒɔint］ n. 接头，接合处，接点
foam ［fəum］ n. 泡沫材料；泡沫橡皮；泡沫塑料；泡沫状物
  e. g. foam material 泡沫材料
seal ［si：l］ vt. 1. 盖章于，盖戳，在…上加盖检验封印；2. 密封
comply ［kəm'plai］ vi. 遵从，依从，服从
bolt ［bəult］ n. 螺栓
replacement ［ri'pleismənt］ n. 代替，替换，更换
foreman ［'fɔ：mən］ n. 工头，领班
announcement ［ə'naunsmənt］ n. 通告，布告，通知；预告

New Phrases

large prefabricated formwork　大型预制模板

anchor shoring and frame　锚固件和框架

erection drawing　安装图

joints of formwork　模板连接处

comply with…　服从，遵从

design drawing　设计图

be short of.　缺乏…

at least　至少

Role Play

State briefly the erection process of aluminum formwork（建筑铝模板）by using the following words：

1. Sequence：

　　1.1 Setting out（by others）由地盘墨斗放线；

　　1.2 Re‑bar to wall（by others）扎墙身铁；

　　1.3 Wall 墙 1.3a E&M for wall（by others）机电留孔，线合等工作 1.3b Embedment installation（by others）留幕墙，外墙预制件，阳台等预留螺丝；

　　1.4 Beam 梁；

　　1.5 Slab 板；

　　1.6 Re-bar to slab（by others）楼面扎铁；1.6a E&M for slab（by others）机电留孔，线合等工作；

　　1.7 Embedment installation（by others）留幕墙，佛沙，阳台等预留螺丝

2. Check vertically 检查铅直度

3. Check level 检查标高

4. Check stub pins are properly wedged 检查销子是否正确地楔入

TEXT A

Formwork（1）

Formwork is the term given to either temporary or permanent moulds into which concrete or similar materials are poured.

Figure 1　Modular steel frame formwork for a foundation

Figure 2　Timber formwork for a concrete pillar

In this building many beams are longer than 4m, the bottom formwork is supported by the steel square support and is made upward-arched 1/1000 of span. After pouring concrete, the weight of concrete makes the bottom formwork become plain that is complied with the specification.

Figure 1

Figure 2

If the constructor plans to install formwork for the upper floor on the existing floor which is newly completed of concreting, the existing concrete floor should reach a required surface strength which is not lower than 1.2N/mm^2, say 72 hours after the concrete pouring and it should be strong enough to bear the load of the upper floor.

When formwork is in removal, the surface, edges and corners of concrete should be maintained well without any damage. Workers like to remove the formwork the earlier the better, but the basic requirement of the specification must be followed, otherwise the quality of concrete can not be guaranteed.

The times to re-use the plywood formwork depend on different areas where it is used. For the key components, only new formwork is adopted. For the ordinary wall the formwork can be used for three times and for the area where the concrete will be covered or backfilled the formwork can be used for six or seven times.

For the sake of safety the most important thing is the timing of removing formwork for the bottom of beam and floor slab. for example, for a cantilevered slab with a span more than 2m. In this case the formwork can be removed after the strength of the concrete reaches 100% of its design strength. In a hot weather and in good curing condition it will need 10 days. If it is an ordinary slab the formwork can be removed much earlier, say 3 days after the 75% of design strength is reached.

There is the same operation for side surface when removing formwork for precast concrete element and formwork of cast‑in‑situ concrete But attention should be paid to the molds for core or holes and the concrete strength should be enough for the surface in order to avoid any collapse or leakage.

It is almost the same requirement to the bottom form of the precast beams and the concrete-in-situ. The only difference is that when the span of the beam is smaller than 4m the removing can be done after the precast concrete beam is in 50% of the designed strength.

On some occasions, the contractor may intend to employ the slip formwork for the project.

Notes

1. 模板工程指在制作、组装、运用及拆除在混凝土施工中用以使混凝土成型的构造设施的工作。使混凝土成型的构造设施称为模板。其构造包括面板体系和支撑体系。面板体系包括面板和所联系的肋条；支撑体系包括纵横围圈、承托梁、承托桁架、悬臂梁、悬臂桁架、支柱、斜撑与拉条等。

2. 早期普遍用木材制作模板。20世纪50年代以后，逐步发展到采用钢材、胶合板、钢筋混凝土，或是钢、木、混凝土等材料混合使用。也有以薄板钢材制作具有一定比例模数的定型组合钢模板。20世纪70年代以后，滑模技术有较大发展。

3. 模板虽然是辅助性结构，但在混凝土施工中至关重要。在水利工程中，模板工程的造价，占钢筋混凝土结构物造价的15%~30%，占钢筋混凝土造价的5%~15%，制作与安装模板的劳动力用量约占混凝土工程总用量的28%~45%。对结构复杂的工程，立模与绑扎钢筋所占的时间，比混凝土浇筑的时间长得多，因此模板的设计与组装工艺是混凝土施工中不容忽视的一个重要环节。

New Words

temporary ['tempərəri] adj. 1. 临时的，暂时的，短时间的 2. 无常的；短暂的

permanent ['pə：mənənt] adj. 1. 永久（性）的，固定的 2. 稳定的；恒定的

mould [məuld] n. 铸模，模型

span [spæn] n. 跨度

concrete ['kɔnkri：t] adj. 固结成的，混凝土制的，水泥的；n. 1. 混凝土；2. 具体物；具体情况；具体概念；vt. 1. 铺以混凝土，以混凝土浇筑；2. 使凝固，使固结；使融洽；vi. 1. 凝固，固结，变坚固；2. 使用混凝土

backfill ['bækfil] vt. 回填（挖掘的洞穴）

cantilever ['kæntili：və] n. 悬臂

New Phrases

modular steel frame formwork for a foundation　模块化的基础钢模框架

timber formwork for a concrete　灌注混凝土的木制（质）模板

bottom formwork　底部模板

upward‐arched　起拱

form removal　拆除模板

plywood formwork　胶合模板

cantilevered slab　悬臂板

design strength　设计强度

concrete-in-situ　现浇混凝土
precast concrete beam　预制混凝土梁
slip formwork　滑模

Role Play

A . Discuss the process of concreting by using the following words：
Standby labors to
   a. Ensure pins/wedges are not dislodged 确保销/楔无松动
   b. Ensure all bracing stay intact 确保没有遗漏斜撑并使其撑牢
   c. Ensure（that）props do not slipped due to vibration 确保所有的支撑在振捣时无滑移
B. Discuss the advantages of aluminum formwork（建筑铝模板）by using the following words：
   1. Environmental friendly（环保）：1.1 Save the trees 节约木材，1.2 Formwork can be re-used 模板可多次再利用
   2. Excellent surface finishes 良好的表面成形
   3. Dimensions variation kept to minimum 尺寸误差最小
   4. Less debris, better house-keeping 杂物较少，易于堆放

Exercises

I. Answer the following questions.

1. What is formwork？
2. How can the constructor install formwork for the upper floor on the existing floor which is newly completed of concrete？
3. When formwork is in removal, what should we pay attention to？
4. For the sake of safety, what is the most important thing when removing the forms？
5. What is the decisive factor when re-using the plywood formwork？

II. Complete the sentences with the given words or expression. Change the form where necessary.

1. More ＿＿＿＿＿＿（temper）workers are employed during the peak period.
2. When ＿＿＿＿＿＿（removal）forms, the surface, edges and corners of concrete should be maintained well without any damage.
3. The existing floor is newly completed of ＿＿＿＿＿＿（concrete）.
4. An ordinary slab the formwork can be removed 3 days later after the 75% of design ＿＿＿＿＿＿（strong）is reached.
5. the construction method should be ＿＿＿＿＿＿（comply）with the specification.

III. Translate the following words or phrases into English.

模块化钢模板的基础框架_____

灌注混凝土的木制（质）模板_____

底部模板_____

起拱_____

拆除模板_____

胶合模板_____

悬臂板_____

设计强度_____

现浇混凝土_____

预制混凝土梁_____

滑模_____

IV. Translate the following sentences into Chinese.

1. After pouring concrete, the weight of concrete makes the bottom formwork become plain that is complied with the specification.

_____

_____

2. For a cantilevered slab with a span more than 2m. In this case the formwork can be removed after the strength of the concrete reached 100% of its design strength. In a hot weather and in good curing condition it will need 10 days.

_____

_____

V. Reading the following materials on aluminium formwork and try to figure it out by referring to the translation.

Project（项目）：ALUMINIUM FORMWORK FORAREA 2 OF DUBAI SPORT CITY （迪拜体育城二区的建筑铝模板）

1. STRIKING OF FORMWORK 拆模

As the specification's requirements of this project, formwork must be dismantled according to the followings：

根据本工程的规范的要求，就按如下所示时间来拆除模板：

1. Side of beams, walls and column (unloaded)：12 hours

一天后拆除梁侧模、墙模和柱模（非承重）

2. Soffit of slab (prop left under)：36 hours (ANALYSIS ON EARLY STRIKING will submit later)

三十六小时后拆除板底模（支撑不拆）

3. Prop to slab (unload)：10 days

十天后拆除板底支撑（非承重）

4. Soffits of beams (prop left under)：36 hours (ANALYSIS ON EARLY STRIKING will submit later)

三十六小时后拆除梁底模（支撑不拆）

5. Prop to beam （unload）: 14 days

十四天后拆除梁底支撑（非承重）

6. Prop to cantilever: 28 days

二十八天后拆除悬臂底支撑

2. DEPLOYING OF FORMWORK 模板配置

1. Main set of system formwork （i. e. all location except stated in bellows）: 1 set

除非以下特别注明，模板主系统为一套。

2. Props under slab: 3 sets

楼板底支撑为三套。

3. Props under beam: 4 sets

梁底支撑为四套。

4. Props under cantilever: 6 sets

悬伸结构底支撑为六套。

TEXT B

Formwork （2）

Formwork comes in five main types:

Traditional timber formwork. The formwork is built on site out of timber and plywood or moisture-resistant particleboard. It is easy to produce but time-consuming for larger structures, and the plywood facing has a relatively short lifespan. It is still used extensively where the labor costs are lower than the costs for procuring re-usable formwork. It is also the most flexible type of formwork, so even where other systems are in use, complicated sections may use it.

Engineered Formwork Systems. This formwork is built out of prefabricated modules with a metal frame （usually steel or aluminum）. It has the wanted surface structure （steel, aluminum, timber, etc.）and can be covered on the application （concrete）side. The two major advantages of formwork systems, compared to traditional timber formwork, are speed of construction and lower life-cycle costs （barring major force, the frame is almost indestructible, while the covering if made of wood, may have to be replaced after a few -or a few dozen -uses, but if the covering is made with steel or aluminum the form can achieve up to two thousand uses depending on care and the applications）.

Re-usable plastic formwork. These interlocking and modular systems are used to build widely variable, but relatively simple, concrete structures. The panels are lightweight and very robust. They are especially suited for low-cost, mass housing schemes.

Permanent Insulated Formwork. This formwork is assembled on site, usually out of insulating concrete forms （ICF）. The formwork stays in place after the concrete has cured, and may provide advantages in terms of speed, strength, superior thermal and acoustic insulation, space to run utilities within the EPS layer, and integrated furring strip for cladding finishes.

Stay-in-Place structural formwork systems. This formwork is assembled on site, usually out of prefabricated fiber-reinforced plastic forms. These are in the shape of hollow tubes，and are usually used for columns and piers. The formwork stays in place after the concrete has cured and acts as axial and shear reinforcement，as well as serving to confine the concrete and prevent against environmental effects，such as corrosion．

New Words

particleboard［′pɑːtikəlˌbɔːd，-ˌbəurd］n. 芯板材；碎木板，刨花板

lifespan［′laifˌspæn］n. 1.（人或动物的）寿命，预期生命期限；2. 存在期；使用期；有效期

procure［prəu′kjuə］vt. .（努力）取得，（设法）获得，得到

prefabricated［priː′fæbrikeitid］adj.（建筑物、船等）预制构件的

indestructible［ˌindi′strʌktəbl］adj. 不能破坏的，不可毁灭的

panel［′pænl］n. 1. 专门小组；2. 面；板；3. 控制板，仪表盘；4.（门、墙等上面的）嵌板，镶板，方格板块

acoustic［ə′kuːstik］adj. 1. 声音的，听觉的；2. 原声的；自然声的

insulation［ˌinsə′leiʃən］n. 1. 隔离，隔绝；绝缘；隔音；2. 绝缘、隔热或隔音等的材料

corrosion［kə′rəuʒən］n. 1. 腐蚀；受腐蚀的部位；2. 腐蚀生成物如绣等；衰败

New Phrases

traditional timber formwork. 传统的木制板模

moisture-resistant 防潮

time-consuming 费时

engineered formwork systems 工程模板系统

re-usable plastic formwork 可重复使用的塑料模板

permanent insulated formwork. 永久绝缘模板

insulating concrete forms（ICF） 绝缘混凝土模板（ICF）

stay-in-place structural formwork systems 永久性结构模板系统

prefabricated fiber-reinforced plastic forms 预制强化纤维塑料模板

Exercises

I. Translate the following English items into Chinese.

Traditional timber formwork. ＿＿＿＿＿＿＿

moisture-resistant ＿＿＿＿＿＿＿

time-consuming ＿＿＿＿＿＿＿

Engineered Formwork Systems _____

Re-usable plastic formwork _____

Permanent Insulated Formwork _____

insulating concrete forms _____

Stay-In-Place structural formwork systems _____

prefabricated fiber-reinforced plastic forms _____

II. Read the following dialogue and try to figure out what they are talking about.

A：In your opinion，what's the use of formwork？

B：The formwork is very important in the project.

A：Please give an example.

B：Without formworks，the concrete will not be cast into its required shape.

A：What's the request of the formwork's rigidity？

B：It must comply with the design request.

A：What is the principle of the formwork design？

B：The principle of the design bases on several points：First the concrete pressure to the formwork，second，the concrete temperature and so on.

A：You are interested in the design of formworks.

B：Yes，because I am a designer.

TRANSLATION SKILLS

常用英汉互译技巧

一、增译法

　　根据英汉两种语言不同的思维方式、语言习惯和表达方式，在翻译时增添一些词、短句或句子，以便更准确地表达出原文所包含的意义。这种方式多半用在汉译英里。

　　1. 汉语无主句较多，而英语句子一般都要有主语。所以在翻译汉语无主句的时候，除了少数可用英语无主句、被动语态或 "There be…" 结构来翻译以外，一般都要根据语境补出主语，使句子完整。

　　2. 英汉两种语言在名词、代词、连词、介词和冠词的使用方法上也存在很大差别。英语中代词使用频率较高，凡说到人的器官和归某人所有的或与某人有关的事物时，必须在前面加上物主代词。因此，在汉译英时需要增补物主代词，而在英译汉时又需要根据情况适当地删减。

　　3. 英语词与词、词组与词组以及句子与句子的逻辑关系一般用连词来表示，而汉语则往往通过上下文和语序来表示这种关系。因此，在汉译英时常常需要增补连词。英语句子离不开介词和冠词。

　　4. 在汉译英时还要注意增补一些原文中暗含而没有明言的词语和一些概括性、注释性的词语，以确保译文意思的完整。

例如：

1. Indeed, the reverse is true.

实际<u>情况</u>恰好相反。（增译名词）

2. 这是这两代计算机之间的又一个共同点。

This is yet another common point <u>between</u> the computers of the two generations. （增译介词）

3. Individual mathematicians often have their own way of pronouncing mathematical expressions and in many cases there is no generally accepted "correct" pronunciation.

每个数学家对数学公式常常有各自的读法，在许多情况下，并不存在一个普遍接受的<u>所谓</u>"正确"读法。（增加隐含意义的词）

4. 只有在可能发生混淆、或要强调其观点时，数学家才使用较长的读法

It is only when confusion may occur, or where <u>he/she</u> wishes to emphasis the point, that the mathematician will use the longer forms. （增加主语）

二、省译法

这是与增译法相对应的一种翻译方法，即删去不符合目标语思维习惯、语言习惯和表达方式的词，以避免译文累赘。增译法的例句反之即可。

又如：

1. You will be staying in this hotel during <u>your</u> visit in Beijing.

你在北京访问期间就住在这家饭店里。（省译物主代词）

2. I hope you will enjoy your stay here.

希望您在这儿过得愉快。（省译主语）

3. 中国政府历来重视环境保护<u>工作</u>。

The Chinese government has always attached great importance to environmental protection. （省译名词）

4. The development of IC made <u>it</u> possible for electronic devices to become smaller and smaller.

集成电路的发展使电子器件可以做得越来越小。（省译形式主语 it）

三、转换法

1. Too much exposure to TV programs will do great harm to the eyesight of children.

孩子们看电视过多会大大地损坏视力。（名词转动词）

2. 由于我们实行了改革开放政策，我国的综合国力有了明显的增强。

Thanks to the introduction of our reform and opening policy, our comprehensive national strength has greatly improved. （动词转名词）

3. 时间不早了，我们回去吧！

We don't have much time left. Let's go back. （句型转换）

四、拆句法和合并法

1. Increased cooperation with China is in the interests of the United States.

同中国加强合作，符合美国的利益。（在主谓连接处拆译）

2. 中国是个大国，百分之八十的人口从事农业，但耕地只占土地面积的十分之一，其余为山脉、森林、城镇和其他用地。

China is a large country with four-fifths of the population engaged in agriculture, but only one tenth of the land is farmland, the rest being mountains, forests and places for urban and other uses. （合译法）

3. Packet switching is a method of slicing digital messages into parcels called "packets," sending the packets along different communication paths as they become available, and then reassembling the packets once they arrive at their destination.

分组交换是传输数据的一种方法，它先将数据信息分割成许多称为"分组"的数据信息包；当路径可用时，经过不同的通信路径发送；当到达目的地后，再将它们组装起来。（将长定语从句拆成几个并列的分句）

五、正译法和反译法

这两种方法通常用于汉译英，偶尔也用于英译汉。所谓正译，是指把句子按照与汉语相同的语序或表达方式译成英语。所谓反译则是指把句子按照与汉语相反的语序或表达方式译成英语。正译与反译常常具有同义的效果，但反译往往更符合英语的思维方式和表达习惯，因此比较地道。

1. 你可以从因特网上获得这一信息。

You can obtain this information on the Internet. （正译）

This information is accessible/available on the Internet. （反译）

2. 他突然想到了一个新主意。

Suddenly he had a new idea. （正译）

He suddenly thought out a new idea. （正译）

A new idea suddenly occurred to/struck him. （反译）

六、倒置法

在汉语中，定语修饰语和状语修饰语往往位于被修饰语之前；在英语中，许多修饰语常常位于被修饰语之后，因此翻译时往往要把原文的语序颠倒过来。倒置法通常用于英译汉，即对英语长句按照汉语的习惯表达法进行前后调换，按意群或进行全部倒置，原则是使汉语译句安排符合现代汉语论理叙事的一般逻辑顺序。有时倒置法也用于汉译英。

如：

1. At this moment, through the wonder of telecommunications, more people are seeing and hearing what we say than on any other occasions in the whole history of the world.

此时此刻，通过现代通信手段的奇迹，看到和听到我们讲话的人比整个世界历史上任何其他这样的场合都要多。（部分倒置）

2. 改革开放以来，中国发生了巨大的变化。

Great changes have taken place in China since the introduction of the reform and opening policy. （全部倒置）

七、包孕法

这种方法多用于英译汉。所谓包孕是指在把英语长句译成汉语时，把英语后置成分按照汉语的正常语序放在中心词之前，使修饰成分在汉语句中形成前置包孕。但修饰成分不宜过长，否则会形成拖沓或造成汉语句子成分在连接上的纠葛。

如：

1. IP multicasting is a set of technologies that enables efficient delivery of data to many locations on a network.

IP 多信道广播是使数据向网络中许多位置高效传送的一组技术。

2. What brings us together is that we have common interests which transcend those differences.

使我们走到一起的，是我们有超越这些分歧的共同利益。

八、插入法

指把难以处理的句子成分用破折号、括号或前后逗号插入译句中。这种方法主要用于笔译中。偶尔也用于口译中，即用同位语、插入语或定语从句来处理一些解释性成分。

如：

如果说宣布收回香港就会像夫人说的"带来灾难性的影响"，那我们将勇敢地面对这个灾难，做出决策。

If the announcement of the recovery of Hong Kong would bring about, as Madam put it, "disastrous effects," we will face that disaster squarely and make a new policy decision.

九、重组法

在进行英译汉时，为了使译文流畅和更符合汉语叙事论理的习惯，在将清英语长句的结构、弄懂英语原意的基础上，彻底摆脱原文语序和句子形式，对句子进行重新组合。

如：

Decision must be made very rapidly, physical endurance is tested as much as perception, because an enormous amount of time must be spent making certain that the key figures act on the basis of the same information and purpose.

必须把大量时间花在确保关键人物均根据同一情报和目的行事，而这一切对身体的耐力和思维能力都是一大考验。因此，一旦考虑成熟，决策者就应迅速做出决策。

十、综合法

指单用某种翻译技巧无法译出时，着眼篇章，以逻辑分析为基础，同时使用转换法、倒置法、增译法、省译法、拆句法等多种翻译技巧的方法。

如：

Behind this formal definition are three extremely important concepts that are the basis for understanding the Internet: packet switching, the TCP/IP communications protocol, and client/server computing.

在这个正式的定义背后，隐含着三个极其重要的概念：分组交换、TCP/IP（传输控制协议/网际协议）通信协议和客户机/服务器计算技术，它们乃是理解因特网的基础。

译　文

第六单元　模板工程

对　话

模板工程检查

咨询工程师：大家都知道，没有模板，混凝土就不能浇筑成形。让我们看看现场模板的安装情况。这块墙体模板较大，你们怎样才能使它固定牢靠？

承　包　方：我们称这种模板为大型预制模板。首先它要安装在有足够空间且排水良好的坚硬场地上。其次，依照安装图，它必须由锚固件和框架支撑。

咨询工程师：你们将采取什么方法防止混凝土从模板连接处溢出呢？

承 包 方：我们用泡沫材料和塑胶条封住连接处。它很管用。

咨询工程师：我认为这儿，大模板穿墙杆拉结螺栓不符合设计图的要求。螺栓直径应为25mm，但是工人却在用12mm的螺栓固定。你能说出替换的原因吗？请在10分钟内回答我。

承 包 方：（5分钟后）真是对不起，我们犯了一个大错。因为25mm直径螺栓一时供应不上，为了避免耽误工期，所以作了替换。我已经让工头把这部分墙模板所有直径为12mm的螺栓换成了25mm的。

咨询工程师：换一下是远远不够的。在合同条件中规定，未经工程师同意，不能改变图纸上的任何东西。依我看，应该解雇决定替换的这名工头以警告工地上所有的人。至少应该对他有所惩罚，向全工地通告这是一个严重的错误以杜绝今后再发生类似情况。

承 包 方：我们会采取严厉措施的，并通告全工地这是一个非常严重的质量问题。另外还要采取一些有力措施以避免此类情况再次发生。

课文 A   模板工程（1）

模板工程这个术语是指内部灌注混凝土或类似材料的临时或永久的筑模。

图1 模块化的基础钢模框架

图2 灌注混凝土的木质模板

在这个建筑物中很多梁的跨度超过4m长，底部模板使用钢支撑并按1/1000跷度起拱。浇筑混凝土后，模板受重，底部变平直，从而达到规范要求的平直度。

如果承包方计划在新浇筑混凝土楼面安装上层楼面模板，那么已建的混凝土楼面应达到不低于1.2N/mm^{2}的表面强度，也就是说在灌注混凝土后的72小时，它应当足够承载上层楼板的荷载。

在拆除模板时，混凝土的表面，边缘和拐角都应当保持完好不受损伤。工人们往往觉得拆除模板越早越好，但一定要遵守工程规范的基本要求，否则混凝土的质量就不能得到保证。

胶合模板重复使用的次数取决于建筑物的不同部位。对于主要部分，只能使用新模板。对于普通墙体，模板可重复使用三次，对于混凝土将被覆盖或回填的部位，模板可重复使用六到七次。

为了安全起见，拆除梁和楼板底部模板的时间是极为重要的。例如，对于跨度超过2m的悬臂板，这种情况下，需在混凝土强度达到设计强度的100%之后拆除模板。在炎热的天气且混凝土凝结条件好的情况下将需要10天。如果是普通板，拆除模板的时间就早多了，也就是说在达到设计强度75%的3天后即可。

对于预制混凝土构件和现浇混凝土的模板，在拆除侧面模板时的操作是相同的，但需要注意筑模的核心和空洞。而且为避免倾倒或损坏，应在混凝土表面达到足够强度时才能拆除。

预制梁和现浇混凝土的底部模板的拆除要求也大体相同。唯一不同的是当梁的跨度小于4m时，预制混凝土梁达到设计强度的50%之后就可以拆除模板。

在有些情况下，承包方可在工程中使用滑模。

课文 B　模板工程（2）

模板主要有五种类型

传统的木模板。这种模板是在现场用木材和胶合板或防潮碎木板制成的。它容易制作，但对于大型建筑来说很费工时，且胶合板还有使用期相对较短的问题。在劳动力成本比生产可重复模板的成本低的地方这种模板被广泛使用。这也是最灵活的模板类型，所以即使使用其他模板类型，在复杂的建筑部位也可能会用到它。

金属模板。这种模板是用金属（通常是钢或铝）预制模具制成，具有木模板、钢模板、铝模板等的表面结构，可用于混凝土的浇筑成型。这种模板与传统的木模板相比有两个主要的优点，一是施工速度快，二是使用周期中成本较低。（除非受到强大的外力，金属模板是不易损毁的。但木模板在使用几次或几十次之后就需要更换，而钢模板或铝合金模板在谨慎使用的情况下其使用次数可达 2000 次）。

可重复使用的塑料模板。这种相扣的模板系统用来建造造型复杂，但相对单一的混凝土建筑。嵌板轻但很坚固。非常适合于造价低廉的大面积住宅项目。

永久绝缘模板。这种模板在现场组装，通常由绝缘的混凝土结构（ICF）制成。这种模板在混凝土凝固后留在原地，可以带来诸多好处，它建造速度快，模板强度高，对外部的温度和声音有阻隔作用，在 ESP 层有安装公用设施的空间而且还可用各种装饰条进行外部装饰。

保留性结构模板系统。这种模板在现场装配通常由预制纤维增强塑料模板制成。它们的形状为空心管状，通常用来建柱和墩。这种模板在混凝土凝固后留在原地起加固轴力和剪力的作用，同时还能封住混凝土使之不受腐蚀等环境影响。

UNIT 7

Reinforcement Works（钢筋工程）

DIALOGUE

Inspection of reinforcement works

E: Firstly please let me know the measures which can enable you to control the quality of the reinforcement works in accordance with the Chinese standard.

C: Yes, of course. I'd like to thank you for your approval of adopting Chinese steel for the partial works of the project. According to our Quality Assurance Program, Before the material was ordered, a group Was sent to carry out an inspection to the steel manufacturer, which included visiting the steel mill to study their production procedures and quality control measures.

E: That's good. But even though the inspection was well done and the result was satisfying, there still should be no negligence in further steps of the works. Let's see what we can do after the reinforcement bar arrives on site.

C: These are the Quality Certificates and Test Reports from the manufacturer. All physical character and chemical components are complied with the specification.

E: That's all right. Now I'd like to discuss the rebar testing with your technician. I hope to be introduced about the sequence of rebar test. (turn to the technician)

T: (Technician): Before doing tests we will inspect the rebar surface. We will check if the size of the rebar is complied with the specification, and if there are any leakages, scars or honeycombs on the surface. After the surface is accepted, the sampled rebars will be tested.

E: What kind of tests do you usually do?

T: The tests most frequently done by us are the physical tests. We take 2 segments of 2 pieces of rebar from each batch of 60t as testing samples. One of the segments will be tension-tested for its yield point, tension strength and the extension rate. The other segment will be tested for its cold bending degree. In case brittle leakage or bad welding performance does occur during test, chemical contentment analysis or other special tests must be done to find out the cause (s).

E: OK. Your description is all right. Thank you.

New Words

reinforcement [ˌriːinˈfɔːsmənt] n. 加强，强化

steel bars for concrete reinforcement 钢筋钢

stretching equipment for prestressing reinforcement 预应力钢筋张拉设备

approval [əˈpruːvəl] n. 1. 赞成，同意；2. 批准，认可

audit [ˈɔːdit] n. 审计，审查，查账

negligence [ˈneglidʒəns] n. 疏忽，玩忽，失职，失误，过失

rebar [riˈbɑː] n. 钢筋；螺纹钢筋

technician [tekˈniʃən] n. 技术人员

leakage [ˈliːkidʒ] n. 漏出物，渗漏物；泄漏量；漏损量

honeycomb [ˈhʌnikəum] n. 麻面，蜂窝，蜂巢

strength [ˈstreŋθ] n. 力量，强度

New Phrases

reinforcement works　钢筋工程

in accordance with　依据，与…一致

Quality Assurance　质量保证

steel manufacturer　钢材生产厂家

steel mill　钢铁厂

place an order　订货

Quality Certificates　产品合格证

physical character　物理特性

chemical components　化学组成成分

be complied with…　符合…

rebar testing　钢筋试验

tension test　拉伸试验

yielded point　屈服点

tension strength　抗拉强度
extension rate　延伸率
cold bending degree　冷弯曲度
a chemical content analysis　化学成分分析

Role Play

Make a brief summary about the inspection of reinforcement works mentioned in the dialogue and discuss with your partner what aspects one should pay attention to while inspecting reinforcement works in the construction site.

TEXT A

Steel Reinforcement Bar

An introduction to types of steel reinforcement bar

1. Classified by mechanical properties

Based on the differences of yield strength and the types, steel reinforcement bar can be classified into four grades of HPB235, HRB335, HRB400 and RRB400. Letter "H", "P", "B" represents "Hot rolled", "Plain", "Bar" respectively. The second letter "R" in the latter three grades is the abbreviation of "Ribbed", and the first letter "R" in the fourth grade stands for "Remained heat treatment".

Steel grade - level symbols

Grade of reinforcement steel	Steel specification	Symbol
I	HPB235	Φ
II	HRB335	$\underline{\Phi}$
III	HRB400	$\underline{\Phi}$
	RRB400	$\underline{\Phi}^R$
IV	HRB540	

2. Classified by processing technology

　　Based on the processing technology, steel reinforcement bar can be classified into types such as hot rolled ribbed steel bar (HRB), remained heat treatment ribbed steel bar (RRB), cold-stretched steel bar, cold drawn low carbon steel wire, steel heat treatment, cold rolled and twisted bar, finishing spiral reinforcement, indented steel wire and stranded steel wire.

　　Hot- rolled steel bar, such as HRB335 and HRB400, is a finished product shaped by hot rolling and cooled naturally.

Remained heat treatment ribbed steel bar（RRB）, such as RRB400, indicates applying water cooling process to the steel bar surface after shaped by hot rolling, then forging the final steel product through tempering treatment by use of the remained heat of the core.

Cold-stretched steel bar is processed at the scene while cold-drawn steel wire is produced at the plant. Prestressing wire basically has to be cold-stretched.

Heat treatment of reinforcement bar is to treat hot-rolled ribbed bar by ways of quenching and tempering so as to improve its strength significantly.

For the project in Dubai, prestressing steel is stretched at the spot and pipe sleeves are placed complying to design requirements. After concreting and the curing of concrete, prestressing steel is stretched again, which should also comply with the design specification.

3. Classified by chemical composition

In this item, steel reinforcement bar can be classified into carbon steel bars and ordinary low alloy steel bars. The mechanical properties of carbon steel bars are related to the content of carbon. Increase in carbon content can enhance the strength and hardness of steel but reduce its plasticity, toughness and welding performance as well. Ordinary low-alloy steel is carbon steel by adding small amount of alloy elements such as manganese, silicon, vanadium and titanium (the content of these are no more than 3% of the total). These alloy elements can improve performances of steel such as the strength and plasticity.

4. Classified by the shape

In this classification, the steel reinforcement can be divided into plain steel bar and deformed steel bar（screw thread, herringbone and crescent）. The surface of plain steel is smooth, HPB235 is plain steel bar, and HRB335, HRB400 and RRB400 are deformed steel bars.

New Words

bar ［bɑːr］ n. 长条，棒，栏杆（常用作护栏）

yield ［jiːld］ vt. （受压）活动，变形，弯曲，折断

represent ［ˌrepriˈzent］ 1. 表现，描绘；2. 代表，象征，表示

roll ［rəul］ vt. & vi. 1. （使）打滚，（使）转动，滚动；2. 卷，把…卷成筒状 vt. 碾平

abbreviation ［əˌbriːviˌeiʃən］ n. 1. 缩写；缩写词；2. 略语；缩写词；缩写形式

rib ［rib］ n. 1. 肋骨，骨架；2. （船或屋顶等的）肋拱，肋材；3. （织物的）凸条花纹，螺纹

stretch ［stretʃ］ vt. & vi. 1. 伸展；拉紧；2. 延伸

twist ［twist］ vt. & vi. 扭，搓，缠绕

strand ［strænd］ n. （线、绳、金属线、毛发等的）股，缕

spiral ［ˈspaiərəl］ adj. 螺旋形的

reinforcement ［ˌriːinˈfɔːsmənt］ n. 巩固，加强，强化

indent ［ˈindent］ vt. 切割…使呈锯齿状

forge ［fɔːdʒ］ vt. 锻造

prestress［′priː′stres］vt. 给…预加应力

quench［kwentʃ］vt. 1.（用水）扑灭（火焰等），熄灭；2. 将（热物体）放入水中急速冷却

temper［′tempə］vt. 1. 使缓和，使温和；2. 使（金属）回火

sleeve［sliː v］n. 1. 衣服袖子；2. 套管，套筒

plasticity［plæ′stisəti］n. 1. 黏性，成形性，柔软性；2. 可塑性，塑性

toughness［′tʌfnis］n. 韧性，坚韧，刚性，健壮性

weld［weld］vt. & vi. 焊接；熔接；锻接

deform［diˈfɔː m］vt. 使变形

herringbone［′heriŋbəun］n. 鲱鱼鱼骨，交叉缝式，人字形

crescent［′kresnt］n. 新月，月牙 adj. 新月形的，逐渐增加的

New Phrases

steel reinforcement bar　钢筋

mechanical property　机械性能

standard yield strength　标准屈服强度

hot rolled　热轧

remained heat treatment　余热处理

hot rolled ribbed steel bar（HRB）　热轧罗纹钢筋

remained heat treatment ribbed steel bar（RRB）　余热处理罗纹钢筋

cold-stretched steel bar　冷拉钢筋

cold-drawn low carbon steel wire　冷拔低碳钢丝

steel heat treatment　热处理钢筋

cold rolled and twisted bar　冷轧扭钢筋

finishing spiral reinforcement　精轧螺旋钢筋

indented steel wire　刻痕钢丝

stranded steel wire　钢绞线

prestressing wire　预应力钢丝

Heat treatment by quenching and tempering　淬火和回火的调质热处理

pipe sleeve　管套

curing（cure）concrete　养护混凝土

carbon steel bar　碳素钢筋

ordinary low alloy steel bar　普通低合金钢筋

carbon content　含碳量

welding performance　焊接性能

plain steel bar　光面钢筋

deformed steel bar　变形钢筋

screw thread　螺纹

Role Play

Discuss with your partner about different classifications of reinforcement bar and their application in the construction field.

Exercises

I. Answer the following questions.

1. Based on the differences in the standard yield strength and the types, how many grades steel reinforcement bar can be divided into? What are they?
2. Are hot rolled ribbed steel bar (HRB) and remained heat treatment ribbed steel bar (RRB) in the same classification when based on their processing technology?
3. What are the mechanical properties of carbon steel bars related to?
4. Can increase in carbon content enhance the strength and hardness of steel?
5. Based on the shape what is the steel reinforcement divided into?

II. Complete the sentences with the given words or expression. Change the form where necessary.

1. In the construction field, the quality of steel reinforcement bars should be in _____ (accord) with the standards of China.
2. All physical character and chemical components of steel reinforcement bars should be _____ (comply) with the technical specification.
3. Classified by the _____ (machine) properties, the types of steel reinforcement bar are HPB235, HRB335, HRB400 and RRB400.
4. Increase in carbon content of carbon steel bars can weaken its welding _____ (perform).
5. Due to shape of steel reinforcement bars, they can be divided into plain steel bar and _____ (deform) steel bar

III. Translate the following words or phrases into English.

钢筋工程_____ 产品合格证_____
质量保证程序_____ 物理特性_____
钢材生产厂家_____ 化学组成成分_____
钢铁厂_____ 拉伸试验_____
屈服点_____ 标准屈服强度_____
抗拉强度_____ 热轧_____
延伸率_____ 余热处理_____
冷弯曲度_____ 热轧钢筋_____
钢筋_____

余热处理钢筋＿＿＿＿＿＿　　　　　冷轧扭钢筋＿＿＿＿＿＿

冷拉钢筋＿＿＿＿＿＿　　　　　　　精轧螺旋钢筋＿＿＿＿＿＿

冷拔低碳钢丝＿＿＿＿＿＿　　　　　刻痕钢丝＿＿＿＿＿＿

热处理钢筋＿＿＿＿＿＿　　　　　　钢绞线＿＿＿＿＿＿

预应力钢丝＿＿＿＿＿＿

淬火和回火的调质热处理＿＿＿＿＿＿　管套＿＿＿＿＿＿

养护混凝土＿＿＿＿＿＿

碳素钢筋＿＿＿＿＿＿　　　　　　　光面钢筋＿＿＿＿＿＿

普通低合金钢筋＿＿＿＿＿＿　　　　变形钢筋＿＿＿＿＿＿

含碳量＿＿＿＿＿＿　　　　　　　　螺纹＿＿＿＿＿＿

IV. Translate the following sentences into Chinese.

1. Remained heat treatment ribbed steel bar （RRB）, such as RRB400, indicates applying water cooling process to the steel bar surface after hot rolling of it, then forging the final steel product through tempering treatment.

2. Heat treatment of reinforcement bar is to treat hot-rolled ribbed bar by ways of quenching and tempering so as to improve its strength significantly.

3. For the project in Dubai, prestressing steel is stretched at the spot and pipe sleeves are placed complying to design requirements. After concreting and curing concrete, prestressing steel is stretched again, which should also comply with the design specification.

V. The following is a brief description of Bao steel. Read it carefully and try your best to figure it out by referring to the Chinese.

High Grade Construction Steel

Bao steel leads its domestic peers in producing structure steel used for high buildings. Bao steel weathering steel possesses the same quality as its international rivals, and is widely used in high buildings. The Bao steel color coated plate is extensively used to build villas, motels and granaries. Our high strength color coated plate product series can be used in large span arch construction. Bao steel has also developed the hot coated aluminum zinc base plate, and the fluorocarbon and high grade polyurethane preprinted galvanized plate, the latter of which has been used in the electricity generating building of China's Great Wall Station at the South Pole.

高级建筑用钢

宝钢钢板在高层建筑钢结构 （structure steel） 中的应用处于国内领先，耐候钢板

（weathering steel）实物质量与世界同类产品相当，并在高层住宅中广泛应用。宝钢彩涂板（color coated plate）被广泛用于建造度假村、移动式宾馆、大型粮仓，高强彩涂板系列产品，可应用于大跨度拱形建筑（large span arch construction）。宝钢还开发了热镀铝锌基板彩涂板（hot coated aluminum zinc base plate）以及氟碳、高性能聚酯等新的表面涂层（fluorocarbon and high grade polyurethane preprinted galvanized plate），采用氟碳表面涂层的彩色钢板已经应用于中国南极长城站发电楼（electricity generating building）。

TEXT B

Construction Technology of Rebar

1. The test of rebar

Rebar to be delivered to site should possess quality certificate or test report. Each bundle of rebar should have labels indicating factory mark, steel grade, heat (batch) number and specifications.

Regular examinations always include inspections of mechanical properties such as static tensile test and cold bending test. By static tensile test, stress-strain curves can be obtained to determine the yield strength, tensile strength, extension rate. Cold bending test indicates the crack-resistance capability of rebar with plastic deformation by cold working at the room temperature. It is a test to measure the resistance to bending deformation of rebar at the room temperature.

For the project in Dubai, it requires that rebar should have a sampling test when it is delivered to the construction site. After being marked, sampled bars will be sent to quality control station to be tested. Only with the test certificate, the rebar can be used at the spot.

2. Bending and cutting of reinforcement rebar

In the process of manufacturing steel at the scene, the rebar bending schedule should be checked carefully against the design so as to avoid errors and omissions and every type of rebar should be tested to be in compliance with the rebar bending schedule.

After these two steps, samples can be produced based on the rebar bending schedule. Only when the samples are tested to be qualified, mass production is permitted. Processed steel should be listed and stacked orderly.

3. The replacement of rebar

If rebar to be used needs replacing in the construction, it is essential to study the intent of design and the properties of the substitution. The provisions in the existing technical specification for steel design should be strictly followed. The principles of replacement include equal strength replacement, equal rebar cross-section and so on. Anyway after the rebar replacement, the structure strength, total cross-section areas and other requirements from the structure, should be maintained as not less than the original. High-tensile steel bar can't substitute the low-tensile ones with the same quantities. When steel bars are substituted in the key parts, the approval of the client and designers should be obtained and a written notice is also required.

4. Processing of rebar

The processing of rebar involves cold tension, cold drawing, straightening, cutting and bending. In the cold working of rebar (including cold tension and cold drawn), cold tension can play the role of straightening and rust removal.

5. Connection of steel reinforcement bars

The connection of steel reinforcement bars involves banding, welding and mechanical connections. Bound connection refers to banding lap joints. Welded connection can be classified into flash butt welding, arc welding, electroslag pressure welding and pressure welding. Mechanical connection can be classified into sleeve cold-pressure joints and screw threaded steel pipe joints.

As for two different grades of steel bars to be welded, the strength of the welding joints must satisfy that of the lower grade. The lapping joint of rebar should be carried out in accordance with the specification and samples from every type of welded rebar should be sent to the quality control station to have a test.

6. Installation and inspection of rebar

The type, grade, size and quantity of the principal rebar should comply with the requirement of design. In addition, rebar should be positioned accurately and fixed reliably. The joints should be in compliance with the specification. The position of welded rebar should possess a certificate issued by quality inspection station and rust can not occur on the surface of the rebar.

Notes

钢筋可翻译为：rebar, reinforcing bar, 或者 reinforcing steel, reinforcement steel, deformed bar.

New Words

rebar [ri′bɑ：] n. 钢筋；螺纹钢筋

deliver [di′livə] vt. & vi. 递送，交付

possess [pə′zes] vt. 1. 具有；2. 占据；3. 有，拥有

tensile [′tensəl] adj. 1. 拉力的，张力的，抗张的；2. 可伸展的，可拉长的，可延展的

omission [əu′miʃən] n. 1. 省略，删节，遗漏；2. 略去或漏掉的事（或人）

intent [in′tent] n. 意图，意向，目的

substitution [ˌsʌbsti′tu：ʃən] n. 1. 代替，代用，替换；2. 代替物，代用品，替换物

straighten [′streitn] vt. & vi. 1. （使）变直，把…弄直；2. （使）变直

arc [ɑ：k] vi. 1. 作弧形运动；2. 形成电弧

electroslag [i′lektrəuslæg] adj. 电渣焊接法的；电渣冶炼法的

rust [rʌst] n. 铁锈 vt. & vi. （使）生锈

New Phrases

construction technology   施工工艺

quality certificate　质量证明书
test report　试验报告
factory mark　厂标
steel grade　钢号
heat（batch）number　炉号
static tensile test　静力拉伸试验
cold bending test　冷弯试验
stress-strain curve　应力-应变曲线
yield strength　屈服强度
tensile strength　抗拉强度
extension rate　伸长率
plastic deformation　塑性变形
cold working　冷加工
at the room temperature　常温下
rebar bending schedule　下料表
rebar cross-section　钢截面面积
high-tensile steel bar　高强度钢筋
bound connection　绑扎连接
lap joint　搭接接头
welded connection　焊接连接
flash butt welding　闪光对焊
arc welding　电弧焊
electroslag pressure welding　电渣压力焊
pressure welding　气压焊
mechanical connection　机械连接
sleeve cold-pressure joint　套筒冷压接头
screw threaded steel pipe joint　螺纹套管钢筋接头
quality control station　质检站

Exercises

I. Translate the following English items into Chinese.

plastic deformation _____

rebar bending schedule _____

rebar cross-section _____

high-tensile steel bar _____

lap joint _____

cold bending test _____

stress-strain curve _____

yield strength _____

tensile strength _____

extension rate _____

welded connection _____

flash butt welding _____

arc welding _____

electroslag pressure welding _____

pressure welding _____

mechanical connection _____

construction technology _____

quality certificate _____

steel grade _____

heat（batch）number _____

static tensile test _____

sleeve cold‐pressure joint _____

screw threaded steel pipe joint _____

quality control station _____

II. Read the following dialogue and try to figure out what they are talking about by referring to the Chinese.

Inspection of reinforcement work

（The supervisor of the project is inspecting reinforcement works. He wants to know how the engineer calculates （计算）the length of each rebar （钢筋）in the concrete and what the principle （原则）of replacement （替换）is if the rebar in the drawing is not available as well as something about rebar fixing （钢筋安装）. The engineer tells him that the formula （公式）of calculating the cutting length is the rebar surface dimension （表面长度）in the drawing minus （减）the bending extension length （弯曲拉伸长度）and plus （加）the length of hooks at the ends, and anyway after the rebar replacement, the structure length, total cross-section areas （整个钢截面面积）and other requirements from the structure should be maintained （保持）as not less than the original （原来的）. As for the last question, the engineer says if the rebar is bearing the tension force （承受拉力）, the fixing length should not be less than 45 times of the diameters （直径）. At last, the supervisor is quite satisfied with the engineer's work, and considers him as an experienced （有经验）and incisive （切中要害）staff. ）

A：Now it's time to go to the rebar yard. Please bring me the rebar bending schedule. How do you calculate the length of each rebar in the concrete?

B：We usually calculate the cutting length by this way：the rebar surface dimension in the drawing minus the bending extension length and plus the dimension of hooks in ends. The bending extension length （measuring deviation）depends on the rebar diameter, bending angle and other different conditions, so it is necessary to have a trial bending for the actual measuring deviation.

A：What is the principle for replacement if the rebar in the drawing is not available but you want to use an alternative rebar?

B：According to the working procedure we will submit our alternative proposal with the calculation for approval first. The principles of replacement include equal strength replacement, equal rebar cross section and so on. Anyway after the rebar replacement, the structure strength, total cross section areas and other requirements from the structure should be maintained as not less than the original.

A：I think you've got the point. Now let's have a discussion about the rebar fixing. In case the diameter 32mm rebar of grade 3 be fixed in C30 concrete, how do you decide the lap length?

B：If the rebar is bearing the tension force, the fixing length should not be less than 45 times of the diameters.

A：Please look at these fixed joints in the cross section. I think there is a problem in your actual fixing operation. Please calculate how many joints should be lapped in this cross section?

B：There are 10 laps in the cross section.

A：What force will the rebars bear in the area and how many rebars are there in total in the cross section?

B：Tension force. I see. There are 30 pieces of rebars in the cross section. The laps in the cross section should be less than 25% of total rebar number. So we must adjust the laps location by replacing 3 rebars without laps at this area. Thank you for your reminding.

对　话

A：现在我们去钢筋加工厂吧。给我看一下钢筋下料表，你们是如何计算混凝土钢筋的长度的？

B：通常切断长度是这样计算的：用图示钢筋表面的长度减去由于弯曲拉伸了的长度，再加上端部弯钩的长度。弯曲拉伸的长度（测量偏差）有赖于钢筋的直径、弯曲角及其他一些不同的条件，所以很有必要通过弯曲试验得到实际的计算偏差。

A：如果图中的钢筋不能用，要替换，替代的原则是什么？

B：根据施工程序，我们将把要替换钢筋的建议及计算结果提交给业主，以取得同意。替而代之的钢筋要与原拟采用钢筋具有同样的强度、相等的截面等等。不管怎样，换过钢筋之后，结构强度、整个钢截面面积及其他结构上的要求应该不小于原来的要求。

A：你说的切中要害。现在我们说说钢筋安装吧。如果直径为 32mm 的三级钢筋用在 C30 的混凝土中，你怎样决定搭接长度呢？

B：如果该钢筋是受拉，搭接长度不应小于直径的 45 倍。

A：请看这个截面的绑扎结头。我看这里的绑扎有问题。请计算一下这个截面上应该有多少根钢筋搭接？

B：这个截面上共有 10 个搭接。

A：在这个面上钢筋要受什么力？总共有多少根钢筋？

B：这个面上受的是拉力，总共有 30 根钢筋。我明白了，截面上搭接个数应少于钢筋数量的 25%。所以我们必须调整搭接的位置，在这个截面上换上 3 根没有搭接的钢筋。谢谢你的提醒。

TRANSLATION SKILLS

英语长句的翻译

在工程英语中，为了明确陈述有关事物的内在特征和相互联系，常采用包含许多子句的复合句，或包含许多附加成分（如定语、状语、主语补足语、宾语补足语等）的简单句。因此，使用长句较多。有些长句所叙述的一连串动作基本上是按动作发生的时间先后或逻辑关系安排的。这与汉语的表达方式一致。这时，可按原文顺序翻译，也就是采用顺译法。例如：In general, drying a solid means the removal of relatively small amounts of water or other liquid from the solid material to reduce the content of residual liquid to an acceptably low value. 可译为：一般来讲，干燥一种固体指的是从固体材料中除去相对少量的水或其他液体，从而使残留液体的含量减少到可接受的低值。但是大多数长句都是较为复杂，因此，首先要懂得如何分析长句。

一、英语长句的分析

一般来说，造成长句的原因有三方面：（1）修饰语过多；（2）并列成分多；（3）语言结构层次多。

在分析长句时可以采用下面的方法：

①找出全句的主语、谓语和宾语，从整体上把握句子的结构。

②找出句中所有的谓语结构、非谓语动词、介词短语和从句的引导词。

③分析从句和短语的功能，例如，是否为主语从句，宾语从句，表语从句等，若是状语，它是表示时间、原因、结果、还是表示条件等等。

④分析词、短语和从句之间的相互关系，例如，定语从句所修饰的先行词是哪一个等。

⑤注意插入语等其他成分。

⑥注意分析句子中是否有固定词组或固定搭配。

例. For a family of four, for example, it is more convenient as well as cheaper to sit comfortably at home, with almost unlimited entertainment available, than to go out in search of amusement elsewhere.

分析：（1）该句的骨干结构为 it is more … to do sth than to do sth else. 是一个比较结构，而且是在两个不定式之间进行比较。（2）该句中共有三个谓语结构，它们之间的关系为：it is more convenient as well as cheaper to … 为主体结构，但 it 是形式主语，真正的主语为第二个谓语结构：to sit comfortably at home，并与第三个谓语结构 to go out in search of amusement elsewhere 作比较。（3）句首的 for a family of four 作状语，表示条件。另外，还有两个介词短语作插入语：for example, with almost unlimited entertainment available，其中第二个介词短语作伴随状语，修饰 to sit comfortably at home.

[译文] 譬如，对于一个四口之家来说，舒舒服服地在家中看电视，就能看到几乎数不清的娱乐节目，这比到外面别的地方去消遣又便宜又方便。

英语习惯于用长的句子表达比较复杂的概念，而汉语则不同，常常使用若干短句，作层次分明的叙述。因此，在进行英译汉时，要特别注意英语和汉语之间的差异，将英语的长句分解，翻译成汉语的短句。在英语长句的翻译过程中，我们一般采取下列的方法。

1. 顺序法

当英语长句内容的叙述层次与汉语基本一致时，可以按照英语原文的顺序翻译成汉语。

例. Even when we turn off the bedside lamp and are fast asleep, electricity is working for us, driving our refrigerators, heating our water, or keeping our rooms air-conditioned.

分析：该句子由一个主句，三个作伴随状语的现在分词以及位于句首的时间状语从句组成，共有五层意思：A. 即使在我们关掉了床头灯深深地进入梦乡时；B. 电仍在为我们工作；C. 帮我们开动电冰箱；D. 加热水；E. 或是室内空调机继续运转。上述五层意思的逻辑关系以及表达的顺序与汉语完全一致。

[译文] 即使在我们关掉了床头灯深深地进入梦乡时，电仍在为我们工作：帮我们开动电冰箱，把水加热，或使室内空调机继续运转。

2. 逆序法

英语有些长句的表达次序与汉语表达习惯不同，甚至完全相反，这时必须从原文后面开始翻译。

例. For our purposes we will say e-commerce begins in 1995, following the appearance of the first banner advertisements placed by ATT, Volvo, Sprint and others on Hotwired. com in late October 1994, and the first sales of banner ad space by Netscape and Infoseek in early 1995.

[译文] 伴随着 ATT、Volvo、Sprint 等公司所做的第一例横幅广告于 1994 年 10 月下旬出现在 Hotwired. com 上，和 1995 年初 Netscape 与 Infoseek 领先出售横幅广告空间，我们会说电子商务是从 1995 年开始的。

3. 分句法

有时英语长句中主语或主句与修饰词的关系并不十分密切，翻译时可以按照汉语多用短句的习惯，把长句的从句或短语化成句子，分开来叙述，为了使语意连贯，有时需要适当增加词语。

例. The number of the young people in the United States who can't read is incredible about one in four.

上句在英语中是一个相对简单的句子，但是如果我们按照原文的句子结构死译，就可能被翻译成："没有阅读能力的美国青年人的数目令人难以置信约为1/4。"这样，就使得译文极为不通顺，不符合汉语的表达习惯，因此，我们应该把它译为：

[译文] 大约有1/4的美国青年人没有阅读能力，这简直令人难以置信。

4. 综合法

事实上，在翻译一个英语长句时，并不只是单纯地使用一种翻译方法，而是要求我们把各种方法综合使用，这在我们上面所举的例子中也有所体现。尤其是在一些情况下，一些英语长句单纯采用上述任何一种方法都不方便，这就需要我们的仔细分析，或按照时间的先后，或按照逻辑顺序，顺逆结合，主次分明地对全句进行综合处理，以便把英语原文翻译成通顺忠实的汉语句子。

例. Napster. com, which was established to aid Internet users in finding and sharing online music files known as *MP3 files*, is perhaps the most well known example of peer-to-peer ecommerce, although purists note that Napster is only partially peer-to-peer because it relies on a central database to show which users are sharing music files.

［译文］Napster. com 建立的目标是帮助因特网用户发现并分享在线音乐文件，即人所共知的 MP3 文件。尽管纯化论者强调：因为它依赖中央数据库来显示哪一位用户正在分享音乐文件，所以 Napster 仅仅是部分对等。但 Napster 或许是对等电子商务最著名的实例。

长难句翻译练习

1. The American economic system is, organized around a basically private-enterprise, market-oriented economy in which consumers largely determine what shall be produced by spending their money in the marketplace for those goods and services that they want most.

［参考译文］美国的经济是以基本的私有企业和市场导向经济为架构的，在这种经济中，消费者很大程度上通过在市场上为那些他们最想要的货品和服务付费来决定什么应该被制造出来。

2. Thus, in the American economic system it is the demand of individual consumers, coupled with the desire of businessmen to maximize profits and the desire of individuals to maximize their incomes, that together determine what shall be produced and how resources are used to produce it.

［参考译文］因此，在美国的经济体系中，个体消费者的需求与商人试图最大化其利润的欲望和个人想最大化其收入效用的欲望相结合，一起决定了什么应该被制造，以及资源如何被用来制造它们。

3. If, on the other hand, producing more of a commodity results in reducing its cost, this will tend to increase the supply offered by seller‑producers, which in turn will lower the price and permit more consumers to buy the product.

［参考译文］另一方面，如果大量制造某种商品导致其成本下降，那么这就有可能增加卖方和制造商能提供的供给，而这也就会反过来降低价格并允许更多的消费者购买产品。

4. In the American economy, the concept of private property embraces not only the ownership of productive resources but also certain rights, including the right to determine the price of a product or to make a free contract with another private individual.

［参考译文］在美国经济中，私有财产的概念不仅包含对生产资源的所有权，也指其他一些特定的权利，如确定一个产品价格和与另一个私人个体（经济单位）自由签定合同的权利。

5. At the same time these computers record which hours are busiest and which employers are the most efficient, allowing personnel and staffing assignments to be made accordingly. And they also identify preferred customers for promotional campaigns.

［参考译文］同时这些计算机记录下哪些时间是最忙的，哪些员工工作效率最高，这样就能相应地做出人员人事安排。而且它们（计算机）也能为促销活动找到那些拥有优先权的顾客。

6. Numerous other commercial enterprises, from theaters to magazine publishers, from gas and electric utilities to milk processors, bring better and more efficient services to consumers through the use of computers.

［参考译文］不计其数的其他商业企业，从剧院到杂志出版商，从公用燃气电力设施到牛奶处理厂，都通过计算机的使用给消费者带来更好、更有效率的服务。

7. Exceptional children are different in some significant way from others of the same age For

these children to develop to their full adult potential, their education must be adapted to those differences.

[参考译文] 残疾儿童在许多关键方面都与其同龄人不同。为了让这些孩子发展其全部的成人后的潜能，他们的教育必须适应这些不同。

8. The great interest in exceptional children shown in public education over the past three decades indicates the strong feeling in our society that all citizens, whatever their special conditions, deserve the opportunity to fully develop their capabilities.

[参考译文] 在过去的 30 年中，公共教育中显示的对残疾儿童的巨大关注表明了我们社会中的一种强烈的情绪，那就是所有的公民，不管其情况有多特殊，都应享有充分发展其能力的机会。

9. It serves directly to assist a rapid distribution of goods at reasonable price, thereby establishing a firm home market and so making it possible to provide for export at competitive prices.

[参考译文] 它（广告）能够直接帮助货物以比较合理的价格被迅速分销出去，因此可以（使公司）建立一个坚固的国内市场，同时也使以具有竞争力的价格提供出口变得可能。

10. Apart from the fact that twenty-seven acts of Parliament govern the terms of advertising, no regular advertiser dare promote a product that fails to live up to the promise of his advertisements.

[参考译文] 除去议会有 27 件法案来规范广告的条件，没有任何一个正式的广告商敢于推销一种商品却不能兑现其在广告中的承诺。

译　文

第七单元　钢筋工程

对　话

钢筋工程检查

咨询工程师：首先请告诉我你们采取了哪些符合中国标准的控制钢筋工程质量的措施。

承　包　方：好的，当然可以。我要感谢你方同意在此项工程的部分工程上采用中国钢。根据我们的质量保证程序，在订购材料之前要对钢材生产厂家进行审查。此项审查包括走访钢铁厂检查他们的生产程序和质量保证办法。

咨询工程师：很好。但是即使做了检查，结果也令人满意，在工程接下来的工作中仍然不能掉以轻心。让我们再看一下钢筋运抵现场后我们能做些什么。

承　包　方：这些是生产厂家的产品合格证和产品检测报告。所有的物理特征和化学成分均符合工程规范。

咨询工程师：好的。现在我想与你们的技术人员讨论一下钢筋实验的情况。我希望你们能把钢筋试验的结果向我介绍一下。（转向技术员）

技　术　员：在进行检测之前，我们将检查一下钢筋的表面。我们要检查钢筋的尺寸是否符合标准。检查表面是否有渗漏物、疤痕或蜂窝。如果表面没有问题，我们再对钢筋进行抽样检测。

咨询工程师：你们通常做哪些方面的检测？

技　术　员：我们最常做的是物理检测。我们从每批次 60 吨的钢材中选取 2 条钢筋的 2 个截断作为检测样本。其中一个截断做拉伸测试来测它的屈服点、抗拉强度和延伸率。另一个要测冷弯曲度。如果在检测过程中有易损渗漏或焊接不好的情况，就必须做化学成分分析或其他的专门检测弄清原因。

咨询工程师：您的介绍很好，谢谢。

课文 A　钢筋工程

钢筋的介绍

1. 按机械性能分类

根据其标准屈服强度的高低和品种的不同，分为 HPB235、HRB335、HRB400、RRB400 四个级别，其中 H、P、B 分别代表热轧（Hot rolled）、光圆（Plain）、钢筋（Bar）；后三个级别钢筋中的第二个字母 R 代表带肋（Ribbed），而第四级别钢筋中的第一个字母 R 代表余热处理（Remained heat treatment）

钢筋级别	牌　　号	符　　号
Ⅰ	HPB235	Φ
Ⅱ	HRB335	Φ
Ⅲ	HRB400	Φ
	RRB400	Φ^{R}
Ⅳ	HRB540	

2. 按加工工艺分类

可分为：热轧钢筋、余热处理钢筋、冷拉钢筋、冷拔低碳钢丝、热处理钢筋、冷轧扭钢筋、精轧螺旋钢筋、刻痕钢丝及钢绞线等。

热轧钢筋是经热轧成型并自然冷却的成品钢筋。如：HPB235、HRB335、HRB400。余热处理钢筋——将钢材热轧成型后立即穿水，进行表面冷却控制，然后利用芯部余热自身完成回火处理所得的成品钢筋。如：RRB400。冷拉钢筋是一种现场的钢筋加工方法。冷拔钢筋是加工厂对钢丝的一种加工方法，预应力钢丝基本上都要进行冷拔。热处理钢筋是将热轧的螺纹钢筋再通过淬火和回火的调质热处理，能显著提高其强度。

本项迪拜工程预应力钢筋现场张拉，按设计要求摆放管套，打完混凝土之后，进行养护混凝土，养护完之后进行张拉，张拉力必须达到设计要求。

3. 按化学成分分类

分为碳素钢筋和普通低合金钢筋。碳素钢筋的机械性能与含碳量多少有关。含碳量增加，能使钢材强度提高，性质变硬，但也将使钢材的塑性和韧性降低，焊接性能也会变差。普通低合金钢筋是在碳素钢的基础上加入少量合金元素（其含量一般不超过总量的 3%），如锰、硅、钒、钛等。这些合金元素可使钢材的强度、塑性等综合性能提高。

4. 按其外形分类

可分为光面钢筋和变形钢筋（螺纹、人字纹及月牙纹）两类。光面钢筋的表面是光圆的，HPB235 钢筋为光面钢筋，HRB335、HRB400 及 RRB400 钢筋为变形钢筋。

课文 B　钢筋工程施工工艺

1. 钢筋的检验

运至工地的钢筋应有出厂质量证明书或试验报告，每捆钢筋应有标牌，注明厂标、钢号、炉号及规格。检查项目常进行机械性能检查，包括：静力拉伸试验和冷弯试验。静力拉伸试验：得出应力—应变曲线，确定屈服强度、抗拉强度、伸长率。冷弯试验是指钢筋在经冷加工（即常温下加工）产生塑性变形时，对产生裂缝的抵抗能力。冷弯试验是测定钢筋在常温下承受弯曲变形能力的试验。

本项迪拜工程要求进厂时候进行抽样检查，将做好标记的样品材料，送往质检站，进行实验检查，只有拿到实验合格证，这批材料才可使用。

2. 钢筋的制作

现场钢筋加工制作时，要将钢筋加工表与设计图复核，检查下料表是否有错误和遗漏，对每种钢筋要按下料表检查是否达到要求，经过这两道检查后，再按下料表放出实样，试制合格后方可成批制作，加工好的钢筋要挂牌堆放整齐有序。

3. 钢筋的替换

施工中如需要钢筋代换时，必须充分了解设计意图和代换材料性能，严格遵守现行钢筋混凝土设计规范的各种规定。替代的钢筋要与原拟定的钢筋具有相同的强度、相等的截面等等。不管怎样更换钢筋之后，结构强度、整个钢截面面积及其结构上的要求应该维持与原来的相同，并不得以等面积的高强度钢筋代换低强度的钢筋。凡重要部位的钢筋代换，须征得甲方、设计单位同意，并有书面通知时方可代换。

4. 钢筋的加工

包括：冷拉、冷拔、调直、切断和弯曲。钢筋冷加工（包括冷拉和冷拔），冷拉可调直和除锈。

5. 钢筋的连接

钢筋的连接分为绑扎连接、焊接连接和机械连接。绑扎连接为绑扎搭接接头；焊接连接分为闪光对焊接头、电弧焊接头、电渣压力焊接头、气压焊接头；机械连接分为套筒冷压接头、螺纹套管钢筋接头。如果有不同级别钢筋进行焊接，焊接点强度必须达到这两根中最低级别钢筋。钢筋进行搭接必须按照规范要求进行。每一种焊接钢筋必须抽样送往质检站。

6. 钢筋的安装与检查

受力钢筋的品种、级别、规格和数量必须符合设计要求。此外，钢筋位置要准确，固定要牢靠，接头要符合规定。焊接钢筋位置必须有质检站的合格证，钢筋表面不能出现铁锈。

UNIT *8*

Concrete Works（混凝土工程）

DIALOGUE

Inspecting Concrete Works

E: Concrete works is a very essential part in construction field and also a very important aspect for this project. We must put our emphasis on it.

C: Yes, we quite agree with you. This is the Quality Assurance Program for the construction. Based on this, we had submitted 13 working procedures about the concrete works for your reference. This is Concrete Mixing Procedure by Auto-Batching plant which describes the main steps of mixing operation using the $40m^3/hour$ batching plant.

E: The procedure is correct. Now I want to have a discussion with your engineer and foreman and see the actual operation. (To a foreman) Usually we say the concrete mixture rate, is calculated on the basis of volume or weight of the material composed?

F: (foreman) It is on the basis of the weight. For example today we use 1510kg of aggregate, 680 kg of sand, 390kg of cement and 200kg of water for one cubic meter of concrete.

E: Please tell me the sequence of loading these materials in the mixer.

F: After the batching plant starts to operate, the aggregate will be loaded first, and then cement, then sand and water.

E: How long is the maximum time for the mixing of concrete which should be reaby for pouring in the formwork?

F: It will depend on the temperature of the concrete and is about 120 minutes.

E: Suppose today, the concrete mixer truck is unable to arrive at the site for pouring concrete, what should you do?

F: If in such hot weather the concrete can not be poured within the time regulated in the working procedure, it will not be used for the permanent works.

E: That's right. Thank you.

New Words

concrete ['kɔnkri:t] n. 混凝土 v. 用混凝土修筑，浇混凝土，凝结

foreman ['fɔ:mən] n. 领班，工头

volume ['vɔlju:m] n. 体积；容积

weight [weit] n. 重量

aggregate ['ægrigit] n. 骨料，集料（合成混凝土或修路等用的）

permanent ['pə:mənənt] adj. 永久的，持久的

New Phrases

Quality Assurance Program 质保文件

working procedure 施工程序

Concrete Mixing Proccdurc 混凝土搅拌工序

Auto-Batching plant 自动搅拌机

concrete mixture rate 混凝土配合比

permanent works 永久性工程

Notes

1. 骨料：混凝土配比成分之一，起骨架作用，也可减少水泥硬化产生的收缩作用。骨料分细骨料和粗骨料两种。其中细骨料粒径 0.16 ~ 5mm，多为河砂、海砂及山砂；粗骨料粒径大于 5mm，有碎石和卵石两种，碎石制作混凝土强度较高，但流动性小。

细骨料：fine aggregate　　　　粗骨料：coarse aggregate

第八单元：混凝土工程 ：搅拌机搅拌混凝土的施工工序，混凝土的运输

Role Play

Discuss with your partner about the gradation（级配）of concrete. Talk about the properties of different concrete and the application of it.

TEXT A

Introduction of Concrete

1. The ingredients of concrete

Concrete is a kind of artificial stone mainly composed of cement (commonly Portland cement) as cementitious materials. Concrete can be produced when cement, water, sand and gravel which are mixed in a reasonable proportion, if necessary, plus chemical additives and mineral admixtures, are stirred evenly, compacted, cured and hardened.

Aggregates make up the bulk of a concrete mixture. Sand, natural gravel and crushed stone are mainly used for this purpose.

Combining water with a cementitious material such as cement forms a cement paste by the process of hydration. The cement paste glues the aggregate together, fills voids within it, and allows it to flow more freely. Before hardening, a cement paste will act as a lubricant which makes the concrete workable to the construction. Less water in the cement paste will yield a stronger, more durable concrete.

2. Grades of concrete strength

The grades of concrete strength are classified by the standard value of cubic compressive strength of concrete. There are 14 grades among the ordinary concrete in China: C15, C20, C25, C30, C35, C40, C45, C50, C55, C60, C65, C70, C75 and C80.

For the project in Dubai Marina, concrete grade C50 is used in the slab floors and grade C75 is used in the column. Both are commercial concrete.

3. The properties of concrete

Concrete has relatively high compressive strength, durability and refractoriness. Abundant raw materials lead to its low cost. The plasticity of concrete is relatively good. Concrete can bond with steel quite well and protect it from rusting.

However, concrete has relatively large weight and significantly lower tensile strength which is about $1/10 \sim 1/20$ of the compressive strength.

New Words

ingredient [in'gri:djənt] n. 1. （混合物的）组成部分；2. （构成）要素，因素
                adj. 构成组成部分的
cementitious [ˌsimen'tiʃiəs] adj. 似水泥的，有黏性的
gravel ['grævəl] n. 沙砾，砾石，石子
compact [kəm'pækt] vt. & vi. 压紧，（使）坚实，把…紧压在一起（或压实）
cure [kjuə] vt. 治愈，治好（人或动物）；养护（混凝土）
glue [glu:] vt. 用胶水将物体粘合，粘牢，粘贴
void [vɔid] n. 空隙，孔隙

lubricant〔ˈluːbrikənt〕n. 润滑剂〔油〕adj. 润滑的
compressive〔kəmˈpresiv〕adj. 有压缩力的；压缩的
durability〔ˌdjurəˈbiliti〕n. 耐久性；耐用性
refractoriness〔riˈfræktəriːnis〕n. 耐火性；耐热度；耐熔度；耐熔性
plasticity〔plæˈstisəti〕n. 可塑性

New Phrases

artificial stone　人造石材
be composed of　由…组成
Portland cement　波特兰水泥
cementitious material　胶凝材料
in a reasonable proportion　按适当比例配合
chemical additives　化学外加剂
mineral admixtures　矿物掺合料
cement paste　水泥浆
concrete strength　混凝土的强度
cubic compressive strength　立方体抗压强度
slab floor　楼板
compressive strength　抗压强度
raw material　原材料
tensile strength　抗拉强度

Role Play

Discuss with your partner about the type of concrete you have encountered in the construction field. What is its advantages and disadvantages?

Exercises

I. Answer the following questions.

1. What is concrete mainly composed of?

2. What makes up the bulk of a concrete mixture and what are mainly used for this purpose?

3. What will be formed when combining water with a cementitious material such as cement?

4. How many grades are there among the ordinary concrete in china?

5. What advantages and disadvantages does concrete have?

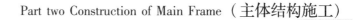

II. Complete the sentences with the given words or expression. *Change the form where necessary.*

1. This product has comparatively high _____ （refractory）.

2. All physical character and chemical components of steel reinforcement bars should.

3. _____ （mine） admixtures can improve the properties of concrete.

4. _____ （Chemistry） admixtures are materials in the form of powder or fluids that are added to the concrete to give it certain characteristics not obtainable with plain concrete mixes.

5. Concrete has relatively high _____ （compress） strength and _____ （durable）.

III. *Translate the following words or phrases into English.*

质保文件_____

施工程序_____

混凝土搅拌工序_____

自动搅拌机_____

混凝土配合比_____

永久性工程 _____

人造石材_____

由…组成_____

波特兰水泥_____

胶凝材料_____

化学外加剂_____

矿物掺合料_____

水泥浆_____

混凝土的强度_____

立方体抗压强度_____

楼板_____

抗压强度_____

原材料_____

抗拉强度_____

IV. *Translate the following sentences into Chinese.*

1. Concrete can be produced when cement, water, sand and gravel which are mixed in a reasonable proportion, if necessary, plus chemical additives and mineral admixtures, are stirred evenly, compacted, cured and hardened.

_____

_____

2. The cement paste glues the aggregate together, fills voids within it, and allows it to flow more freely.

_____

3. Concrete has relatively high compressive strength, durability and refractoriness.

4. However, concrete has relatively large weight and significantly lower tensile strength which is about 1 / 10 ~ 1 / 20 of the compressive strength.

V. Read the following passage to know more about what the reinforced concrete is and try to figure out what it talks about.

Reinforced Concrete（钢筋混凝土）

1. To offset the limitation of plain concrete, it was found possible, in the second half of the nineteenth century, to use steel with high tensile strength to reinforce concrete, chiefly in those places where its small tensile strength would limit the carrying capacity of the member.

2. The reinforcement, usually round steel rods with appropriate surface deformations（变形）to provide interlocking, is placed in the forms in advance of the concrete. When completely surrounded by the hardened concrete mass, it forms an integral part of the member.

3. The resulting combination of two materials, known as reinforced concrete, combines many of the advantage of each: the relatively low cost, good weather and fire resistance, good compressive strength, and excellent formability（可模锻性）of concrete and the high tensile strength and much greater ductility and toughness than steel. It is this combination which allows the almost unlimited range of uses and possibilities of reinforced concrete in the construction of buildings, bridges, dams, tanks, reservoirs, and a host of other structure.

Phrases for reference：

plain concrete　素混凝土
tensile strength　抗拉强度
reinforced concrete　钢筋混凝土
carrying capacity　承载能力
interlocking　粘结力
compressive strength　抗压强度
ductility　延展性
toughness　韧性

　　1. 为了弥补素混凝土的局限性，在十九世纪后半叶，人们发现可以使用具有高抗拉强度的钢筋来增强混凝土，主要用于那些由于混凝土较低的抗拉强度限制了构件的承受能力的地方。

　　2. 在浇筑混凝土之前，把表面适当变形的圆形钢筋放入模板，钢筋表面变形是为了增加粘结力。当钢筋被硬化的混凝土包裹后，钢筋就成为构件的一部分了。

　　3. 两种材料组成的复合材料称为钢筋混凝土，它具有两种材料的许多优点：混凝土的廉价、较高的耐火性和耐候性、较高的抗压强度，成型性能好、较高的拉伸强度，较大的延展性和韧性钢的成形性。正是由于这些优点的结合使钢筋混凝土几乎能不受限制地广泛应用于修建房屋、桥梁、水坝、储水池、水库和其他许多建筑结构当中。

TEXT B

Concrete Construction

1. Mixing concrete

Mixing concrete refers to the process of evenly mixing and combining water, cement, fine and coarse aggregate. The process of mixing should increase the compressive strength and plasticity of the resulting concrete. The mixing time, which is variable with different types of mixers and workability of concrete, is essential to the quality of the concrete.

2. The transportation of concrete

The time for transporting the concrete should not exceed the initial setting time of concrete and the road for transportation should be smooth. Concrete pump may be employed for large equipment bases and multi-storey buildings, which need large volume concreting and require stable pouring rate.

For the project in Dubai Marina, the time spent on transporting and pouring ready-mixed concrete type C50 and type C75 should not be more than two hours. The concrete isn't allowed to be delivered at high temperature.

3. Pouring concrete

For the project in Dubai Marina, it is required that construction joints, retarder and sufficient carpenters and masons should be made available before concrete casting. Meanwhile. three sample blocks from each concrete tanker must be tested. If in hot weather, ice may be added and mixed with concrete before it being cast.

4. Curing concrete

After the concrete has been placed, it should be covered and sprayed with water within 12 hours. After the concrete strength reaches $1.2N/mm^2$, without making significant compact on concrete, workmen can stand on it and erection of scaffold and formwork are allowed.

5. The quality inspection of concrete

This step involves quality inspection during concreting and after concrete curing. Concrete should be checked at least twice for each work shift.

Spot checks may be carried out in case of special circumstance. Quality should be checked at any time when mixing concrete. For the quality inspection after curing concrete, it mainly refers to the cubic compressive strength.

For the project in Dubai Marina, test blocks sampled from pouring concrete should be sent to the laboratory for a test. In case of the insufficient concrete strength, the designing institute should make a redesign just to get the concrete works in question consolidated. Concrete with significantly insufficient strength should be knocked off and poured again.

New Words

transport [træns′pɔːt] vt. （用交通工具）运输，运送，输送

retarder [ri′tɑːdə] n. 阻滞剂，缓凝剂，减速器

carpenter [′kɑːpintə] n. 木工，木匠

mason [′mesən] n. 石匠，砖瓦匠

spray [sprei] vt. & vi. 喷，喷洒，向…喷洒

erection [′irekʃən] n. 建立，建造，竖立，安装

scaffold [′skæfəld] n. 脚手架

New Phrases

mixing concrete 搅拌混凝土

fine and coarse aggregate 粗细骨料

the transportation of concrete 混凝土的运输

the initial setting time of concrete 混凝土的初凝时间

concrete pump 混凝土泵

multi-storey buildings 高层建筑

ready-mixed concrete 商品混凝土/预拌混凝土

pouring concrete 混凝土的浇筑

construction joint 施工缝

test blocks of concrete 混凝土试块

work shift 工作班

spot check 抽查

Exercises

I. Read the following dialogue and try to figure out what they are talking about by referring to the words given.

Inspection of Concrete Pouring 混凝土浇筑的检查

E：Can you continue the concrete pouring after three hours suspension?

C：No. It is not allowed. Since it is hot weather we can not continue concreting operation after stopping for more than the regulated period.

E：What should you do in this case?

C：We must make a construction joint. The concrete surface will be chiseled and cleaned by compressed air or jetting water, and also water and cement mortar are sprayed, then the new concrete can be poured. The rebar should not be touched during vibration.

E：Can you make construction joints at any place during concreting?

C：No. The location of construction joints should be decided in accordance with the works procedure. Generally speaking the construction joints in column should be horizontally made in top of foundation or under beams or slab, and in walls, should be vertically made.

New Words for reference

suspension [sə'spenʃən] n. 1. 暂停，中止，暂缓；2. 推迟，延期

joint [dʒɔint] n. 接合板、休口板

chisel ['tʃizəl] n. 凿子，錾子 vt. & vi. 凿，雕；镌

jet vt. 喷射

mortar ['mɔːtə] n. 灰浆

spray [sprei] vt. & vi. 喷，喷洒，向…喷洒

vibration [vai'breiʃən] n. 振动，颤动

in accordance with 与…一致，依照

Generally speaking 一般而言

II. The following is a brief description of building materials. Read it carefully and try your best to figure it by referring to the Chinese.

Building materials （建筑材料）

The materials are the basic elements of any building. Building materials can be classified into three groups, according to the purposes they are used for. Structural materials （结构材料） are those that hold the building up, keep it rigid, form its outer covering of walls （外墙） and roof, and divide its interior into rooms. In the second group are materials for the equipments inside the building, such as the plumbing, heating and lighting systems. Finally there are materials that are used to protect or decorate other materials.

Steel and concrete are the most widely used structural materials today. Steel is truly an all-round material. It is nearly as durable as stone. But it must be painted to prevent it from rusting. In modern construction steel is used for the supporting framework of large buildings.

Cement is an important building material. Among various Portland cement （硅酸盐水泥中）, the following varieties are now generally available from the markets in the industrialized countries.

（1）ordinary Portland cement, which is the cheapest.

（2）rapid hardening cement, which is slightly more expensive than（1）.

（3）sulphate-resisting cement.

（4）air-entraining cement, which greatly improves the frost（霜、冰点以下的温度）resistance of the concrete.

（5）low-heat cement for massive construction such as dams.

（6）high-alumina cement, which reaches Portland 28-day strength in 24 hours with corresponding high heat. Its color is normally black.

（7）another high-alumina cement, which is used for furnace linings, is white. It is several times more expensive than the black variety.

The above-mentioned cements are widely used on the construction site. Now let's talk about pipes. Pitch fiber pipels（沥青纤维管）is an easily-joined pipe and it is as strong as stoneware pipes（粗陶管）, but it is not so resistance to all corrosive or hot liquids. Asbestos cement pipes（石棉水泥管）, on the other hand, can be used for liquids with almost any purpose.

The more expensive asbestors sheet is nailable, almost as hard as wood and fully fireproof. The cheaper sheet is easily broken by shock or pressure or under the effect of a flame. Plastics have been widely used for a variety of accessory roles（配件）in buildings including drainpipes, panels and decorative ceilings. Composite materials（合成材料）are gaining importance in building homes. A modern material in house building is glass-reinforced polyester resin（玻璃纤维聚酯树脂）. Panels（面板）of this material are composites themselves. Materials used for doors and windows frames are timber, steel and aluminum alloys（合金）.

New Words

purpose〔'pə:pəs〕n. 目的；意图

plumbing〔'plʌmiŋ〕n. 1. 建筑物的管路系统；2. 自来水管道

decorate〔'dekəreit〕vt. 装饰

　　e. g. decorate with ribbons. 用丝带装饰。

durable〔'djuərəbl〕adj. 持久的，耐用的

framework〔'freimwə：k〕n. 构架；结构

cement〔si'ment〕n. 水泥

rust〔rʌst〕n. 铁锈 vt. & vi.（使）生锈

sulphate〔'sʌlfeit〕n. 硫酸盐

entrain〔in'trein〕v. 使空气以气泡状存在于混凝土中；乘火车

alumina〔ə'lju：minə〕n. 氧化铝，矾土

furnace〔'fə：nis〕n. 熔炉，火炉

resistant〔ri'zistənt〕adj. 有抵抗力的，抵抗的，阻止的，抗…的，耐…的

corrosive〔kə'rəusiv〕adj. 腐蚀性的；侵蚀性的 n. 腐蚀性物品

asbestos〔æs'bestəs〕n. 石棉 adj. 石棉制的；含石棉的

fireproof〔'faiə'pru：f〕vt.. 使防火，使耐火

accessory〔æk'sesəri〕n. 附件，配件，附属物 adj. 1. 非主要的；副的；2. 辅助的

drainpipe ['dreinpaip] n. 排水管

panel ['pænl] n. 镶板；板条；护墙板；窗玻璃片；建筑用四分板；木工用线板

composite ['kɔmpəzit] adj. 混合成的，综合成的，复合的 n. 合成物；复合材料

polyester [ˌpɔli'estə (r)] n. 聚酯纤维，涤纶

resin ['rezin] n. 1. 树脂，松香；2. 合成树脂

New Phrases

building material 建筑材料

be classified into 分（类）为…

structural material 结构材料

portland cement 波特兰水泥，普通水泥，硅酸盐水泥

ordinary Portland cement 普通硅酸盐水泥

rapid-hardening cement 快硬水泥

sulphate-resisting cement 耐硫酸盐水泥

air-entraining cement 掺气水泥；加气水泥

low-heat cement 低热水泥

high-alumina cement 高铝水泥

furnace lining 炉衬

pitch fiber 沥青纤维管

asbestos cement pipe 石棉水泥管

composite materials 合成材料

glass-reinforced polyester resin 玻璃纤维聚酯树脂

aluminum alloy 铝合金

建筑材料

材料是所有建筑的基本要素。根据用途建筑材料可以分成三类。结构材料形成建筑骨架，具有刚度，包括外墙、房顶，把内部分隔成若干间隔的材料。第二类是房子内部所需设备的材料，比如：卫生管道、供热和照明设备。最后还有一类材料是用来保护或装饰其他材料的。

钢筋混凝土是当今用途最广泛的结构材料，钢的确适合各种用途，它和石头一样坚硬，但必须刷上漆以防锈。在现代施工中钢被用来做大型建筑物的框架。

水泥是一种重要的建筑材料，在各种硅酸盐水泥中，在工业化国家的制造厂一般可以买到下面几种：

（1）普通硅酸盐水泥，这是最便宜的；

（2）快硬水泥，比普通硅酸盐水泥略贵；

（3）耐硫酸盐水泥；

（4）加气水泥，大大改善混凝土的抗冻性；

（5）低热水泥，用于大体积建筑，如大坝；

（6）高铝水泥，通常为黑色，高铝水泥经过 24 小时即可达到硅酸盐水泥 28 天内才能达到的强度，同时发出高热；

（7）用作炉衬的高铝水泥，呈白色，它比黑色高铝水泥要昂贵几倍。

以上提到的水泥广泛用在建筑工程上，我们再看看管道，沥青纤维管易于接合，也和粗陶管一样很坚固，但是耐受腐蚀性液体或高温液体的能力不太强。石棉水泥管几乎可以用于任何目的，包括各种液体，较贵的石棉水泥板可以受钉，大致像木板一样坚固，而且十分耐火。比较便宜的石棉板受震受压或遇火都易毁坏，塑料在房屋的配件中有各种广泛用途，包括排水管、屋面板及装饰性天花板。合成材料的重要性在房屋建造上已日益明显，一种现代房屋建造材料是玻璃纤维聚酯树脂，这种材料制成的面板本身是复合物。用来作门窗的建筑材料有木材、钢、铝合金。

TRANSLATION SKILLS

被动语态翻译

一、英语中使用被动语态大大多于汉语。

由于科技英语的主要目的是表述科学发现、科学事实、实验报告和各种说明等，这就使得科技英语中以客观陈述为主，被动语态在科技英语文章使用得更为广泛，以体现科学性和客观性。

例 1：Once the flower has been pollinated and fertilized, the plant provides the newly formed seeds with food materials, which will be needed when they themselves germinate.

花一旦授了粉并受了精，植株就会对新生种子提供养料贮藏，以备种子未来萌芽之需。

例 2：Once the overall program strategy has been clearly established, then the syntactic details of the language can be considered. Such an approach is often referred to as "top-down" programming.

一旦清楚地制定了全面的编程策略，然后便考虑该语言的句法细节。这种方法经常称作"自顶向下"的程序设计法。

例 3：This equilibrium is completely destroyed when the virgin soil is brought into cultivation. 未垦土壤一经种植，这种平衡就完全遭到破坏。

例 4：Several approaches to the problem of ladle skull slag or deoxidation-scum removed was being tried.

罐内结壳，熔渣或脱氧浮渣清除问题的几项解决方案正在实验中。

另外，在被动句中，by 短语有时表达方式、方法或手段，而不只表达行为的发出者（doer）。

例 1：The temperature of the liquid is raised by the application of heat.

加热可以提高液体温度。

例 2：Useful facts may be collected either by making careful observation or by setting up experiment.

通过仔细的观察或做实验可以收集到有用的数据。

二、翻译时，可以采用以下技巧：

1. 翻译成汉语的主动句

将英语被动结构翻译成汉语主动结构时，可进一步分为以下几种情况：

（1）英语被动结构的主语

英语原文中的主语在译文中仍做主语。在采用此方法时，我们往往在译文中使用了"加以"，"经过"，"用……来"等词来体现原文中的被动含义。

例1：Other questions will be discussed briefly.

其他问题将简单地加以讨论。

例2：In other words mineral substances which are found on earth must be extracted by digging，boring holes，artificial explosions，or similar operations which make them available to us.

换言之，矿物就是存在于地球上，但须经过挖掘、钻孔、人工爆破或类似作业才能获得的物质。

例3：Nuclear power's danger to health，safety，and even life itself can be summed up in one word：radiation.

核能对健康、安全，甚至对生命本身构成的危险可以用一个词—辐射来概括。

（2）将英语原文中的主语翻译为宾语，同时增补泛指性的词语（人们，大家等）作主语。

例1：It could be argued that the radio performs this service as well，but on television everything is much more living，much more real.

可能有人会指出，无线电广播同样也能做到这一点，但还是电视屏幕上的节目要生动、真实得多。

例2：Television，it is often said，keeps one informed about current events，allows one to follow the latest developments in science and politics，and offers an endless series of programmes which are both instructive and entertaining.

人们常说，电视使人了解时事，熟悉政治领域的最新发展变化，并能源源不断地为观众提供各种既有教育意义又有趣的节目。

例3：It is generally accepted that the experiences of the child in his first years largely determine his character and later personality.

人们普遍认为，孩子们的早年经历在很大程度上决定了他们的性格及其未来的人品。

另外，下列的结构也可以通过这一手段翻译：

It is asserted that…	有人主张……
It is believed that…	有人认为……
It is generally considered that…	大家（一般人）认为
It is well known that…	大家知道（众所周知）……
It will be said …	有人会说……
It was told that…	有人曾经说……

（3）将英语原文中的 by，in，for 等做状语的介词短语翻译成译文的主语，在此情况下，英语原文中的主语一般被翻译成宾语。

例1：A right kind of fuel is needed for an atomic reactor.

原子反应堆需要一种合适的燃料。

例2：By the end of the war, 800 people had been saved by the organization, but at a cost of 200 Belgian and French lives.

大战结束时，这个组织拯救了八百人，但那是以二百多比利时人和法国人的生命为代价的。

例3：And it is imagined by many that the operations of the common mind can be by no means compared with these processes, and that they have to be acquired by a sort of special training.

许多人认为，普通人的思维活动根本无法与科学家的思维过程相比，而且认为这些思维过程必须经过某种专门的训练才能掌握。

（4）翻译成汉语的无主句

例1：Great efforts should be made to inform young people especially the dreadful consequences of taking up the habit.

应该尽最大努力告诉年轻人吸烟的危害，特别是吸烟上瘾后的可怕后果。

例2：By this procedure, different honeys have been found to vary widely in the sensitivity of their inhibit to heat.

通过这种方法分析发现不同种类的蜂蜜对热的敏感程度也极为不同。

例3：Many strange new means of transport have been developed in our century, the strangest of them perhaps the hovercraft.

在我们这个世纪内研制了许多新奇的交通工具，其中最奇特的也许就是气垫船了。

例4：New source of energy must be found, and this will take time⋯

必须找到新的能源，这需要时间⋯⋯

另外，以"it"为形式主语的被动语态句型是科技英语中的一种典型句型。翻译时应加以注意。

如：It is hoped that ⋯　　　　　　　　　希望⋯⋯

It is reported that ⋯　　　　　　　　据报道⋯⋯

It is said that ⋯　　　　　　　　　　据说⋯⋯

It is supposed that ⋯　　　　　　　　据推测⋯⋯

It may be said without fear of exaggeration that ⋯　可以毫不夸张地说⋯⋯

It must be admitted that ⋯　　　　　　必须承认⋯⋯

It must be pointed out that ⋯　　　　　必须指出⋯⋯

It will be seen from this that ⋯　　　　由此可见⋯⋯

（5）翻译成带表语的主动句

例1. The decision to attack was not taken lightly.

进攻的决定不是轻易做出的。

例2. On the whole such an conclusion can be drawn with a certain degree of confidence, but only if the child can be assumed to have had the same attitude towards the test as the other with whom he is being compared, and only if he was not punished by lack of relevant information which they possessed.

总的来说，得出这种结论是有一定程度把握的，但必须具备两个条件：能够假定这个孩子对测试的态度和与他比较的另一个孩子的态度相同；他也没有因为缺乏别的孩子已掌握的有关知识而被扣分。

（注意上述翻译技巧在该句翻译中的综合运用。）

2. 译成汉语的被动语态

英语中的许多被动句可以翻译成汉语的被动句。常用"被"，"给"，"遭"，"挨"，"为……所"，"使"，"由……"，"受到"等表示。

例 1. Early fires on the earth were certainly caused by nature, not by Man.

地球上早期的火肯定是由大自然而不是人类引燃的。

例 2. These signals are produced by colliding stars or nuclear reactions in outer space.

这些讯号是由外层空间的星球碰撞或者核反应所造成的。

例 3. Natural light or "white" light is actually made up of many colours.

自然光或者"白光"实际上是由许多种颜色组成的。

例 4. The behaviour of a fluid flowing through a pipe is affected by a number of factors, including the viscosity of the fluid and the speed at which it is pumped.

流体在管道中流动的情况，受到诸如流体黏度、泵送速度等各种因素的影响。

例 5. They may have been a source of part of the atmosphere of the terrestrial planets, and they are believed to have been the planetesimal-like building blocks for some of the outer planets and their satellites.

它们可能一直是行星的一部分大气的来源。它们还被认为是构成外部行星以及其卫星的一种类似微星的基础材料。

例 6. Over the years, tools and technology themselves as a source of fundamental innovation have largely been ignored by historians and philosophers of science.

工具和技术本身作为根本性创新的源泉多年来在很大程度上被科学史学家和科学思想家们忽视了。

例 7. Whether the Government should increase the financing of pure science at the expense of technology or vice versa（反之）often depends on the issue of which is seen as the driving force.

政府是以减少技术的经费投入来增加纯理论科学的经费投入，还是相反，这往往取决于把哪一方看作是驱动的力量。

例 8. The supply of oil can be shut off unexpectedly at any time, and in any case, the oil wells will all run dry in thirty years or so at the present rate of use.

石油的供应可能随时会被中断；不管怎样，以目前的这种消费速度，只需 30 年左右，所有的油井都会枯竭。

译　文

第八单元　混凝土工程

对　话

混凝土工程检查

咨询工程师：混凝土工程是施工现场必不可少的一部分，也是此项工程非常重要的一个方面，我们必须对此加以重视。

承　包　商：是的，我很同意你的说法，这是本施工项目的质保文件。在此基础上，我们还递交了 13 项有关混凝土工程的施工程序供你参考。这是自动搅拌机的混凝土搅拌工序，说明了使用 40m³/小时搅拌机操作的主要步骤。

咨询工程师：程序是正确的。现在我想和你们的工程师及工长讨论一下有关实际操作。（对工长说）通常我们说的混凝土配合比是根据混合材料的体积计算还是根据重量计算的？

工　　　长：是根据重量计算的。比如今天我们用 1510kg 的骨料，680kg 的沙子，390kg 的水泥和 200kg 的水来搅拌出一立方米的混凝土。

咨询工程师：请跟我说一下往搅拌机里装填这些材料的顺序。

工　　　长：在搅拌机开始工作后，先装骨料，然后装水泥，再装砂子和水。

咨询工程师：从混凝土搅拌完毕到灌入模板最大的时间限度是多长？

工　　　长：这要看混凝土的温度，大约 120 分钟吧。

咨询工程师：假如今天，混凝土搅拌车不能到达现场来灌注混凝土，你们说该怎么办？

工　　　长：如果是像这样炎热的天气，混凝土不能在施工程序规定的时间内灌注，那么它就不能用于永久性工程了。

咨询工程师：你说的很对，谢谢。

课文 A　混凝土介绍

1. 混凝土的组成

普通混凝土是以水泥（通常为波特兰水泥）为主要胶凝材料，与水、砂、石子，必要时掺入化学外加剂和矿物掺合料，按适当比例配合，经过均匀搅拌、密实成型及养护硬化而成的人造石材。

在混凝土中，砂、石及碎石起骨架作用，称为骨料；

水泥与水形成水泥浆，水泥浆包裹在骨料表面并填充其空隙。在硬化前，水泥浆起润滑作用，赋予拌合物一定和易性，便于施工。水泥浆硬化后，则将骨料胶结成一个坚实的整体。

2. 混凝土的强度等级

混凝土强度等级是以立方体抗压强度标准值划分，目前中国普通混凝土强度等级划分为 14 级：C15、C20、C25、C30、C35、C40、C45、C50、C55、C60、C65、C70、C75 及 C80。本项迪拜码头工程楼板用 C50，柱用 C75 用来打柱子，均为商品混凝土。

3. 混凝土的材料性质

混凝土有很多的优点：如抗压强度高；耐久、耐火性能好；原材料丰富、成本低；

具有良好的可塑性；与钢筋粘结良好，可以保护钢筋不会锈蚀等。

但混凝土也有它的缺点：自重很大；抗拉强度很低，约为抗压强度的 $1/10 \sim 1/20$。

课文 B　混凝土工程施工

1. 混凝土的搅拌

混凝土搅拌，是将水、水泥和粗细骨料进行均匀拌和及混合的过程。同时，通过搅拌还要使材料达到强化、塑化的作用。混凝土的搅拌时间与混凝土的搅拌质量密切相关，随搅拌机类型和混凝土的和易性不同而变化。

2. 混凝土的运输

运输中的全部时间不应超过混凝土的初凝时间。混凝土的运输道路要求平坦，对于浇筑量大、浇筑速度比较稳定的大型设备基础和高层建筑，宜采用混凝土泵。本迪拜码头项目 C50、C75 商品混凝土从出场时间算起，从运输出发点到浇筑完成要求不超过两个小时，不允许在高温下运输。

3. 混凝土的浇筑

本迪拜码头项目中，要求混凝土浇筑时，要做好施工缝的准备和准备缓凝剂，木工及泥瓦工人手要充足。且混凝土在浇筑前必须做试块，一般一车混凝土做三个试块。在天热情况下，可以在浇筑的混凝土加入冰块，搅拌后浇筑。

4. 混凝土的养护

在混凝土浇筑完毕后，应在 12h 以内加以覆盖和浇水，养护至其强度达到 $1.2N/mm^2$ 以上，才准在上面行人和架设支架、安装模板，但不得冲击混凝土。

5. 混凝土的质量检查

混凝土质量检查包括施工过程中的质量检查和养护后的质量检查。每一工作班至少检查两次。

如遇特殊情况还应及时进行抽查，混凝土搅拌时应随时检查。混凝土养护后的质量检查，主要指混凝土的立方体抗压强度检查。

本迪拜码头项目中，要求浇筑时做的试块，要送往实验室做检测。如果混凝土强度不足，要由设计院重新设计加固，严重不足的则必须敲掉重新浇筑。

UNIT *9*

Inspection of Safety（安全检查）

DIALOGUE

Safety patrol

E：Firstly, I'd like to know the organization for safety works.

C：At the beginning of the project, we have appointed a very qualified and experienced person as Safety Officer who has sufficient time, authority and responsibility to ensure the safety program. The safety officer with his three assistants has an office in project management. There are totally ten persons working full time for safety matters. Each of them is responsible for each working section with around 150 to 200 workers.

E：That's good. As you know, It is equally important to set up safety organization as well as to give people on-site safety education. Could you pleas give me a brief introduction to your complete training program for safety?

C：Since the setting up of the site, our Safety Training Program has been carried out on the basis of the Chinese Construction Ministry Standard JGJ 59-99.

E：What are the contents of the workers' training class?

C：The contents include, but are not limited to, jobsite, safety policy employee responsibility under China Labor Law, company's safety regulations, construction accidents and reporting, electrical safety, personal safety equipment, scaffolding, trenching and excavation, crane safety, respiratory protection, fire protection and prevention, toxic substances, first aid and emergency aid procedure, and so on.

E：That's good. Now we can go to the work area for a safety inspection to see if the safety regulations are strictly implemented or not. Let's start with the helmet, the personal protective equipments. It's a pity that that not everyone has the helmet and protective footwear.

C：Since the weather in this country is very hot, local people feel uncomfortable with shoes and helmet even if they know these are useful in protection of their health and safety.

E：You must take strong measures to ensure that everybody wears safety shoes and helmet. Besides, people working in dusty area must wear the respirators.

C：OK. I think our scaffolding is quite satisfying.

E：No. I am still not satisfied with the working conditions above ground. Some working tables, which are 2 meters high above the ground, have no ladders. And in a few places there are too many materials piled on the scaffolding.

C：It is really a dangerous operation, we will get it rectified. An instruction will be given to the working section now.

Notes

1. 会话背景与指南：建筑行业是发生工伤事故比较高的一个行业。由于国际工程往往集中了不同国家的技术和雇用大量的当地劳务人员，思想观念和工作方式的不同，加之所存在的语言障碍（language barrier），施工中出现事故的可能性就更大。强调安全并不会影响工程的进度。在国外，雇主与劳动力之间的关系是一个敏感的问题（sensitive issue）。如果承包商重视工人的健康与安全工作，工人的工作积极性就高，工作的效率也就高。反之，若工地常常发生工伤事故（accidents at site），这不仅会降低工人的工作效率，而且很可能在当地招募不到所需的劳动力，从而影响工程的顺利开展。

2. 对于危险场所，要标有汉语和当地语书写的警告牌（warning signs）。在进场道路和现场内的道路危险路段，也应设有限速（speed limit）标志与相应的警告牌。

New Words

sufficient［sə'fiʃənt］adj. 1. 足够的，充足的；2.【逻辑学】（条件）必然的

content［'kɔntent］n. 1. 所容纳之物，所含之物；2.（书等的）内容，目录；3. 容量，含量；
4.（书、讲话、节目等的）主题；主要内容

regulation［ˌregju'leiʃən］n. 1. 管理，控制；2. 规章，规则，章程，规章制度，法规

scaffold［'skæfəld，-ˌəuld］n. 脚手架

trench［trentʃ］n. 深沟，地沟

excavation［ˌekskə'veiʃən］n. 发掘；挖掘；开凿

respiratory［'respərəˌtɔːri:］adj. 呼吸的，呼吸用的

respirator ['respə₁reitə] n. 1. 口罩，防毒面具；2.（人工）呼吸机
inspection [in'spekʃən] n. 1. 检查，视察；2. 检验；审视；3. 检阅
rectify ['rektifai] vt. 改正，矫正

New Phrases

Safety Officer   安全主任
be responsible for 对…负责
working section   施工队
safety organization   安全工作人事结构
Chinese Construction Ministry   中国建设部
jobsite safety policy   现场安全策略
China Labor Law   中国劳动法
safety regulations   安全制度
construction accidents and reporting   施工事故和报告
electrical safety   电气安全
personal safety equipment   个人安全设备
crane safety   起重机安全
respiratory protection   呼吸防护
fire protection and prevention   防火
toxic substances   有毒物质
first aid and emergency aid procedure   急救和紧急措施

Role Play

Discuss with your partners about the measures we should take to ensure the safety in the construction field. Talk about the potential danger in the site and the measures to avoid it.

TEXT A

Working at Height

Controls relating to working at height or in confined areas (e. g. Permit-to-work, task risk assessment) are effective in reducing injuries by raising awareness of the hazards and ensuring the correct work methods are followed and the proper precautions are taken.

Mandatory use of safety equipment (harnesses, safety nets) to properly protect workers from falls, posting of permits, and regular inspections of the job site are commonly employed techniques.

A. Ladders

1. Ladders are primarily for access only.

2. Before use, check that the ladder is in good condition.

3. Ladders must be tied and/or footed at all times.

4. Ladders must extend 1 meter above the working platform to provide handholds when mounted/dismounting.

5. As an angle guide, ladders must be one-out for every four up.

B. Scaffolding

1. All scaffolding must be erected, altered or dismantled by a trained, competent and certified scaffolder.

2. Fall arrest equipment must be used by scaffolders if working above 4 metres with unprotected edges.

   (For other personnel, this limit is usually 2 metres)

3. Scaffolds must be inspected by a competent person and reports entered into the Scaffolding Log.

a. Before first use.

b. After substantial alterations.

c. Following strong winds or collision.

d. At regular intervals not exceeding 7 days.

4. Never work on scaffold unless minimum platform width is 4 boards, with handrail, intermediate rail and toe board fitted.

5. Minor works may be carried out without handrails but only if a full harness is worn and anchored.

6. Access must be by a secured ladder.

7. Do not take up boards, move handrails or remove ties to gain access for work.

Changes must only be made by a competent scaffolder.

C. Mobile Scaffold Tower

1. Must be erected by a trained, competent and certified person, in accordance with manufacturer's recommendations.

2. Must be erected on firm level ground, free from underground services.

3. Area beneath must be cordoned off by suitable means or signage.

4. Working platforms must have handrail, intermediate rail and toe boards fitted. Access must be by internal ladders.

D. Use of Safety Nets

During roof work, a safety harness is used as a means of protecting the person from falling. However, it is not always practical for roofers to be continuously clipped on, due to the lack of a secure point. The actual use of the harness system by construction workers on such roof work is quite low-this is due to the discomfort and restrictions in using the harness. Failure to use the harness is a common complaint on construction work at sites. To counter these problems the use of safety nets should be considered. These are installed under the entire area at which work at height is taking place. It is important to note that the harness system should still be in use and that edge protection is still required on roofing work. The installation of the nets should only be carried out by a competent contractor.

E. Inspection of Safety Harnesses

All Safety Harnesses (including those worn by contractors) should be checked prior to use for the following：

a) That the traceability label is adequately attached to the product

b) Check the webbing and ropes for：

.. Cuts, tears

.. Excessive wear

.. Burns, chemical attack

.. Hardening of the fibres

.. Sewing must be free of cuts

c) Check the metal fittings for ：

.. Sharp edges

.. Excessive wear

.. Correct operation

.. Distortion

F. Working at heights of 2 meters (6 feet) or higher above the ground cannot proceed unless：

1. a fixed platform is used with guard or hand rails, verified by a competent person, or fall arrest equipment is used

2. a proper anchor, mounted preferably overhead

3. full body harness using double latch self locking snap hooks at each connection

4. synthetic fiber lanyards

5. shock absorber

6. fall arrest equipment will limit free fall to 2 meters (6 feet) or less a visual inspection of the fall arrest equipment and system is completed and any equipment that is damaged or has been activated is taken out of service

7. person (s) are competent to perform the work

(extracted from CSI-TF3 A Compilation Study of Good Practices in Health & Safety in the Cement Industry)

Notes

1. 高处作业安全防护"三宝"：由于建筑行业的特殊性，高处作业中发生的高处坠落、物体打击事故的比例最大。许多事故案例都说明，由于正确佩戴了安全帽、安全带或按规定架设了安全网，从而避免了伤亡事故的发生。事实证明，安全帽、安全带、安全网是减少和防止高处坠落和物体打击这类事故发生的重要措施。由于这三种安全防护用品使用最广泛，作用又明显，人们常称之为"三宝"。作业人员必须正确使用安全帽，调好帽箍，系好帽带；正确使用安全带，高挂低用。

2. CSI：水泥可持续性发展倡议组织（Cement Sustainability Initiative）基于对商业可持续发展的共同追求，汇聚了全球 18 个重要的水泥生产商，其水泥产量约占全球水泥总产量的 30%。迄今为止，CSI 仍然是全球最大由单个行业独自推出的可持续性项目之一。

New Words

hazard［ˈhæzəd］n. 1. 危险，公害；2. 危害物；3. 危险的根源

precaution［priˈkɔːʃən］n. 预防措施；预防；防备

handhold［ˈhændˌhəuld］n. 扶手，把手点

dismantle［disˈmæntl］vt. 拆开，拆卸

scaffolder［ˈskæfəldə］n. 脚手架工

alteration［ˌɔːltəˈreiʃən］n. 1. 改动，更改，改变；2. 变化；改变

handrail［ˈhændreil］n. 栏杆，扶手

harness［ˈhɑːnis］n.（防止坠落或摔倒的）背带，保护带

anchor［ˈæŋkə］vt. & vi.（把…）系住，（使）固定

cordon［ˈkɔːdn］vt. 封锁；用警戒线围住

signage［ˈsainidʒ］n. 指示牌；标志牌

harden［ˈhɑːdn］vt. & vi.（使）变硬；（使）坚固；（使）硬化

distortion［diˈstɔːʃn］n. 扭曲；变形；失真，歪曲

New Phrases

confined areas　密闭空间

permit-to-work　工作许可证

task risk assessment　工作风险分析

fall arrest equipment　防止坠落设施

at regular interval　定期

intermediate rail　中间栏杆

toe board　踢脚板

mobile scaffold Tower　可移动的脚手架

prior to…　在…之前

traceability label　可追溯性标签

synthetic fiber lanyard　合成纤维的系索

shock absorber　减震器

Role Play

Based on the content of the passage, can you make a summary about the measures we should take to ensure the safety while we are working at height? Discuss with your partner and report it to the class.

Exercises

I. Answer the following questions.

1. Should all scaffolding must be erected, altered or dismantled by a trained, competent and certified scaffolder?

2. If the platform width of scaffold is 3 boards, without handrail, intermediate rail and toe board fitted, can people work on it safely?

3. Mobile scaffold tower can be erected by any worker in construction site, isn't it?

4. Due to the discomfort and restrictions in using the harness. Failure to use the harness is a common complaint on construction work at sites. To counter these problems, what might be considered?

5. Before working at heights of 2 meters (6 feet) or higher above the ground, what should we consider?

II. Complete the sentences with the given words or expression. Change the form where necessary.

1. Ladders are _____ (primary) for access only.

2. Ladders must extend 1 meter above the working platform to provide handholds when _____ (dismount).

3. Changes of mobile scaffold must only be made by a competent _____ (scaffold).

4. _____ (inspect) of Safety Harnesses should be done prior to the use.

5. The _____ (install) of the nets should only be carried out by a competent contractor.

III. Translate the following words or phrases into English.

施工队_____   工作许可证_____

中国建设部_____   工作风险分析_____

安全制度_____   防止坠落设施_____

电气安全_____   可移动的脚手架_____

呼吸防护_____   减震器_____

防火_____

IV. Translate the following sentences into Chinese.

1. Controls relating to working at height or in confined areas (e. g. Permit-to-work, task risk assessment) are effective in reducing injuries by raising awareness of the hazards and ensuring the correct work methods are followed and that the proper precautions are taken.

_____

_____

_____

2. The actual use of the harness system by construction workers on such roof work is quite low – this is due to the discomfort and restrictions in using the harness. Failure to use the harness is a common complaint on construction work at sites.

_____

_____

_____

V. *The following is about occupational health and safety. Read it carefully and try your best to figure it out by referring to the Chinese.*

Manual Handling

Due to the repetitive nature of some of the tasks related to cement production, it is very important to ensure that the correct training is given to employees in relation to manual handling.

Size up the job first. If you think it is too heavy, get helpor use a crane or fork lift

Look out for sharp edges, splinters and nails

Pull out or knock down projecting nails before you pass material on or throw it out for scrap

Don't try to carry a load you cannot see over. Remove obstructions before lifting

Stack goods carefully and tidily on trucks and trailers

When lifting heavy objects, use your legs as much as possible to save your back muscles

Get a good grip of the articles

Keep your back straight and chin in

Slacken and bend your knees

Take up a firm stand, lift steadily and do not twist your body

When lifting or guiding pieces of equipment, watch for nipping points.

Lifts utilizing cranes, hoists, or other mechanical lifting devices will not commence unless：

.. an assessment of the lift has been completed and the lift method and equipment has been determined by a competent person（s）

.. operators of powered lifting devices are trained and certified for that equipment

.. rigging of the load is carried out by a competent person（s）

.. lifting devices and equipment have been certified for use within the last 12 months（at a minimum）

.. load does not exceed dynamic and/or static capacities of the lifting equipment

.. any safety devices installed on lifting equipment are operational

.. all lifting devices and equipment have been visually examined before each lift by a competent person（s）

（extracted from CSI-TF3 A Compilation Study of Good Practices in Health & Safety in the Cement Industry）

人 工 搬 运

在水泥生产中有一些重复性的工作，因此对从事人工搬运的人员进行正确培训非常重要。

　　对工作进行估计，如果你认为太重，则寻求帮助—使用起重设备和叉车

　　注意尖锐的边缘，碎片和钉子

　　在处理物料和丢弃废弃物的时候拔出或楔入凸出的钉子

　　如果不清楚所搬运的物品，则不要搬运。在搬运之前取出障碍物

　　在车辆和拖车上仔细堆放物品并整理整齐

　　当提升重物时，尽量用腿以保护腰

　　抓牢所持物品

　　保持背部挺直，收下颚

　　屈膝

　　站稳，稳稳地站起来不能扭腰

　　在搬运或调整设备位置时，注意夹点

　　在使用起重机，导链，或其他机械起重装置时必须符合下列要求：

.. 完成对起重进行评估，由有资质的人员决定使用的对起重方式和设备

.. 使用起重设备的人员经过培训并取证

.. 由有能力的人员对吊装物进行固定

.. 起重设备的使用许可证使用许可必须在 12 个月以内（至少）

.. 起重物重量不超过起重设备动态和静态的能力

.. 起重设备上的装置是可以操作的

.. 所有起重装置和设备在使用之前必须由相关人员检查

TEXT B

What Do the Best Companies Do for Safety and Health?

1. Clearly describe what people are expected to do for safety

　　Every level of employee, from the most senior executive to the newly hired worker, clearly understands what is expected. There are specific, demanding standards for each person in all major work activities. Without adequate standards, there can be no meaningful measurement, evaluation, correction or commendation of performance.

2. Make safety a line management responsibility and accountability

　　Safety is better served when it is so ingrained into every activity that it becomes impossible to ignore it. There is little talk of doing things the safe way and more talk of doing things the right way. Safety is equal to all considerations of production, costs and quality. This is reflected in performance appraisals, salary adjustments, and promotions.

3. Incorporate safety into the business process as an operational strategy

　　Leaders around the world increasingly recognize that a well-managed safety system provides an operational strategy to improve overall management. But in recent years a significant number of major applying the tools and techniques of good safety management gives them not only reduced injuries and illnesses but also measurable improvements in efficiency, quality and productivity.

As an example of generalized OHS Policy the attached policy is used by a CSI company.

The Group Health & Safety Policy requires all our local managers to：

. . Comply with all applicable Health & Safety Legislation

. . Provide a healthy and safe workplace for all employed（both Direct and Contracted Employees）

. . Continuously improve towards Best Industry Health &Safety Practice

The Group H&S Policy also requires all employed（both Direct and Contract Employees）to：

. . Work in a healthy and safe manner as required by law and as directed by management

（extracted from CSI-TF3 A Compilation Study of Good Practices in Health & Safety in the Cement Industry）

Notes

1. OHS：OCCUPATIONAL HEALTH & SAFETY（OHS）职业健康与安全

New Words

specific［spi'sifik］adj. 1. 明确的，确切的，详尽的；2. 具体的，特有的，特定的

demanding［di'mændiŋ］adj. 1. 工作要求高的，需要高技能（或耐性等）的，费力的；2. 要求极严的；苛求的；难满足的

adequate［'ædikwit］adj. 1. 充分的，足够的；2. 适当的，胜任的

commendation［'kɔmən¡deiʃən］n. 奖，奖品；表扬；嘉奖状

responsibility［ri¡spɔnsə'biliti］n. 1. 责任；2. 责任感，可信赖性；3. 职责

accountability［ə¡kauntə'biliti］n. 1. 有责任，有义务，可说明性；2. 应作解释

ingrain［in'grein］vt. 使根深蒂固

ignore［ig'nɔː］vt. 1. 不顾，不理，忽视；2. 对…不予理会

promotion［prə'məuʃən］n. 1. 提升，晋级；2. 宣传，推销；3. 推广，促进

incorporate［in'kɔːpəreit］vt. 1. 包含，加上，吸收；2. 把…合并，使并入

efficiency［i'fiʃənsi］n. 1. 效率，效能，功效；2. 提高功效的方法

generalize［'dʒenərəlaiz］vt. & vi. 概括，归纳，推论

applicable［'æplikəbl］adj. 适当的；合适的

New Phrases

senior executive 高级管理人员

line management 直接管理

performance appraisals 奖励

salary adjustments 薪酬调整

operational strategy 运行策略

Exercises

I. The following is a brief description of Typical Injury Causes & Types. Read it carefully and try your best to figure it outby referring to the Chinese.

Typical Injury Causes & Types

Main causes are Slips, Trips and Falls (29%), Falling or Moving Objects (19%) and Lifting, Overload and Exertion (18%). These three causes account for 66% of the total accidents.

Injuries By Cause:

Caught in Fixed Machinery 9%

Vehicles, Mobile Plant 6%

Falling or Moving Objects 19%

Slips, Trips, Falls 29%

Injuries by Heat or Chemicals 1%

Lifting, Overload or Overexert 18%

Hand Tools 6%

Other or Multiple Causes 12%

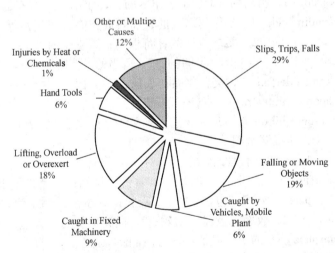

Injuries By Cause

Most Injuries are to Arms and Hands (32%), Legs and Feet (25%) and Back (13%)

.. These injuries are 71% of the total

Typical Injury Categories and Ages

.. Plant Operators (39%) and General Operatives (33%) are the most vulnerable.

.. 30 – 39 is the most injury prone age range (33%), followed by 20 – 29 (25%), and 40 – 49 (24%)

(extracted from CSI-TF3 A Compilation Study of Good Practices in Health & Safety in the Cement Industry)

典型的伤害致因和类型

主要原因包括滑倒、绊倒和坠落（29%），下降或搬移（19%）和起重，超重和拉伤（18%）。这三个原因占事故总数的66%。

伤害原因：

被固定的机械伤害占9%

车辆和移动设备占6%

下降或搬移占（19%）

滑倒，绊倒或跌倒占29%

高温或化学品致伤占1%

起重，超载或用力过度占18%

手动工具占6%

其他因素致伤占12%

很多工伤伤及手臂和手（32%），腿和脚（25%），背（13%）

·· 这些伤害占所有工伤的71%

典型伤害的种类和年龄

·· 设备操作人员（39%）和普通员工（33%）是最易受伤人群

·· 30~39岁是最易受伤的年龄段（占33%），其次是20~29岁（占25%）和，40~49岁（占24%）

TRANSLATION SKILLS

定语从句翻译

英语中，定语从句分成限制性从句与非限制性从句两种。他们在英语中的位置一般是在其所修饰的先行词后面。限定性定语从句与非限定性定语从句的区别只是在于限制意义的强弱。而汉语中定语作为修饰语通常在其所修饰的词前面，并且没有限制意义的强弱之分，因此，限制与非限制在翻译中并不起十分重要的作用。英语中多用结构复杂的定语从句，而汉语中修饰语则不宜臃肿。所以，在翻译定语从句时，一定要考虑到汉语的表达习惯。如果英语的定语从句太长，无论是限制性的或非限制性的，都不宜译成汉语中的定语，而应用其他方法处理。常见的定语从句翻译有以下几种方法。

一、前置法

把定语从句翻译到所修饰的先行词前面，可以用"的"来连接。既然定语从句的意义是作定语修饰语，所以在翻译的时候，通常把较短的定语从句译成带"的"的前置定语，翻译在定语从句的先行词前面。

例1：He who has never tasted what is bitter does not know what is sweet.

没有吃过苦的人不知道什么是甜。

例2：Space and oceans are the new world which scientists are trying to explore.

太空和海洋是科学家们努力探索的新领域。

例3：His laughter, which was infectious, broke the silence.

他那富有感染力的笑声打破了沉寂。

二、后置法

把定语从句翻译在所修饰的先行词后面，翻译为并列分句。英语的定语从句结构常常比较复杂，如果翻译在其修饰的先行词前面的话，会显得定语太臃肿，而无法叙述清楚。这时，可以把定语从句翻译在先行词后面，译成并列分句。翻译时可以用两种方法来处理。

1. 重复先行词

由于定语从句的先行词通常在定语从句中充当句子成分，如果单独把定语从句翻译出来的话，常常需要重复先行词，还可以用代词代替先行词来重复。

例1：I told the story to John, who told it to his brother.

他把这件事告诉了约翰，约翰又告诉了他的弟弟。

例2：We wish to express our satisfaction at this to the Special Committee, whose activities deserve to be encouraged.

在我们对特别委员会表示满意，特别委员会的工作应该受到鼓励。

例3：You, whose predecessors scored initial success in astronomical research, have acquired a greater accomplishment in this respect.

你们的先辈在天文学研究方面取得了初步的成功，而你们现在则在这一方面获得了更大的成就。

例4：Although he lacks experience, he has enterprise and creativity, which are decisive in achieving success in the area.

他虽然经验不足，但很有进取心和创造力，而这正是在这一领域获得成功的关键。

2. 省略先行词

如果把定语从句翻译在先行词后面，在"通顺、完整"的前提下，有时候可以不用重复先行词。

例1：It is he who received the letter that announced the death of your uncle.

是他接到那封信，说你的叔叔去世了。

例2：They worked out a new method by which production has now been rapidly increased.

他们制定出一种新方案，采用之后生产已迅速得到提高。

3. 融合法

把定语从句和它所修饰的先行词结合在一起翻译。融合法是指翻译时把主句和定语从句融合成一句简单句，其中的定语从句译成单句中的谓语部分。由于限制性定语从句与主句关系较紧密，所以，融合法多用于翻译限制性定语从句，尤其是"there be"结构带有定语从句的句型。

例1：There is a man downstairs who wants to see you.

楼下有人要见你。（原句中的主句部分there is a man 翻译成"有人"，然后将定语从句译成句子的谓语部分。）

例2：In our factory, there are many people who are much interested in the new invention.

在我们工厂里，许多人对这项新发明很感兴趣。（原句中的主句部分there are many people 翻译成"许多人"，作译文的主语，然后将定语从句译成句子的谓语部分。）

例3：We used a plane of which almost every part carried some indication of national identity.

我们驾驶的飞机几乎每一个部件都有一些国籍标志。（原句的主句较简单，整句句子的重点是在定语从句中，因此，翻译时将主句译成主语，而将定语从句译成句子的谓语部分。）

例4：She had a balance at her banker's which would have made her beloved anywhere.

她在银行里的存款足以使她到处受到欢迎。（原句的主句较简单，整句句子的重点是在定语从句中，因此，翻译时将主句译成主语，而将定语从句译成句子的谓语部分。）

4. 分译法

分译法是指将主句和从句分开翻译的一种方法，主要用于较长的非限制性定语从句里。采用这种方法可避免句子的冗长和累赘。这种方法一般采用主句在前，从句在后的翻译形式，将句子翻译成两个相对独立的小分句。

（1）译出关系代词或关系副词

根据逻辑的需要，在翻译前，我们首先应该弄清关系词所指代的内容，进而按照先行词的词义来进行翻译。

例1：He has learned French, which he thinks is the most beautiful language in the world.

他学过法语，他认为法语是世界上最美的语言。

例2：This is a college of science and technology, the students of which are trained to be engineers or scientists.

这是一所科技大学，该校学生将被培养成工程师或科学工作者。

另外，在英语中常常会把需要强调的内容放于句首，而汉语中却习惯把附加性说明的定语部分翻译成后置型的并列分句，以求在形式上突出主句的内容。

例1：She suddenly thought of her husband, who had left her and their children behind and had never been heard of.

她丈夫早就抛弃了妻儿一直杳无音信，现在她突然想起了他。

例2：The men suddenly awakened to the fact that there were beauty and significance in these trifles, which they had so long trodden carelessly beneath their feet.

以前，它们一直被这些人漫不经心地踩在脚下，现在这些人突然意识到这些小玩意儿的美丽和意义了。

（2）不翻译关系代词或关系副词

有些定语从句表面上是非限制性定语从句，但在意义上却已经和主句融为了一体。在翻译时，应该将引导定语从句的关系词省略，从而使句子的意思显得更为连贯。

例1：After dinner, the four key negotiators resumed their talks, which continued well into the night.

晚饭后，四个主要谈判人物继续进行会谈，一直谈到深夜。

例2：His wife, Betty, is Shanghai-born Chinese who left China at the age of eight, and whose book "Moon", tells of her sister's life in China.

他妻子贝蒂是一位出生在上海的华人，八岁离开中国，写过一本名叫《月》的书，记叙了她妹妹在中国的生活。

（3）译成相对独立的小分句

有些定语从句在修饰关系上与先行词之间关系显得较为疏远，这时，我们通常会将定语从句译成独立的句子。

例1：One was a violent thunderstorm, the worst I had ever seen, which obscured my objective.

有一次暴风骤雨，猛烈的程度实在是我平生所鲜见的。这场暴风雨遮住了我的目标。

例2：Nevertheless the problem was solved successfully, which showed that the computations were accurate.

不过问题还是圆满地解决了，这说明计算是很精确的。

译　文

第九单元　安全检查
对　话

安全检查

咨询工程师：首先，我想了解一下安全工作的组织机构。

承　包　方：从工程一开始我们就指定了一个适合本岗位，有资格，有经验的人作为安全负责人，他有充分的时间并对确保安全工作负有责任。安全负责人和他的三个助理的办公室在项目管理部门。共有十个人全职负责安全方面的工作。他们中的每个人负责某一个工段，其中有大约150到200名工作人员。

咨询工程师：很好。正如你所知，设立安全机构并对人员进行现场安全教育是非常重要的。你能给我简要地介绍一下你们整个的安全培训方案吗？

承　包　方：从场地建设之日起，我们就根据原国家建设部 JGJ59—88 标准开始执行安全培训方案了。

咨询工程师：对工人培训课程的内容是什么？

承　包　方：内容不仅仅限于以下内容：现场工作安全措施，中国劳动法员工的责任，公司安全措施，施工事故及报告，电气安全，人员安全设施，脚手架，沟渠挖掘，起重机安全使用方法，呼吸防护，火灾预防，有毒物质预防，急救及紧急事件救助措施等等。

咨询工程师：很好。现在我们一起去工地进行安全检查看看这些安全规定是否能够严格执行。让我们从安全帽这类个人防护设备开始吧，很遗憾，不是每个人都佩戴安全帽，穿着安全鞋。

承　包　方：因为这个国家的天气很热，即使知道安全鞋安全帽对安全很重要，但是他们还是觉得穿戴上不舒服。

咨询工程师：你们必须采取强有力的措施确保每个人都要穿安全鞋和戴安全帽。此外，在灰尘大的地方工作人员必须戴防毒口罩。

承　包　方：好的。我想我们的脚手架会让你感到满意。

咨询工程师：不。我对地面以上的工作条件仍然不够满意。有些在地面以上2米高的工作平台没有梯子。而且脚手架上有些地方堆放的材料太多。

承　包　方：这样施工的确很危险，我们必须整改。我们这就给各工段采取安全措施。

课文 A　高空作业

　　高空作业或密闭空间作业的控制措施（例如工作许可证，工作风险分析），通过提高隐患意识和确保采用正确的工作方式和正确的预防措施，可以有效地减少伤害。

　　通过强制使用安全设施（安全带和安全网）可以保护员工避免从高处坠落，张贴工作许可证，定期检查工作现场等是通常采用的技术（见附件高处作业数据表）

　　A 梯子

　　1. 梯子只是用来登高。

　　2. 在使用前，检查梯子能正常使用。

　　3. 梯子必须固定好。

　　4. 梯子必须高出工作平台一米以上，方便在上下梯子时作为扶手。

　　5. 作为角度的要求，梯子水平和垂直方向的角度应控制在 1:4。

　　B 脚手架

　　1. 脚手架必须由经过培训具有资质的架子工搭建、改变或调整。

　　2. 在 4 米高处工作没有边缘防护的情况下，脚手架工必须使用防止坠落的措施。（对于其他人员，这个限制通常是 2m）

　　3. 脚手架必须由有能力的人员进行检查，检查的结果放在脚手架的标签里面。

　　　　a. 第一次使用

　　　　b. 发生了实质的改变

　　　　c. 在强风或撞击之后

　　　　d. 定期进行（不超过 7 天）

　　4. 脚手架工作平台最低的宽度是 4 块板，配置扶手，中间栏杆和踢脚板。

　　5. 如果进行小量的工作可以没有护栏但是必须戴好全身式安全带并挂好。

　　6. 上下必须通过固定好的梯子。

　　7. 施工中不能为了方便拿起踏板，移开护栏或解开连接点；任何更改必须由有资质的架子工来做。

　　C 可移动的脚手架

　　1. 必须由具有资质的施工人员搭建，参照建造商的建议。

　　2. 搭建在坚固的地面上，离开地下设施。

　　3. 利用适当的方式或标识对地下区域进行警戒。

　　4. 工作平台必须有护栏，中间横杆和踢脚板。必须通过中间梯子上下。

　　D 使用安全网

　　在屋顶工作时，安全带是避免人员高处坠落的一种手段，但是，由于缺乏固定点，要求使用者每时每刻都拴挂安全带并不现实。施工人员使用安全带的几率很低，这是由于使用安全带不舒服和其局限性所致。在我们建筑现场不使用安全带是一种常见现象。通过使用安全网可以解决这些问题。安全网应该安装在所有高处作业的区域的下方。另外，高空作业时必须同时使用安全带，在屋顶工作仍旧需要边缘防护。必须由具备资质的人员安装安全网。

　　E 安全带检查

　　在使用安全带（包括合同方人员使用的）之前必须进行检查：

　　　　a）产品上必须有可追溯性标签

b）检查安全带和安全绳看是否有：

被切开或撕开

过度磨损

烧坏，化学侵蚀

纤维硬化

连接处是否脱线撕裂

c）检查金属部件

锋利的边缘

过度磨损

纠正操作

变形

F 在 2 米以上的高度工作必须符合下面要求：

1. 固定的平台必须有护栏或扶手，经有资质的人员检验，或有防止坠落设施：

2. 一个位于上方的合适的固定点

3. 安全带使用双重保险，连接处使用自锁挂钩

4. 合成纤维的系索

5. 减震器

6. 安全带可以容许向下坠落 2 米以内（6 英尺）

对防止坠落设施进行外观检查，看是否有损坏的或松动的部件

7. 具有从事此项工作资质的人员

（摘自水泥工业健康和安全管理实践研究汇编）

课文 B　最好的公司在健康和安全方面是如何做的？

1. 清楚地阐述人们在安全方面该做的事情：

每个层次的员工，从最高的执行委员到新雇佣的员工，清楚地了解自己该做的事情。在主要的工作活动中对所有人员都应该有具体严格的要求。没有完善的标准，就无法对业绩进行衡量，评价奖励或纠错。

2. 让安全成为直接管理层的责任和义务

当安全成为每一项工作根深蒂固的一部分，让人无法忽略时，就会产生很好的效果。人们很少说安全地去工作，但经常说正确地工作。考虑产品成本和质量的同时必须考虑安全。这可以体现在奖励加薪和升职等方面。

3. 将安全和业务经营活动结合在一起作为公司的运行策略

全球的领导者越来越认识到一个优秀的安全管理系统能提供一套运行策略来提高公司整体管理水平。这些年来许多大的公司发现，应用好的安全管理工具和技术给他们带来的不仅是减少伤害和职业病，同时在效率、质量和生产力方面都有明显提高。

作为一个实例，下面是 CSI 公司使用的 OHS（职业安全与健康）的策略。

集团的健康和安全方针要求所有当地经理做到：

1. 遵循所有可适用的健康和安全法律。

2. 为所有员工提供一个健康和安全的工作环境（包括在编员工和合同人员）。

3. 持续改进实现工业最佳健康和安全的实践。

4. 集团健康和安全同样要求所有员工（包括在编员工和合同工）做到以健康和安全的方式进行工作，遵守法律及管理规则。

（摘自水泥工业健康和安全管理实践研究汇编）

UNIT 10

Quality Control （质量控制）

DIALOGUE

（*Quality is one of the critical factors to ensure the success of a construction project. Due to the recent quality defects in the construction, a special meeting is held.*）

E： I have recently noticed that your performance with regard to compliance with the specifications and quality has slackened. On 18th and 19th of this month, I spent some time observing the placing of concrete for the ground floor. I carried out a slump test at the placement location with the help of your testing engineer and found that the water / cement ratio was not in accordance with the specification.

C： I believe quality is the life of the whole works and our first priority in its achievement. About the placement of the ground floor, we suspended the pouring operation and cleared the unqualified mix away when such problems as you described had occurred. At the same time, our technician looked into the cause and found that the electronic control system of the batch plant was out of order. We will repair it and the pouring operation will be resumed soon.

E： When do you plan to do the repairs?

C： Tomorrow. We will draw a lesson from these matters and strengthen our quality assurance system.

E：I also want to draw your attention to the water curing of concrete and storage of construction materials，especially the reinforcing steel.

C：We will pay more attention to those activities. It's true that we are facing a pressing completion time and have to expedite the construction progress，but we will certainly not do it at the cost of the project's quality. I believe that efforts on both sides will result in not only a timely product but also a high-quality one.

Notes

1. 会话背景与指南：竣工工程质量的好坏直接关系到工程是否达标（the intended goal）。投入使用后工程的效益是否能得到最大程度的发挥。因此，在工程的实施阶段，业主往往会派遣自己的技术监理人员到现场的各工作面去监督承包商的工程工作。

对于一个国际承包商（international contractor）来说，承建工程质量的优劣直接影响到他在国际工程承包界的信誉（reputation in the international contracting industry）。如果由于承包商的原因而发生重大的质量事故，那么他将失去信誉，失去更多承建工程的机会（business opportunity），从而难于立足于国际工程承包市场（international contracting market）。

在施工工程的过程中，承包商要辨证的处理质量、进度和费用之间的关系。越是在工期紧的情况下，越不能忽视质量，否则，很可能欲速则不达（the more haste, the less speed）。万一出现质量问题，要及时改正，虚心接受业主人员的批评意见。对于一个国际承包商来说，一个优质的工程就是其最好的广告（a high-quality product is the best advertisement for an international contractor）。

2. slump test 坍落度试验也可以说 slump consistency test。Slump：坍塌，坍落（度），工程中常见的术语还有：slump block（坍落试验堆），slump cone（坍落度筒），slump meter（坍落度计）。

New Words

critical［'kritikəl］adj. 决定性的，关键性的，危急的

slacken［'slækən］vt. & vi. 1.（使）松弛；2.（使某物）放慢，迟缓；3. 松懈下来，变迟缓

priority［prai'ɔriti］n. 1. 优先权，重点；2. 优先考虑的事；3.（车辆的）优先通行权

placement［'plesmənt］n.（对物件的）安置，放置

resume［ri'zju：m］vt. & vi. 重新开始；重新获得；（中断后）又继续

　　e. g. resume the work（复工），resume the talk（恢复谈判），resume the journey（又继续赶路）

storage［'stɔ：ridʒ］n. 1. 贮存，贮藏；2. 储藏处，仓库

expedite［'ekspiˌdait］vt. 1. 加快进展；2. 迅速完成

New Phrases

construction project　建设项目
quality defect　质量缺陷
with regard to　关于
compliance with　遵守
slump test　坍落度试验
water / cement ratio　水灰比
in accordance with sth　按照…
unqualified mix　不合格的拌合料
pouring operation　浇筑作业
look into sth　研究，调查 e. g. Look into the cause　调查原因
quality assurance system.　质量保证体系
water curing of concrete　混凝土水养护
construction material　建材
reinforcing steel　钢筋
at the cost of　以…为代价

Role Play

Discuss with your partner about the importance of the quality of works and what measures might be taken to ensure the high quality of works.

TEXT A

Quality Control and Quality Assurance (1)

QA/QC Procedure of the Project in Dubai Marina (1)
General Requirement

Where specifically stated herein, the Main Contractor (or his sub-contractors/suppliers) shall establish, document and maintain a Quality Assurance and Quality Control system capable of verifying to the satisfaction of the Engineer that all materials and workmanship, whatever their sources, conform to the requirements of this Performance Specification. Should the main Contractor or any of his sub-Contractors be certified to BS 5750 or ISO 9000/1, then these Works should be mentioned accordingly.

Quality of Materials and Supply

Unless otherwise stated or approved by the Engineer all materials used in the Works shall be new and of the best quality as specified in the Contract.

All materials and equipment specified in the contract documents which are to be incorporated in the Works must be obtained from or through a Dubai Emirate supplier and or manufacturer who must be registered and licensed by the Dubai Municipality. If such specified materials or equipment is not available from the Dubai Emirate market, then any other source is acceptable.

Materials delivered to the site for the purpose of Works, shall be accompanied by a "certificate of Guarantee" signed by the authorized representative of the manufacturer. Such Certificate shall state that the materials specifications and test results are in compliance with the specified requirement of the pertinent designations of the most recent edition of BSI, ASTM or any other approved equivalent National Standard unless otherwise directed. Falsification of such Certificates, Materials, Specifications or Test Results shall be just cause for the rejection of the materials.

The Contractor shall select rock quarries and shall submit laboratory tested and accepted samples, within sufficient time before their due, in order for the Engineer to determine their conformity within the related specifications. The Contractor shall exercise a continuous quality control upon the extracted material to confirm its suitability for use.

No material shall be supplied on the site before the Engineer's approval of the type of equipment which the Contractor intends to use in the quarry, and for the method of work. The Contractor shall arrange visits to the quarry, factories and /or workshops where the materials are manufactured, if the Engineer desires to do so before or during the approval process or any time during the progress of the work.

The Engineer's acceptance of the materials does not relieve the Contractor of his total responsibility to carry on with additional investigations in order to obtain and supply during the progress of the Works uniform material conforming to the specifications.

（Extracted from structural specification of multi-story residential building on plot 9AB, Dubai Marina ）

Notes

1. BS: abbr. British Standard 英国标准
2. ISO: abbr. International Organization for Standardization 国际标准化组织
3. BSI: abbr. （1） British Standard Institution 英国标准协会
            （2） British Standards Institution 英国标准机构
4. ASTM abbr. （1） American Society of Testing Materials 美国材料实验
            （2） American Society for Testing Materials 美洲试验材料协会
5. 长句分析: 句中……the Main Contractor （or his sub-contractors/suppliers） shall establish, document and maintain a Quality Assurance and Quality Control system capable of verifying to the satisfaction of the Engineer that all materials and workmanship, whatever their sources, conform to the requirements of this Performance Specification.
主语: the Main Contractor （or his sub-contractors/suppliers）
谓语: establish, document and maintain

宾语：a Quality Assurance and Quality Control system 其后置定语为：capable of verifying to the satisfaction of the Engineer

宾语从句：that all materials and workmanship, whatever their sources, conform to the requirements of this Performance Specification. 其修饰的先行词为主句宾语的中心词 "system"。

New Words

verify ['verifai] vt. 1. 证实，核实；2. 查对；核准

workmanship ['wɜːkmənʃip] n. 技艺，工艺，手艺

certified ['sɜːtifaid] adj. 1. 被鉴定的；2. 被证明的，有保证的

specify ['spesifai] vt. 1. 指定；2. 具体说明，把…写入说明书，详细列举

incorporate [in'kɔːpəreit] vt. 1. 包含，加上，吸收；2. 把…合并，使并入
         vi. 1. 包含，吸收；2. 合并，混合

emirate [e'miərit] n. 酋长国

license ['laisəns] vt. 批准，许可，颁发执照 n. 执照

municipality [mjuˌnisi'pæliti] n. 市政当局，自治市，自治区，自治市或区的政府当局

compliance [kəm'plaiəns] n. 服从，听从，顺从；依照

pertinent ['pɜːtinənt] adj. 有关的；中肯的；恰当的；相宜的

designation [ˌdezig'neiʃən] n. 1. 名字，称号；2. 选派，指定，委任

equivalent [i'kwivələnt] adj. 1. 相等的，相当的；2.（数量、度量、价值、力量、意义、重要性等)均等的;同等重要的,等量的;等价的,等值的

falsification [ˌfɔlsəfə'keʃən] n. 弄虚作假；歪曲

due [djuː] adj. 1. 应支付［给予］的；2. 应有的，应得到的；3. 到期的；4. 适当的，正当的，适宜的；5. 由于；因为；6. 适当的，恰当的，合适的
   n. 1. 应有的权利，应得到的东西；2. 应缴款
   adv. 正向；正对着
   prep. 1. 该由…所得，应向…支付；2. 应得，被欠

quarry ['kwɔːri] n.（采）石场；露天矿场

conformity [kən'fɔːmiti] n. 依照，遵从；符合，一致

uniform ['juːnifɔːm] adj. 全都相同的，一律的，一致的，统一的

New Phrases

a Quality Assurance and Quality Control system　质量保证与质量控制系统

be capable of　有…的能力

conform to…　符合，遵照

Performance Specification　性能说明书，设计任务说明书

certificate of Guarantee　保单，保证书

National Standard　国家标准
rock quarry　采石厂

Role Play

What are the requirements mentioned in the text with regard to the quality of works? Based on what you have learnt in your professional courses, what other requirements should be given in order to ensure the quality of the works?

Exercises

I. Answer the following questions.

1. What should the Main Contractor（or his sub-contractors/suppliers）establish, document and maintain in the QA/QC procedure?

2. What should all materials and workmanship conform to in this project?

3. What are the requirements of the supplier or the manufacturer of the materials and equipment in this project?

4. What should the certificate of Guarantee state?

5. If the Engineer desires to visit the quarry, factories and／or workshops where the material is manufactured, what should the contractor do?

II. Complete the sentences with the given words or expression. Change the form where necessary.

1. Quality is the life of the whole works and the first _____（prior）to be considered.

2. We should pay special attention to the _____（store）of construction materials, especially in rainy days.

3. The materials specifications and test results should be in _____（comply）with the approved National Standard.

4. Based on the laboratory test results of samples, the Engineer can determine their _____（conform）within the related specifications.

5. All materials and workmanship should conform to the requirements of the mentioned _____（perform）Specification.

III. Translate the following words or phrases into English.

建设项目_____

质量缺陷_____

坍落度试验 _____

水灰比_____

不合格的拌合料_____

浇筑作业_____
质量保证体系_____
混凝土水养护_____
建材_____
质量保证与质量控制系统_____
设计任务说明书_____
保证书_____
国家标准_____
采石厂_____

IV. Translate the following sentences into Chinese.

1. Where specifically stated herein, the Main Contractor (or his sub-contractors/suppliers) shall establish, document and maintain a Quality Assurance and Quality Control system capable of verifying to the satisfaction of the Engineer that all materials and workmanship, whatever their sources, conform to the requirements of this Performance Specification. Should the main Contractor or any of his sub-Contractors be certified to BS 5750 or ISO 9000/1, then these Works should be mentioned accordingly.

_____
_____
_____
_____

2. All materials and equipment specified in the contract documents which are to be incorporated in the Works must be obtained from or through a Dubai Emirate supplier and or manufacturer who must be registered and licensed by the Dubai Municipality.

_____
_____

TEXT B

Quality Control and Quality Assurance (2)

Quality of Materials and Supply (2)

Wherever in the Specifications tests on materials, tests on completed work and construction control tests are called for or implied, they shall be carried out according to, and the materials shall comply with, the requirements of the Specifications (latest edition) with the latest standards listed below as the priority:

a. UAE and DM standards.

b. International standard such as ISO.

c. Standards such as BSI and DIN.

d. Others as stated in the Specification such as ASTM, etc.

Where specific material or equipment is referred to in the Contract, it is intended only to indicate the acceptable standard. The Contractor may offer alternative materials or equipment of an equal standard. The contractor must submit a statement listing proposed alternatives together with such information and samples as the Engineer may need to satisfy himself that the alternatives offered are of equal quality to the items specified. The cost of submitting such samples will be borne by the Contractor.

The contractor will be required to produce documentary evidence that all materials which are not available in the local market and which have to be imported have been ordered sufficiently in advance to ensure that no delay to the Engineer. A material tracking schedule shall be submitted periodically as required by the Engineer, which consists of the details of submittals, approvals, placement of order and the requirement of the item in the work. The Contractor shall be responsible for delays as a consequence of delayed ordering.

Should the Engineer discover in the Works any material other than those approved, he may order their removal from the site and replacement with approved materials at no cost to the Employers and in compliance with Standard Specifications.

All specified materials incorporated in the Works shall be fixed or applied strictly in accordance with the manufacturer's printed instruction.

The Bills of Quantities shall NOT be used as a basis for ordering materials and the Contractor is entirely responsible for assessing the quantities of materials to be ordered.

All materials or manufactured items shall be carefully loaded, transported, unloaded and stored in an approved manner, protected from damage and exposure to weather or dampness during transit and after delivery to the Site. Damaged material or manufactured items damaged during and after fixing in position shall be removed, repaired or replaced by the Contractor at his own expenses.

（Extracted from structural specification of multi-story residential building on plot 9AB, Dubai Marina）

Notes

1. UAE abbr. United Arab Emirates （亚洲）阿拉伯联合酋长国
2. DM：Design Manual 设计手册
3. Standards such as BSI and DIN.
4. 长句分析：在句中：A material tracking schedule shall be submitted periodically as required by the Engineer, which consists of the details of submittals, approvals, placement of order and the requirement of the item in the work.
主语：A material tracking schedule
谓语：shall be submitted
状语：periodically；as required by the Engineer
非限定性定语从句：which consists of the details of submittals, approvals, placement of order and the requirement of the item in the work

New Words

imply〔im′plai〕vt. 1. 暗示，暗指；2.（思想、行为等）必然包含，使有必要

　　　　　　　　　vt. & vi. 说明；表明

alternative〔ɔ：l′tə：nətiv〕adj. 两者（或两者以上）择一的，二择其一的，可从数个中

　　　　　　　　　　　　任择其一的；（两种选择中）非此即彼的

　　　　　　　　　　　　n. 可供选择的事物；可供选择的机会；替换物，替代品

bear〔bɛə〕vt. & vi. 承担，负担（过去式：bore；过去分词：borne/born）

sufficiently〔sə′fiʃəntli〕adv. 足够地，充分地

periodically〔piəri′ɔdikli〕adv. 1. 周期性地；2. 定期地

placement〔′pleismənt〕n. 1. 安置；2.（对物件的）安置，放置

consequence〔′kɔnsikwəns〕n. 结果，后果

order〔′ɔ：də〕n. 1. 次序，顺序；2. 订购，订货；订单

　　e. g.　place an order 定购（货物）

assess〔ə′ses〕vt. 1. 估价，估计；2. 评定，核定，评估

dampness〔′dæmpnis〕n. 湿气，潮湿

transit〔′trænsit〕n. 搬运；载运；运输

New Phrases

carry out . 实行，执行；实现，完成

in advance　预先，事先

refer to　提及；涉及，谈到，提到

a material tracking schedule　原材料跟踪计划

as a consequence of…　作为……结果

Exercises

I. Read the following passage and try to answer the questions given at the beginning.

Questions：

1. How do you understand the term quality control? Give examples.

2. What are involved when exercising quality control and achieve quality assurance?

3. What tasks governs basically the construction of a designed system?

4. What role does quality control play in design, materials selection and construction?

5. Can you make a summary of quality control and quality assurance by combining the content of the passage and your experience?

Quality Control and Quality Assurance

Quality control assures the reliability of performance of the designed system in accordance with assumed and expected reserve strengths in the design. To exercise "quality control" and achieve "quality assurance" encompasses monitoring the roles and performance of all participates: the client or owner, the designer, the concrete producer, the laboratory tester, the constructor, and the user. In summary, a quality assurance system needs to be provided based on the exercise of quality control at various phases and interacting parameters of a total system.

Construction of a designed system is governed basically by five primary tasks: planning, design, materials selection, construction and use.

Quality assurance is necessary to satisfy the user's needs and rights. It ensures that the activities influences the final quality of a concrete structure.

In order to plan the successful execution of a proposed constructed system, all main and sub activities have to be clearly defined.

Quality control in design aims at verifying that the designed system has the safety, serviceability and durability required for use, to which the system is intended as required to be the applicable codes, and that such a design is correctly presented in the working drawings and the accompanying specification. The degree of quality control depends on the type of system to be constructed: the more important the system, the more control that is required. As a minimum, a design must always be checked by an engineer other than the originating design engineer.

It has to be emphasized at the outset that the quality of materials such as reinforced concrete is not determined only by compressive or tensile strength tests. Many other factors affect the quality of the finished product such as water/cement ratio, cement content, creep and shrinkage characteristics, freeze and thaw properties, and other durability aspects and conditions.

Construction is the execution stage of a project, which can be used to satisfying all design and specification requirements within prescribed time limits at minimum cost. To achieve the desired quality assurance, the construction phrase has to be proceeded by an elaborate and correct preparation stage, which can be part of the design phrase. The preparation of planning phrase is very critical since it gives an overall clear view of the various activities involved and the possible problems that could arise at the various phrases of execution.

New Words for reference

encompass [en'kʌmpəs] vt. 1. 围绕，包围；2. 包含，包括，涉及（大量事物）

participant [pɑː'tisipənt] n. 参加者，参与者

parameter [pə'ræmitə] n. （限定性的）因素，特性

serviceability [ˌsəːvisə'biliti] n. 有用性，适用性

compressive or tensile strength tests　抗压或抗拉强度

water/cement ratio　水灰比

cement content　水泥用量

creep and shrinkage characteristics　徐变和收缩特性

freeze and thaw properties　冻融性

prescribe［priˈskraib］vt. & vi. 规定，指定遵守

II. Try to translate the following passage into Chinese by referring to the dictionary and make a better understanding about quality control.

Quality control

As with cost control, the most important decisions regarding the quality of a completed facility are made during the design and planning stages rather than during construction. It is during these preliminary stages that component configurations, material specifications and functional performance are decided. Quality control during construction consists largely of insuring conformance to these original designs and planning decisions.

While conformance to existing design decisions is the primary focus of quality control, there are exceptions to this rule.

First, unforeseen circumstances, incorrect design decisions or changes desired by an owner in the facility function may require re-evaluation of design decisions during the course of construction. While these changes may be motivated by the concern for quality, they represent occasions for re-design with all the attendant objectives and constraints.

As a second case, some designs rely upon informed and appropriate decision making during the construction process itself.

With the attention to conformance as the measure of quality control during the construction process, the specification of quality requirements in the design and contract documentation becomes extremely important. Quality requirements should be clear and verifiable, so that all parties in the project can understand the requirements for conformance. Much of the discussion in this chapter relates to the development and the implications of different quality requirements for construction as well as the issues associated with insuring conformance.

TRANSLATION SKILLS

词汇的翻译

专业英语文章的主要内容是阐述事理，其特点一般是平铺直叙、逻辑性强，公式、数据和专业词汇较多。因此，翻译专业英语文章时对译文的要求就更严格，要做到说理清楚，逻辑正确，公式、数据和词义的选择准确无误，专业词语应与汉语相应的词语保持一致。现就专业英语中专业词语的基本翻译方法归纳如下：

一、词义的选择

有些词在普通用语和专业用语中的词义区别较大，而且同一个词在不同专业性质的篇目中，词义可能又不一样。翻译这类词必须根据文章的内容来确定词义，然后选用与之相当的汉语来表达所译内容。如以下单词：

例词：	专业意义	普通意义
character	字符	性格；品质
location	存储单元	位置；定位
memory	存储器	记忆；回忆
driver	驱动器	驾驶员；传动器
carry	进位	搬运；携带
power	功率	幂；能量
field	字段	原野；田地

二、新词语的译法

对于一些科技英语新词语，就要根据原词的涵义，采用科学灵活的方法译成相应的汉语。

1. 音译：音译就是按术语的发音译成读音与原词大致相同的汉字。

例如：radar	雷达 （无线电定位术）
TOEFL	托福 （Test of English as a Foreign Language 托福考试）
Hacker	黑客 （从网络中擅自存取的人）
Nanometer	纳米 （长度单位 10 亿分之一米）
clone	克隆 （无性繁殖）
Modules	模块 （组件）
sonar	声纳 （声波导航和测距设备）
hertz	赫兹 （频率单位）

2. 意译：意译是对原词所表达的具体事物和概念进行仔细推敲，以准确译出该词的科学概念。也就是按科技新词语的词义译出。

例如：microcomputer	微 （型计算） 机
teleprompter	电传打字机
microprocessor	微处理器
gramophone	留声机
cutting—edge technology	前沿技术
videophone	可视电话
high—tech sector	高科技板块
guided missile	导弹
think tank	智囊团
IT 产业 （Information Technology）	信息技术产业

3. 形译：用英语常用字母的形象来为形状相似的物体定名。翻译这类术语时，一般采用形译法。

例如：T-square	丁字尺
A-bedplate	A 形底座
D-valve	D 形阀
M-wing	M 形机翼

4. 混合式翻译：混合式翻译是指，在科技文献中某些商标、牌号、型号和表示特定意义的字母、单词均可直接使用原文，只译普通名词。

例如：B-52 E bomber	B-52 E 轰炸机

BASIC Language	BASIC 语言（初学者通用符号指令码）
Ada Language	Ada 语言（行动数据自动化系统）
X ray	X 射线（伦琴射线，x 光）
C network	C 形网络（网络系统）
N – region	N 区（电子导电区）

三、在科技文献中常常会碰到一些非英语单词、短语和缩略语（主要为拉丁语）。翻译这类词时应查阅有关书刊，采用新的通行译法。

例如：e. g.（exempli gratis）= for example 例如

i. e.（id est）= that is 即，就是

e. r.（en route）= on the way 在途中

versus（vers，vs.） 与……相比，依赖

et. al. = on the others 以及，其他，等

vice versa（v. v.） 反过来，反之亦然

tc.（et cetera）= and so on/and so fourth 等等

Vide ante 见前

idem 同上，同前

inter 在……中间

Viz（videlicet）= namely 就是，正是

N. B.（nota bene） 注意

译　文

第十单元　质量检查

对　话

（质量是建设项目成败的决定性因素之一。由于最近在施工中存在质量缺陷，特召开了一次专门会议。）

咨询工程师：我最近注意到你们在遵守工程规范和质量的情况方面不尽如人意。在本月的 18 号和 19 号，我花了些时间检查地面混凝土的浇筑情况。在你们检测工程师的帮助下在浇筑现场进行了一个坍落度实验，我发现水灰比不符合工程规范的要求。

承　包　方：我相信质量是整个工程的生命，也是我们在工作中的首要问题。关于浇筑地面这件事，我们在你说明的问题发生之后就停止了浇筑作业并且清除了不合格的拌和料。同时我们的技术人员查明了问题原因，发现配料场的电子控制系统出了问题。我们会安排修理以便浇筑作业尽快重新开始。

咨询工程师：你们计划什么时候去修理？

承　包　方：明天。我们会从这事情中吸取教训，加强我们的质量保证体系。

咨询工程师：我提醒你们对混凝土水养护和施工材料，尤其是钢筋的贮存，也要引起

注意。

承　包　方：我们一定对以上事宜多加注意。的确，我们正面临工期缩短，又要加快施工进程，但我们决不会以牺牲工程的质量为代价来完成任务。我相信在我们双方的共同努力下，我们不仅能够按时完工而且保证质量上乘。

课文 A　质量控制和质量保证 （1）

迪拜码头项目中的质量保证和质量控制程序总体要求

在此特别规定，主要承包商（或分包商/供货商）要建立能够令咨询工程师满意的质量与质量控制系统，以文件的形式体现出来并且保持执行，保证所有的材料和工艺，无论其来源如何都能遵照其设计任务说明书的要求。如果主承包商和他的任何分包商都得到 BS5750 或 ISO9000/1 认证，那么这些工程也应被相应提及。

材料及供货的质量

除非另外说明或由咨询工程师批准，工程所用全部材料应按合同指定是新近生产的且质量上乘。

所有在合同文件中说明的，用于各项工程之中的材料和设备都必须从迪拜酋长国的供货商或生产商那里或通过他们购买。这些供货商或生产商必须有迪拜市政当局注册并颁发许可证。如果指定的材料和设备无法在迪拜酋长国买到，则可以采用其他途径购买。

运送到施工现场为工程所用的材料必须有一份由生产商授权的代表签名的保证书。这份保证书应说明材料规格和检测结果，均符合 BSI，ASTM 或任何其他同等的经批准的国家标准最新版本中有关规定所指定的要求，除非另外说明，如证书，材料，规格或检测结果上有弄虚作假的情况，则立即停止使用该材料。

承包商应在预期使用之前充足的时间里选择采石厂并提交经实验室检测和被接受的样品，以使咨询工程师测定其是否符合相关的要求。承包商应对选取的材料采用连续不断的质量控制办法来证明其适合使用。

在咨询工程师对承包商在采石场使用的设备以及工作办法批准之前不允许将材料运抵现场。在批准之前，批准过程中以及工程进行的任何时间，如果咨询工程师要求，承包商都应安排其到生产资料的采石场，工厂或车间进行视察。

咨询工程师同意使用材料并不能减轻承包商对材料所付的总责任。在工程进行期间承包商应采取其他的调查方式购买到并供给统一的与规范相符的材料。

（摘于迪拜码头 9AB 地段多层住宅楼的结构要求）

课文 B　质量控制和质量保证 （2）

材料和供给的质量 （2）

要求所用材料进行规范检测，已完工工程的检测以及施工控制检测都应按规范（最新版本）的要求执行，使用的材料必须符合工程规范。以下是需要首先执行的最新标准：

a. 阿拉伯联合酋长国标准和设计手册标准。

b. 国际标准，例如 ISO

c. BSI 标准和 DIN 标准

d. 工程规范中所列的其他标准，例如 ASTM 等等合同中特别提及的材料和设备是可以接受的唯一标准。合同中可能给出同等标准下的其他可供选择的材料和设备，承包商必须递交一份说明，列出计划选择何种产品以及其相关材料及样品，因为咨询工程师需要证明一下所选择的产品是否与合同说明的产品质量相同。递交此类样本的费用由承包商负责。

对于所有在当地市场无法买到，必须进口的材料，承包商应向咨询工程师提交书面材料证明并且在预先充足的时间内订购以确保不会延误使用。要按咨询工程师的要求定期递交原材料跟踪计划表，包括订单递交、同意、投放的详细情况以及工程中产品的要求。对于没有及时订购所导致的工程延误由承包方负责。

如果咨询工程师发现在工程中有任何未经批准的材料使用，可以命令将这批材料从现场运走并更换批准使用的材料，依照工程规范标准业主不承担任何费用。

用于工程中所有指定的材料都应严格地依照生产商印发的说明安装和使用。

工程量单不应作为订购材料的依据，承包商应对需要订购材料数量的估计负全责。

所有材料及产品都应小心装载、运输、卸下并按批准的办法贮存，在运输期间和运送到现场后要避免损坏，风吹日晒或受潮。

在安装期间及以后如有损坏的材料或产品应立即拆除，修理或更换，所产生的费用由承包方负担。

UNIT *11*

Roofing Works（屋面工程）

DIALOGUE

Inspection of Roof and Water Proofing

E: I was once told by a building contractor that the most complaints he received were from the roofing leakage, is that correct?

C: No. It is already a history. But I understand what you mean. Anyhow enough attention should really be put/paid to the roof（ing）construction.

E: Now we would like to know the main steps of waterproofing for precast concrete panel roof. What are the working scopes for the designing institute and contractor respectively in the waterproofing drawing?

C: According to the contract, the drawings provided by the designer are purely indicative as to the general areas to be waterproofed and in no way should they be taken to present accurate details of junctions at walls and windows or at skirting, etc. We have prepared the detailed drawings with technical specification as sample of materials, and submitted it one week ago.

E: Before you start the waterproofing works, how will you do for the surface preparation?

C: All surfaces to be waterproofed shall be thoroughly roughened, then it follows with a good cleaning to remove any dust or oil or other laitance material that would affect bonding.

E：How do you deal with the defects on concrete surface before waterproofing starts?

C：All holes, cracks, honeycomb, construction joints, or other defects on surface must be cut out, cleaned, saturated with water and pointed up with non-shrink mortar following the application procedure recommended by the manufacturer.

E：Your description sounds correct. But the most important thing is to operate strictly complied with the specification and procedures. Any negligence will cause water leakage . We have had too many lessons.

C：We are quite aware of this. We will strengthen our supervision on the works for every building. If any water leakage happens, the supervisor and workers in charge will be penalized severely.

E：But do not forget to give them necessary training before the works starts. Since some special materials will be used, it is important to apply the waterproofing strictly in accordance with the instructions from manufacturers.

C：Yes, we will.

Notes

1. 会话背景与指南：屋面工程包括屋面结构以上的屋面找平层（roofing screed coat）、隔气层（moisture barrier/ air-insulation layer）、保温层（thermal barrier/insulation layer/thermal insulation）、防水层（waterproof layer）、保护层（protective layer）和使用面层（surface course），是房屋建筑的一项重要的分部工程。其施工质量的优劣，不仅关系到建筑物的使用寿命，而且直接影响其使用功能。

2. 屋面防水工程施工前应对图纸进行审核，了解屋面施工图中的防水细部构造，并编制屋面防水工程施工方案或技术措施方案。使用的防水材料应通过技术鉴定并且必须符合设计要求。防水材料进入现场后，应抽查复试，达到技术指标才可使用。屋面防水工程必须由防水专业队施工。

屋面防水施工应注意事项：

（1）严禁在雨天进行卷材和保温施工。

（2）卷材防水层的找平层要符合质量要求，达到规定的干燥程度。

（3）在屋面拐角、天沟、水落口、屋脊、卷材搭接、收头等节点部位，要仔细铺平贴紧、压实、收头牢靠、符合设计要求和屋面防水工程技术规范等有关规定，在屋面拐角、天沟、水落口、屋脊等部位要加铺卷材附加层。

（4）卷材铺贴时要避免过度拉紧和皱折，基层与卷材间排气要充分，向横向两侧排气后用辊子压平粘实。

（5）卷材搭接宽度和铺贴要顺直，同时要严格按照基层所弹标线施工。

（6）铺设保温层时要保护好防水层。

New Words

complaint ［kəm'pleint］ n. 1. 抱怨，诉苦，埋怨，不满；2. 投诉

leakage ［'li：kidʒ］ n. 1. 漏，漏出；2. 漏出物，渗漏物

waterproof ［'wɔ：təpru：f］ adj. 不透水的，防水的 vt. 使防水；使不透水 n. 防水衣物

respectively ［ris'pektivli］ adv. 分别；各自；顺序为；依次为

indicative ［in'dikətiv］ adj. 表明；标示；显示；暗示

junction ［'dʒʌnkʃən］ n. 联结点，会合点，枢纽

skirting ［'skə：tiŋ］ n. 裙料，壁脚板

roughen ［'rʌfən］ vt. & vi. （使）变得粗糙；（使）变得不平

laitance ［'leitəns］ n. 水泥乳，浮浆皮（混凝土表面的乳白色浆）

bond ［bɔnd］ n. 1. 联系，关系；2. 连接，接合，结合

crack ［kræk］ vt. & vi. （使…）开裂，破裂 n. 裂缝，缝隙

honeycomb ［'hʌnikəum］ n. 蜂窝，蜂巢

saturate ［'sætʃəreit］ vt. 1. 浸湿，浸透；2. 使…大量吸收或充满某物

manufacturer ［'mænjuˌfæktʃərə］ n. 制造商，制造厂，制造者，生产商

negligence ［'neglidʒəns］ n. 1. 疏忽，玩忽，失职，失误，过失；2. 不修边幅

supervision ［ˌsju：pə'viʒən］ n. 监督，管理

penalize ［'pi：nəlaiz］ vt. 对…予以惩罚

New Phrases

precast concrete panel roof　预制混凝土板屋顶

surface preparation　表面处理

concrete surface　混凝土表面

construction joints　施工缝

non-shrink mortar　无收缩砂浆

water leakage　漏水

in accordance with　按照…

Role Play

Discuss with your partner about types of roof you have encountered in China and talk about their advantage and disadvantage, e. g. sharply-pointed ridge roof, flat surface roof etc.

TEXT A

Build-up Reinforced Bitumen Membrane Inverted Roof Covering

Location:

O Tower: Tower roof and mechanical floor, 42th and 44th floor outdoor terrace,

O Podium: 1st and 2nd floor outdoor terrace, roof deck

  – Drawing reference (s): (GA) A. 101, 102, 142, 144, 145, 146, (21), (34), (41) and (47) series drawings and relevant details.

  – Base: concrete screed laid to falls minimum 50mm

Preparation: Smooth and free from any protrusions

  – Waterproof covering: 4mm APP modified reinforced bituminous membrane.

Manufacturer: 'DAKTECH', Testudo mineral or approved equal.

First layer: 4mm thick APP modified bituminous membrane polymer reinforced

Attachment: partially bonded to manufacturers recommendations

  – Insulation: 50mm extruded polystyrene insulation with aluminum foil to top surface.

  – Filter layer: geotextile filter layer to approval

  – Surface protection/Security:

  – 50mm limestone chipping ballast to all other areas as shown on drawings.

GENERAL REQUIREMENTS

ROOFING GENERALLY

  – Unless specified otherwise, lay roof covering in accordance with BS 8217 to provide a secure, free draining and completely weather tight roof.

  – Ancillary products and accessories, where not specified, to be types recommended for the purpose by the membrane manufacturer.

  – Use operatives trained in the application of built-up membrane roofing and who have attended a recognized training scheme. Submit evidence of training to Engineer on request.

  – Maintain fully trained operatives on site throughout the installation period.

ADVERSE WEATHER

  – Store rolls of membrane indoors until they are to be used immediately.

  – Provide temporary covers and drainage as required to keep unfinished areas of the roof dry.

  – Suspend work in severe or continuously wet weather unless an effective temporary roof is provided over the working area.

  – If unavoidable wetting of the construction does occur, take prompt action to minimize and make good any damage.

(Extracted from specification for build-up felt roof coverings of multi-story residential building on plot 9AB, Dubai Marina)

New Words

build – up［ˈbildʌp］adj. 组合的

bitumen［biˈtuːmən］n. 沥青，柏油

membrane［miˈmentəu］n. 薄膜

podium［ˈpəudiːəm］n. 平台

inverted［inˈvəːtid］adj. 反向的，倒转的

protrusion［prəˈtruːʒən］n. 伸出，突出

mineral［ˈminərəl］n. 矿物；矿石；

polymer［ˈpɔləmə］n. ＜化＞聚合物（体）adj. 聚合的

insulation［insəˈleiʃən］n. 1. 隔离，隔绝；绝缘；隔声；2. 绝缘、隔热或隔声等的材料

geotextile n. 土工织物

limestone［ˈlaimˌstəun］n. 石灰岩

chipping［ˈtʃipiŋ］n. 碎屑，破片

ballast［ˈbæləst］n. 道砟材料

accessory［ækˈsesəri］n. 附件，配件，附属物

gauge［geidʒ］n. 厚度，直径

flashing［ˈflæʃiŋ］n. 防水板，遮雨板

perimeter［pəˈrimitə］n. 1. 周边，周围，边缘；2. 周长

plinth［plinθ］n. ＜建＞（柱的）底座；基座

track［træk］n. 轨道

ancillary［ˈænsəˌleriː］adj. 1. 辅助的，补充的；2. 附属的，附加的

drainage［ˈdreinidʒ］n. 1. 排水，放水；2. 排水系统，下水道

New Phrases

built-up membrane roofing　组合薄膜屋面

tower roof　塔顶

mechanical floor　设备层

outdoor terrace　室外平台

concrete screed　混凝土找平层

APP：abbr. Application　应用；已被批准的；已被承认的；良好的；有效的

modified reinforced bituminous membrane　加强型改性沥青薄膜

first layer　底层

modified bituminous membrane　改性沥青薄膜

modified bituminous membrane polymer reinforced　加强型聚合物改性沥青薄膜

extruded polystyrene insulation　挤塑聚苯乙烯绝缘

aluminum foil　铝箔

filter layer　过滤层，渗透层
geotextile filter layer　土工织物过滤层

Role Play

Discuss with your partner about the construction procedure of the roof and the measures to ensure the waterproofing of it based on what you have learnt in the dialogue and text.

Exercises

I. Answer the following questions.

1. Where can the type of roof covering mentioned in the passage be applied?

2. What preparation should be made before constructing the roof?

3. What are the requirements of accessories?

4. When encountering adverse weather, how should the contractor deal with the works?

II. Complete the sentences with the given words or expression. Change the form where necessary.

1. The residents are _____ (complaint) about the roofing leakage.

2. The surfaces to be waterproofed are quite _____ (roughen).

3. Heat _____ (insulate) in building is quite important in the north part of China.

4. The _____ (manufacture) in this region provides high quality bitumen.

5. The _____ (supervise) of the Engineer can guarantee the quality of Works.

III. Translate the following words or phrases into English.

预制混凝土板屋顶_____

表面处理_____

施工缝_____

无收缩砂浆_____

漏水_____

组合薄膜屋面_____

设备层_____

混凝土找平层_____

底层_____

改性沥青薄膜_____

铝箔_____

土工织物过滤层_____

IV. *Translate the following sentences into Chinese.*

1. All other accessories necessary to complete the installation in accordance with the membrane manufacturer's recommendations.

2. Use operatives trained in the application of built-up membrane roofing and who have attended a recognized training scheme. Submit evidence of training to Engineer on request.

3. Provide temporary covers and drainage as required to keep unfinished areas of the roof dry.

4. If unavoidable wetting of the construction does occur, take prompt action to minimize and make good any damage.

TEXT B

Water Proofing for Precast Reinforced Concrete Panel

The concrete panel roof fixed on purlins in this project has four layers of waterproofing.

The first layer is a sort of oil plus the asphalt felt which is sealed into the joints between the concrete panels and sprayed on the surface of the panels. This layer of oil or asphalt felt is for avoiding steam from inside building to get into the insulation layer above. The asphalt material should be lapped at least 50mm thick when it is laid on the concrete panel and up 150mm thick on joints with wall and arch-shaped elements. The softening point of the asphalt material must be higher than 50℃ (centigrade degree).

Block or panel made of foam concrete or foam bitumen which is light and low heating conductive material are usually used for the insulation layer after the asphalt felt.

For the third layer of the waterproofing, cement grouting mortar is a 50mm thick layer of 1: 3 cement mortar or 1:8 bitumen mortar with a thickness of 20 – 25 mm. the surface is rough for receiving the top layer another layer of asphalt felt.

Bitumen paste material is used to paste the asphalt felt on the plastering. After the cement mortar is dry enough, say, around 15% – 20% water content, the bitumen paste material will be heated to 240℃ (centigrade degrees) and then sprayed on the plastering for pasting of the asphalt felt.

One should not lay down the asphalt sheets from the upper to the lower if there is a slope on the roof while he should begin from the eaves, the lowest place of the roof, and parallel to the ridge, lapped at least 70mm. the vertical joints of each layer should be alternated at least 500mm. finally the small gravel (3 – 5mm grading) are spread and pasted on the asphalt felt for protection.

As to the waterproof in the area where the pipes penetrate through floors or roofs, all pipes of whatever nature passing through roofs and floors are to be sealed around with asphalt collar up to at least 150mm above finished slab level and properly dressed around the pipes with angle fillet at bottom. The surface of the pipes should be thoroughly cleaned and painted with an approved bituminous solution before the asphalt is applied. Finally all pipes penetrating waterproofed areas must be sealed effectively.

Notes

1. 长句分析：As to the waterproof in the area where the pipes penetrate through floors or roofs，all pipes of whatever nature passing through roofs and floors are to be sealed around with asphalt collar up to at least 150mm above finished slab level and properly dressed around the pipes with angle fillet at bottom.

状语：As to the waterproof in the area

where the pipes penetrate through floors or roofs 为定语从句修饰先行词"area"

as to：至于

主语：all pipes of whatever natural passing through roofs and floors

　　　各种穿过屋顶和地板的管道

谓语：are to be sealed around with… and dressed

翻译：对于各种穿过屋顶和地板的管道，都要在比最终饰面至少高 150mm 的区域内用沥青密封，底部由楞条适当环绕。

New Words

purlin［'pə：lin］n. 檩桁条

asphalt［'æsˌfɔ：lt］n. 1. 沥青，柏油；2.（铺路等用的）沥青混合料

felt［felt］n. 毛毡；毡制品；油毛毡

lap［læp］vt. 使形成部分重叠；部分叠盖 vi. 折叠 部分重叠；

foam［fəum］n. 1. 泡沫，泡沫材料；2. 泡沫橡胶，海绵橡胶；3. 泡沫剂（用于洗涤、
　　　　　　　　剃须、灭火等）

grout［graut］vt. 用薄泥浆填塞

mortar［'mɔ：tə］n. 砂浆，灰浆

thickness［'θiknis］n. 厚；厚度

eaves［i：vz］n. 屋檐

parallel［'pærəlel］adj. 1.（指至少两条线）平行的；2. 类似的，相对应的；3. 并行的

alternate［ɔ：l'tə：nit］adj. 1. 轮流的，交替的；2. 间隔的；3. 代替的
　　　　　　　　　　　vt. & vi. 其他读音：［'ɔ：ltə：neit］（使）交替，（使）轮换

gravel［'grævəl］n. 沙砾，砾石，石子

penetrate［penitreit］vt. & vi. 渗透

collar［'kɔlə］n. 圈；衣领，领子

New Phrases

precast reinforced concrete panel roof　预制钢筋混凝土板屋顶

asphalt felt　沥青油毡

concrete panel　混凝土面板

insulation layer　绝缘层

softening point　软化点

foam concrete　泡沫混凝土

foam bitumen　泡沫沥青

low heating conductive material　低导热性材料

cement grouting mortar　灌浆水泥砂浆

cement mortar　水泥砂浆

bitumen mortar　沥青砂浆

plastering　抹灰

bitumen paste material　沥青粘合材料

water content　含水量

finished slab　最终饰面

Exercises

I. Read the following passage and try to answer the questions given at the beginning.

Questions：

1. If you have a chance to build a house for yourself，what kind of roof do you prefer?

2. What factors may influence your decision in constructing the roof according to the passage?

3. What are the two main types of roof? And please state their advantages respectively.

4. Please state the construction of traditional roof and a trussed rafter roof in your own words by combining the information provided in the passage and what you have learnt in your building operation class.

5. What other factors may limit or constrain your construction of the roof?

Roof Construction

The design of the roof and preparation required to secure it to the main structure will be detailed on your construction drawings. The roof was first considered when foundations were poured，and it was at that very early stage that the importance of wall strengths and their relation to the roof became apparent. That initial assessment should have enabled you to arrive at the current stage of construction with a suitable and solid base on which the roof can now be placed.

Roof Types

There are two main types of roof and the one you have chosen to build is likely to reflect how you intend using the space it will provide. Traditional roof designs offer greater flexibility because they are constructed with substantial timber beams，whilst the lightweight trussed rafter type is easier to lift into place.

The basic principle of the traditional roof construction is to bring load-bearing cross walls up into the roof space to support horizontal running purlins. These are large section timbers onto which the rafters are fixed at regular intervals, to support the roof coverings. When large spans are involved, the purlins can be replaced with lightweight steel beams, and timber is then placed on top of these, so that rafters can be fixed.

A trussed rafter roof is the lightweight alternative and ideal if the void is only going to be used for minor storage. This type of construction relies on an array of small bracing timbers, rather than large single beam. The amount of timber involved virtually fills the void, making it fairly useless, but the frames can be lifted into position easily. Once seated on top of the walls, the frames are connected using galvanized metal plates, and diagonally braced according to the manufacturer's instructions.

Roof frames can be created in a plethora of different shapes and materials and each one will have its own set of pertinent calculations for load bearing and fixing. Your architect will have recommended a particular type of construction based on cost, style and function, in accordance with local planning restrictions and building regulations. The profile of your roof may therefore already have been determined by earlier limitations or constraints forced upon you by external authorities.

(extracted from http：//www. howtobooks. co. uk/property/self-build/roof. asp)

Words and Phrases for Reference

wall strength　墙壁强度

substantial［səb'stænʃəl］adj. 1. 坚固的；结实的 2. 大量的，可观的

timber［'timbə］n.（用于建筑或制作物品的）树木，林木

beam［bi：m］n. 梁，横梁

lightweight trussed rafter　轻型桁架拱（桁架式缘子）

load – bearing cross walls 承载横壁（横隔墙；横墙）

span［spæn］vt. 建造跨越（某物的）桥或拱

lightweight steel beams　轻型钢梁

an array of　一排；一群；一批

bracing［breisiŋ］timbers　支撑梁

metal plates　金属薄板

diagonally［dai'ægənəli］adv.　斜对地；斜地

braced［breist］adj. 拉牢的

a plethora of　过多、过剩

pertinent［'pə：tinənt］adj. 有关的；中肯的；恰当的；相宜的

II. Translate the following passage into Chinese by referring to Dictionary and try to make a better understanding about roof construction.

Metal Decking Roof

The construction of metal for the roof deck should be in accordance with the technical specification and complied with the ASTM （American Society for Testing and Materials）. The hot dip galvanized metal deck is 0. 0454 inch minimum thick with two coats and profiled channel of 1 – 1/2 inch minimum depth. It is important that all necessary accessories such as closure pieces, sump pans, flashings and other items as required should be fabricated of the same material and completed as the metal decking units, with the thickness as recommended by the deck manufacturer. The mental decking material should be handled, hauled and delivered in a way which would prevent bending, denting, scratching, or damaging of any kind.

Many metal decks are installed with screws between deck and purlins. But in this project it is installed by welding. After the installation, tests for waterproofing and uplifting force should be done.

Words and Phrases for Reference

dip ［dip］ vt. 浸

galvanize ［'gælvə₁naiz］ vt. 用锌镀 （铁）

profile ［'prəufail］ vt. 描…的轮廓

fabricate ［'fæbrikeit］ vt. 制造，装配，组装

haul ［hɔː l］ vt. & vi. 拖，拉

dent ［dent］ vt. 使产生凹痕

screw ［skruː］ n. 螺丝钉

metal decking roof　金属板屋顶

technical specification　技术规范

ASTM （American Society for Testing and Materials） 美国试验和材料学会

hot dip galvanized metal deck　热镀锌钢盖甲板

profiled channel　压槽

closure pieces　封闭板

sump pans　集水板

TRANSLATION SKILLS

英译汉中非谓语动词及状语从句的译法

一、英译汉非谓语动词的译法

英语中非谓语动词包括分词、不定式和动名词。动名词与名词具有类似的功能，在翻译时可以参考名词性从句或抽象名词的译法。下面，我们主要通过一些实例说明动词不定式和分词的翻译方法。

例 1. Americans do not like to be called materialistic because they feel that this unfairly accuses them of loving only material things and of having no religious values.

美国人不喜欢被称为物质主义者，因为他们认为指控他们只重物质利益，没有宗教价值观是不公正的。（不定式作宾语）

例 2. The writer's purpose may be simply to inform, or to make readers aware of similarities or differences that interesting and significant in themselves.

作者的目的或许只是想告诉读者或者让读者意识到（存在于比较对象之间的）很有趣、值得注意的相似和不同之处。（不定式作表语）

例 3. The aim of science is to describe the world in orderly language, in such a way that we can, if possible, foresee the results of those alternative courses of action between which we are always choosing.

科学的目的在于用规律的语言来描述世界。这样，如果可能的话，我们就能预见到可供选择的两个行动方案的结果。我们经常遇到这种选择。（不定式作表语）

例 4. It is the business of the scientist to accumulate knowledge about the universe and all that is in it, and to find, if he is able, common factors which underlie and account for the facts that he knows.

科学家要做的事就是积累有关宇宙和宇宙中的一切事物的知识，而且要是可能的话，找出那些既能构成科学家所知事实的基础，又能解释这些事实的共同因素。（不定式作主语）

例 5. It is a difficult task to compare two systems of education which stem from different roots and often produce contrasting effects.

两种教育制度体系源于不同的根基，并常常产生对照鲜明的不同效果，因而，要将它们作一比较，确非易事。（不定式作主语）

例 6. This tendency to escalate a situation into its worst possible conclusion is what I called awfulizing, and it can be a key factor in tipping the balance toward illness or health.

把一种情况逐渐地想象为最坏的结果，我称之为"杞人忧天"，这或许能打破你体内平衡，或使你患病，或使你健康。（不定式作定语）

例 7. As never before, the nations of the world demonstrated a willingness to put aside ideological and individual differences to confront a common threat.

世界各国决心要把意识形态分歧和各自的不同意见放在一边而来正视这个共同的威胁，这在以前从来没有过。（不定式作定语）

例 8. To communicate precisely what you want to say, you will frequently need to define key words.

要准确表达想要表达的内容，就经常需要对关键词进行释义。（不定式作状语）

例 9. To make calculations manageable even by computers, most of the models suppose either that the oceans are a shallow, motionless swamp or that they don't exist at all.

为了使这些计算甚至可以用普通的计算机来处理，大多数模型要么假设海洋是既浅又静止的沼泽，要么假设它们根本不存在。（不定式作状语）

例 10. We can have greater confidence in the reality of a healing system that is beautifully designed to meet most of its problems.

我们对下述事实应抱有充分而信心：人体的健康机制十分精妙，足以应付大部分疾病。（不定式作状语）

例 11. Having disproved and disputed the theory for more than two decades, some biologists are now embarking an undertaking to interpret it in a new approach.

20 多年来，某些生物学家一直对该理论持否定与争议的态度，现在他们正在开始一项研究，以新的方法解释这一理论。（现在分词做状语）

例 12. The first cause of the liberation of women was the development of effective birth – control methods, freeing women from the endless cycle of childbearing and rearing.

妇女的解放首先起因于有效的节育措施的出现，从而将女人从生养孩子的无尽循环中解放出来。（现在分词做状语）

例 13. At every crossways on the road that leads to the future, each progressive spirit is opposed by thousands of men appointed to guard the past.

在通往未来道路的每一个十字路口上，每一个具有进步思想的人都会遭到受命维护过去的千千万万名卫道士的反对。（过去分词做定语）

例 14. The very first flight of Spacelab, manned by an international team of scientist-astronauts, demonstrated that a Nobel-prize-winning theory on the function of the inner ear was incorrect.

正是这第一座由跨国科学家和宇航员操作的太空试验站，证明了一项曾获诺贝尔奖的关于人体内耳作用的理论是不正确的。（过去分词做定语）

例 15. But the details of this movement ——what causes it, how it relates to other processes occurring in the ocean at the same time, and how it interacts with the earth's atmosphere —— remain sketchy.

但这种洋流的详细情况 ——诸如什么导致了这种洋流，它与伴随它的其他海洋特征有什么联系以及它与地球的大气是怎样相互作用的 ——都还不太清楚。（现在分词做定语）

二、英 译 汉 状语从句的译法

英语状语从句表示时间、原因、条件、让步、目的等等，英语状语从句用在主句后面的较多，而汉语的状语从句用在主句前的较多，因此，在许多情况下，应将状语从句放在主句前面。下面我们通过一些实例说明它们常用的翻译方法。

例 1. When the levels reached 6 percent the crew members would become mentally confused, unable to take measures to preserve their lives.

当含量达到 6% 时，飞船上的人员将会神经错乱，无法采取保护自己生命的措施。（时间状语从句）

例 2. When censorship laws are relaxed, dishonest people are given a chance to produce virtually anything in the name of "art".

当审查放宽时，招摇撞骗之徒就会有机可乘，在 "艺术" 的幌子下炮制出形形色色的东西来。（时间状语从句）

例 3. When tables and other materials are included, they should be conveniently placed, so that a student can consult them without turning over too many pages.

当书中列有表格或其他参考资料时，应当将这些内容编排在适当的位置，以便使学生在查阅时，不必翻太多的书页。（时间状语从句）

例 4. This happens when a fact is discovered which seems to contradict what the "law" would lead one to expect.

每当发现一个事实使人感到与该定律应得出的预期结论相矛盾的时候，就发生这种情况。（时间状语从句）

例 5. Now since the assessment of intelligence is a comparative matter we must be sure that the scale with which we are comparing our subjects provides a valid or fair comparison.

既然对智力的评估是比较而言的，那么我们必须确保，在对我们的对象进行比较时，我们所使用的尺度能提供"有效的"或"公平的"比较。（原因状语从句）

例 6. The policies open to developing countries are more limited than for industrialized nations because the propereconomies respond less to changing conditions and administrative control.

由于贫穷国家的经济对形势变化的适应能力差一些，政府对这种经济的控制作用也小一些，所以发展中国家所能采取的政策比起工业化国家来就更有局限性。（原因状语从句）

例 7. For example, they do not compensate for gross social inequality, and thus do not tell how able an underprivileged youngster might have been had he grown up under more favorable circumstances.

例如，他们（测试）并不对社会总的不平等做出补偿，因此，测试不能告诉我们，一个社会地位低下的年轻人如果生活在较为优越的条件下，会有多大的才能。（结果状语从句）

例 8. It also plays an important role in making the earth more habitable, as warm ocean currents bring milder temperature to places that would otherwise be quite cold.

由于温暖的洋流能把温暖的气候带给那些本来十分寒冷的地区并使之变暖，因此，海洋在使我们这个地球更适合人类居住方面也扮演一个重要的角色。（原因状语从句）

例 9. Electricity is such a part of our everyday lives and so much taken for granted nowadays that we rarely think twice when we switch on the light or turn on the radio.

电在我们的日常生活中所占的地位是如此重要，而且现在人们认为电是想当然的事，所以我们在开电灯或开收音机时，就很少再去想一想电是怎么来的。（结果状语从句）

例 10. The first two must be equal for all who are being compared, if any comparison in terms of intelligence is to be made.

如果要从智力方面进行任何比较的话，那么我们对所有被比较者来说，前两个因素必须是一致的。（条件状语从句）

例 11. Although television was developed for broadcasting, many important uses have been found that have nothing to do with it.

虽然电视是为了广播而发明的，但是电视还有许多与广播无关的重要用途。（让步状语从句）

例 12. Though the cost of the venture would be immense, both in labour and power, many believe that iceberg towing would prove less costly in the long run than the alternative of desalination of sea water.

这种冒险的代价，不管是在人力还是在能源消耗方面，都将是巨大的。然而，许多人认为，冰山牵引最终会证明比选择海水脱盐法花费要少。（让步状语从句）

例 13. Therefore, although technical advances in food production and processing will perhaps be needed to ensure food availability, meeting food needs will depend much more on equalizing economic power among the various segments of populations within the developing countries themselves.

因此，尽管也许需要粮食生产和加工方面的技术进步来确保粮食的来源，满足粮食需求更多的是取决于使发展中国家内部的人口各阶层具有同等的经济实力。（让步状语从句）

例 14. Whether the characters portrayed are taken from real life or are purely imaginary, they may become our companions and friends.

无论书中描述的角色来自真实生活还是来自纯粹的想象，他们都可能成为我们的伙伴和朋友。（让步状语从句）

例15. By many such experiments Galileo showed that, apart from differences caused by air resistance, all bodies fall to the ground at the same speed, whatever their weight is.

伽利略经过多次这类实验证明，一切物体，不论其重量如何，除了因空气阻力引起的差别外，都是以同样的速度落向地面的。（让步状语从句）

译　文

第十一单元　屋面工程
对　话

屋顶和防水检查

咨询工程师：我曾经听一个建筑承包商说他接到的投诉绝大多数都是屋顶渗漏方面的，是这样吗？

承　包　商：不，那已经是历史了。但是我明白你的意思。不管怎样，屋顶的建造确实需要给予足够的重视。

咨询工程师：现在我想知道预制混凝土板屋顶防水的主要步骤。设计部门和承包方在防水图纸方面各自的工作范围是怎样的？

承　包　商：根据合同，设计者提供的图纸只是对需要做防水总区域的说明，它们不可能有非常准确的细节，如墙和窗的接缝，墙裙及软金属屋面折缝等等。我们已经做好了详细的图纸附带诸如材料样本的技术规范，一周前就已经递交上去了。

咨询工程师：在做防水工程前，表面的准备工作你们是怎么做的？

承　包　商：所有需要做防水的表面都要彻底地粗抹灰，然后用水好好冲洗去除灰尘、油和其他影响粘结的浮浆皮材料。

咨询工程师：在做防水之前你们怎么处理混凝土板表面的缺陷？

承　包　商：对于表面所有的洞，裂缝，蜂窝，施工缝或其他缺陷我们都会按照生产商建议的操作步骤将其清除、净化，用水浸透再用不收缩砂浆填平。

咨询工程师：你的描述听起来很有道理。但最重要的是要严格地遵守操作规范和操作步骤。任何疏忽都可能会导致漏水发生。我们有过太多的这样的教训。

承　包　商：我们很清楚这一点。我们会加强每一座楼这方面的监理工作。如果有任何漏水事件发生，负责的监理和工人都要被严厉处罚。

咨询工程师：但是在工程开始前不要忘记给他们作必要的培训。因为要用到一些特殊的材料，严格地遵守供应商的要求来进行防水工作是非常重要的。

承　包　商：是的，我们会的。

课文 A　倒置式沥青薄膜防水屋面

位置

O 塔楼：塔顶和设备层，42 层和 44 层室外平台。

O 平台：1 层和 2 层室外平台，屋面。

参考图纸：（GA）A．101，102，142，144，145，146，（21），（34），（41）和（47）系列图纸及相关材料。

找坡层：混凝土找坡，最小 50mm 厚。

基层：混凝土砂浆层铺设至少 50mm 厚，且表面应光滑平整。

防水层：经批准使用合格的 4mm 厚改性沥青薄膜。

生产商：'DAKTECH'，Testudo 矿石或经批准的同等材料。

底层：经批准使用的合格的 4mm 厚加强型聚合物改性沥青薄膜。

结合层：可采用生产商的建议。

保温层：50mm 厚挤塑聚苯乙烯泡沫塑料板。

隔离层：无纺聚酯纤维布。

保护层：按图纸所示部位铺设 50mm 厚碎石灰石。

基本要求

屋顶基本要求

—如无特别说明，需遵照 BS8217 铺设屋顶，以保证其安全，排水通畅且完全不受天气侵扰。

—无特别说明的附件及配件均应采用薄膜生产商所推荐的类型。

—所安排的操作人员需经过组合式薄膜楼顶应用正规培训。按要求向咨询工程师提交培训证明。

—在工程施工期间，保证现场经过培训的操作人员充足。

不利天气

—将薄膜卷存放于室内，到使用时才拿出。

—按要求提搭设临时遮棚和排水沟使未完工的屋顶保持干燥。

—遇到大雨及连续下雨的天气要停止施工除非有较好的临时遮棚。

—如果在施工中不可避免地被雨淋到，要及时采取措施将损失降至最小并将认真修复损害处。

（摘自迪拜码头 9AB 地块高层住宅楼组合式油毡屋顶的操作规范）

课文 B　预制钢筋混凝土板屋顶的防水

此项工程中檩条上的混凝土面屋顶有四层防水层。

第一层是一种油加在混凝土层面与沥青油毡之间的一种油，其作用是黏结牢固。这层油和油毡是为了避免建筑物内部的蒸汽进入上面的隔热层。沥青在混凝土板上至少要铺 50mm 厚，在与墙的接缝处及拱形处至少要达到 150mm 厚。沥青材料在大于 50℃（摄氏度）的温度下会软化。

用泡沫混凝土或泡沫沥青制成的砌块和盖板重量轻且属低热导材料，通常用于油毡之上的隔热层。

对于防水层的第三层，灌浆水泥砂浆可用厚度为 50mm 的 1:3 水泥砂浆层或厚度为 20~25mm 的 1:8 的沥青砂浆层。表面粗糙以利铺盖另一层油毡。

　　用沥青粘合材料来粘接抹灰层上的油毡。在水泥砂浆层干到一定程度，也就是说含水量在 15%~20% 左右的时候，将沥青粘合材料加热到 240℃（摄氏度），然后洒在抹灰层上粘牢油毡。

　　如果屋顶是斜坡的不应从上至下铺设油毡，而应从屋顶的最低处屋檐开始，平行铺到屋脊，至少铺 70mm 厚。每一层的垂直接缝应该间隔至少 500mm，最后铺撒小碎石（3~5mm）粘到油毡上起防护作用。

　　在管子穿过楼板和屋顶需要防水的地方，对于穿过屋顶和地板的各种材质的管道周围都应用沥青环状封住，沥青厚度在最终饰面上至少 150mm 且底部形成一个圆角围在管子周围。在涂沥青之前管子表面应当彻底清洁并刷上经批准使用的沥青溶液。最后必须将全部由管道穿透的防水部分有效地密封。

Part three
Final–Stage Works (后期工程)

UNIT *12*

Apparatus Works（设备工程）

DIALOGUE

Inspect of Piping and Electrical Woks

E：Can you tell me the scope of piping works belonging to the Civil Works?

C：The piping works include the systems for fresh water supply, rain water drainage, sewer water drainage and fire fighting works.

E：Now I want to know some details about the piping works. Firstly I would like to know the preparation for the piping works, for example, the material procurement, as many sorts of material should be clarified, purchased and stored ready for the works.

C：Yes, you are right. We have submitted all specifications of the main material used for pipeline and they are approved by the consultant, such as galvanized steel pipes for fresh water supply system, unplasticized P. V. C. pipes for flush water supply system, plastic covered copper tube for hot water from electric water heater to outlet, ductile iron pipes for fire service system, cast iron pipes for rainwater and waste water drainage system and so on.

E：What standard are these materials complied with?

C：They are manufactured in accordance with the B. S. （British Standard）

E：Now let's turn to the electrical works. I think you are clear about the interface of the electrical works between the civil works contractor and the erection contractor.

C：Yes. Our electrical works belong to the civil works scope. It covers the power supply system outside the building and the lighting system inside and outside the buildings.

E：What about your installation procedures for the works?

C：The procedures will involve details about the receiving, unloading, storage, removal from storage, hauling, cleaning, installation on foundations and other necessary steps to place all equipment into successful operation.

E：Do you assemble any equipment?

C：Yes. Our installation works include complete assembly of equipment shipped unassembled, dismantling and reassembling of equipment to make adjustments, and provision of personnel and equipment for testing and placing the equipment into operation.

E：I think you should add a procedure for the equipment protection. It is very important that the equipment should be protected from damage of any kind from the time it is unloaded until it is ready for initial operation.

C：It can be done. For assurance of the quality of installation and testing we will invite the manufacturer's representative to inspect and advise while the works is going on.

Notes

1. P. V. C. Poly Vinyl Chloride 聚氯乙烯
2. P. V. C pipe：聚氯乙烯塑料管

New Words

pipe［paip］n. 管子，管道 vt. 1. 以管输送；2. 传送，传输

drainage［'dreinidʒ］n. 1. 排水，放水；2. 排水系统，下水道；3. 废水，污水，污物

sewer［'suːə］n. 污水管，下水道

clarify［'klærifai］vt. 澄清；说明，阐明

galvanize［'gælvə₁naiz］vt. 用锌镀（铁）

plasticize［'plæstisaiz］v. 使成可塑体

flush［flʌʃ］vt. & vi. 冲刷，清除

copper［'kɔpə］n. 1. 铜；2. 铜币

ductile［'dʌktəl］adj. 可延展的，有韧性的

interface［'intəfeis］n. 接口，界面，分界面

installation［₁instə'leiʃən］n. 安装，设置，装置

haul［hɔːl］vt. 运送

assemble［ə'sembl］vt. 装配，组合，组装

assembly［ə'sembli］n. 装配，组装，总成

dismantle［dis'mæntl］vt. 拆开，拆卸

reassemble［ˌriːəˈsembəl］vt. 重新组装
initial［iˈniʃəl］adj. 1. 最初的，开始的，第一的；2. 原始的，初期的

New Phrases

piping works 　管道工程

fresh water supply 　自来水供应

rainwater drainage 　雨水排放

sewer water drainage 　下水道排放

fire fighting works 　消防

galvanized steel pipe 　镀锌钢管

unplasticized P. V. C. pipe 　硬 P. V. C 管

flush water supply system 　冲洗用水系统

plastic covered copper tube 　带塑料外壳的铜管

electric water heater 　电热水器

draw off 　1. 排出，抽出(某物)，拉走(某人)；2. （使）撤离，（使）后退；3. 使转移掉

draw off point 　出水处

ductile iron pipe 　可伸展铁管

fire service system 　消防系统

cast iron pipes 　铸铁管道

rainwater and waste water drainage system 　雨水及废水排放

electrical works 　电气工程

civil works contractor 　土建承包商

erection contractor 　安装承包商

power supply system 　配电系统

lighting system 　照明系统

Role Play

What role does the pipe works play in water supply and drainage system in a building? Discuss this problem with your partner based on what you have learnt in your professional courses by referring to the new words mentioned in this dialogue.

TEXT A

Water Supply and Drainage

Aiming to ensure safe exploitation of the future building and satisfy sanitary needs of future residents, the following systems will be mounted:

- System of cold drinking-water;
- Circulative system of hot drinking-water;
- Fire-extinguishing system;
- System of collection and disposition of domestic drains;
- System of collection and disposition of rain and thaw water.

WATER-SUPPLY

Domestic water-supply

Drinking-water in the building will be used for residents' sanitary needs and extinguishing indoor fires.

Drinking-water will be supplied to the building from outside water networks. Water-metering unit-common water-meter for the whole building, fitting for closing and control etc. -will be installed in the basement of the building, in a lighted and heated technical room. After installation of common meter, meters of cold and hot water will be installed in commonly used premises-landings-for individual users. Readings of these meters will be recorded in computer system for controlling the building.

Water-improvement equipment-mechanic, water softening deironing filters-will be installed in the building. This will ensure perfect quality of water, long-time exploitation of sanitary devices, system of heating and hot water-supply and equipment as well as residents' health and hygiene.

Hot water will be prepared in the thermal unit of the building to satisfy residents' needs. System of hot water is circulative which will ensure quick flow of hot water to a specific point of use. Dryers and coil pipes will be mounted in bathrooms.

Inside water-supply pipelines will be mounted of highest-quality pipes and connecting parts intended for drinking-water.

Fire-water-supply

Fire taps will be mounted in the basement and landings of the building. This will ensure quick localization and extinguishing fire foci. Water for extinguishing fires will be supplied from outside water-supply networks.

DRAINAGE SYSTEMS

Systems of domestic drains and rain drains will be formed in the building.

System of domestic drains

Domestic drains form due to residents' sanitary activity. These drains will be collected by internal supports and discharged into outside domestic drainage networks.

Pipelines of domestic drainage will be constructed of cast-iron or plastic drainage pipes absorbing noise. This will ensure comfortable operation of the system.

System of rain drains

Rain water and thaw water will be removed from roofs and terraces of the building into outside domestic drainage networks. Removal of other conditionally clean drains from other systems of the building (heating equipment, etc) into inside rain drainage pipeline from which the water is drained into outside drainage pipeline is also projected.

As the parking lot will be built in the basement, the floor-level of which is below the level of ground water, this water will be collected and removed to outside networks by pumps. Aiming not to pollute environment with drains from the parking lot, oil products will be removed from these drains before draining them into outside networks. Oil separator will be mounted outside the building.

Notes

1. 建筑给水排水工程是给水排水工程的一个分支，也是建筑安装工程的一个分支。主要是研究建筑内部的给水以及排水问题，保证建筑的功能以及安全的一门学科。主要分为：建筑给水系统，建筑排水系统（含雨水以及污水，废水），消火栓给水系统，自动喷淋灭火系统，景观系统，热水系统，中水系统等。

2. 建筑内部给水系统按用途基本上可分为三类：

（1）生活给水系统：要求水质必须严格符合国家规定的饮用水质标准。（2）生产给水系统：生产用水对水质、水量、水压以及安全方面的要求由于工艺不同，差异很大。（3）消防给水系统：消防用水对水质要求不高，但必须按建筑防火规范保证有足够的水量与水压。

3. 建筑内部排水系统的分类

建筑内部排水系统根据接纳污、废水的性质，可分为三类：

（1）生活排水系统：我国目前建筑排污分流设计中是将生活污水单独排入化粪池，而生活废水则直接排入市政下水道。（2）工业废水排水系统：用来排除工业生产过程中的生产废水和生产污水。生产废水污染程度较轻，如循环冷却水等。生产污水的污染程度较重，一般需要经过处理后才能排放。（3）建筑内部雨水管道：用来排除屋面的雨水，一般用于大屋面的厂房及一些高层建筑雨雪水的排除。

New Words

exploitation [ˌeksplɔiˈteiʃən] n. 开发；开采；开拓

sanitary [ˈsæniˌteriː] adj. 1. 清洁的，卫生的，保健的；2. 卫生的，环境卫生的，公共卫生的

mount [maunt] vt. 1. 准备，安排，组织开展；2. 安置

resident [ˈrezidənt] adj. 定居的；常驻的；（在某地）居住的

circulative [ˈsəːkjuleitiv] adj. 循环的，促进循环的，流通的

extinguish [iksˈtiŋgwiʃ] vt. 使熄灭，扑灭

disposition ［ˌdispə'ziʃən］ n. 安排；布置；排列

install ［in'stɔːl］ vt. 1. 安装；2. 安顿，安置

premise ［'premis］ n. 1. 前提，假定；2. ［复数］房屋，房屋连地基，生产经营场所

hygiene ［'haidʒiːn］ n. 卫生学，保健学

dryer ［'draiə］ n. 1. 干燥机，干燥器，烘缸；2. 干燥剂，催干剂，速干剂

drain ［drein］ vt. & vi. （使）流干，排空，放光；（使）逐渐流走 n. 排水沟，排水管

discharge ［dis'tʃɑːdʒ］ vt. & vi. 放出；流出

absorb ［əb'sɔːb］ vt. 吸收（液体、气体等）；吸收（热、光、能等）

thaw ［θɔː］ vi. （冰、雪及冷冻食物）溶化，溶解 n. 融化，解冻

New Phrases

system of cold drinking-water   冷饮水系统

circulative system of hot drinking-water   热饮水循环系统

fire-extinguishing system   灭火系统；消防系统

system of collection and disposition of domestic drains   住户排水的收集与处置系统

system of collection and disposition of rain and thaw water   雨水与融水的收集与处置系统

water-metering unit   水表装置

common water-meter   普通水表

meters of cold and hot water   冷、热水表

water-improvement equipment   水净化设备

water softening deironing filter   水软化除铁过滤器

coil pipe   盘管；盘曲管

fire tap   消防栓

cast-iron or plastic drainage pipes   铸铁或塑料排水管

oil separator   油水分离器

Role Play

Discuss the classification of water supply and drainage in a building based on what you have learnt in your professional courses by referring to the new words mentioned in this passage.

Exercises

I. Answer the following questions.

1. What systems will be mounted in order to ensure safe exploitation of the future building and satisfy sanitary needs of future residents?

2. What are the two classifications of water supply in a building?

3. What will be formed as the drainage system in the building?

4. There are two kinds of water-meters mentioned in this passage, and what are they? Where

are they installed?

    5. What will the water softening deironing filters ensure in a building?

    6. What will be removed from these drains in order not to pollute environment with drains from the parking lot?

II. Complete the sentences with the given words or expression. Change the form where necessary.

    1. The piping works include the systems for fresh water supply, rain water _____ （drain）, fire fighting works and etc.

    2. The _____ （erect） of formwork is quite complicated.

    3. The contractor is quite clear of the _____ （install） procedure of piling works.

    4. _____ （circulate） system of hot drinking-water will ensure quick flow of hot water to a specific point of use.

    5. Water for _____ （extinguish） fires will be supplied from outside water-supply networks.

III. Translate the following words or phrases into English.

管道工程_____　自来水供应_____
雨水排放_____　电热水器_____
电气工程_____　土建承包商_____
安装承包商_____　配电系统_____
照明系统_____　冷饮水系统_____
普通水表_____　油水分离器_____

IV. Translate the following words or phrases into Chinese.

sewer water drainage _____ fire fighting works _____

galvanized steel pipes _____

unplasticized P. V. C. pipes _____

flush water supply system _____

plastic covered copper tube _____

draw off point _____

ductile iron pipe _____

fire service system _____

cast iron pipe _____

rainwater and waste water drainage system _____

circulative system of hot drinking-water _____

fire-extinguishing system _____

system of collection and disposition of domestic drains _____

system of collection and disposition of rain and thaw water _____

water metering unit _____

meters of cold and hot water _____

water improvement equipment _____

water softening deironing filter _____

cast iron or plastic drain _____

V. Translate the following sentences into Chinese.

1. We have submitted all specifications of the main material used for pipeline and they are approved by the consultant, such as galvanized steel pipes for fresh water supply system, unplasticized P. V. C. pipes for flush water supply system, plastic covered copper tube for hot water from electric water heater to draw off point, ductile iron pipes for fire service system, cast iron pipes for rainwater and waste water drainage system and so on.

_____

_____

2. Our installation works include complete assembly of equipment shipped unassembled, dismantling and reassembling of equipment to make adjustments, and provision of personnel and equipment for testing and placing the equipment into operation.

_____

_____

3. Water-improvement equipment-mechanic, water softening deironing filters-will be installed in the building. This will ensure perfect quality of water, long time exploitation of sanitary devices, system of heating and hot water-supply and equipment as well as residents' health and hygiene.

_____

_____

_____

VI. Try to Write.

Direction: You are required to write a letter of complaint according to the following information provided. You may refer to the given words and samples.

Letters of Complaint（投诉信）

投诉信是指向提供服务货物的一方进行投诉，说明对服务或产品的质量不满的原因，并要求对方进行赔偿或者退货。写信时要把不满意或要求索赔的理由说清楚，语气要肯定，但是不宜过于生硬或使用伤害对方的语言。在投诉产品质量时（Complaining about the Quality of Products），详细说明情况后，要明确地表明自己的主张。

Sample

Nov. 11. 2010.

Dear Mr. Suzuki,

For the water softening deironing filters we received on July 15, at the time of inspection five

（5）pieces were found damaged, as fully described in the attached report made by our inspector. We request that you send five（5）new pieces as replacements as soon as possible.

We cannot understand how this kind of mistake could occur at your end. We have to ship the goods back to your company by freight at your expense and we ask that you refund the US＄15,000 which we have already paid you. Please remit this amount to our account（A/C No. 1012379）with the Midori Bank, Ltd. Minato Branch, Tokyo. Please note that we hereby also reserve the right to claim any damaged arising out of your wrong shipment.

A quick refund will be highly appreciated.

Sincerely yours,

John Smith

TEXT B

Central Station Air-conditioning System

Central station conditioning systems serving large buildings in the United Kingdom have generally been designed so as to provide an all-year round heating and cooling facility. The requirement of simultaneous heating and cooling is most necessary in the transition seasons. However, energy-efficient buildings being designed at present that comply with the new building regulations on insulation standards, are less sensitive to solar heat gain. Furthermore analysis of building thermal characteristics indicates that in the transition seasons the cooling load is minimal.

If the building's thermal characteristics are such that the spring and autumn cooling requirement are low enough to be satisfied by the free cooling effects of the ventilation air, the function of both conventional boiler and chiller plant can be performed by an air-to-water heat pump. The heat pump would use external air as a heat source for heating during winter operation, and dissipation of heat gain when operating as a chiller during summer operation.

With the traditional mistrust of changeover control of the central air-conditioning plant, conventional design solutions have been based upon the non-changeover operation of two-and four-pipe induction or fan coil systems, etc. with non-changeover controlling both the boiler plant and the chiller plant operate to provide simultaneous heating and cooling throughout the year. This type of operation was required by building with large glazed area, where spring and autumn solar gain would be excessive. However, buildings designed under the new regulation effect a much greater degree of gain attenuation and are in some cases quite capable of sustaining stable space conditions with a changeover operation. The reduction of glazed areas to approximately 30 percent of the wall area is a major factor influencing the thermal performance of these building through the critical transitional months of spring and autumn.

Notes

1. 户式中央空调的工作原理

a. 冷（热）水机组的基本工作过程是：室外的制冷（热）机组对冷（热）媒水进行制冷降温（或加热升温），然后由水泵将降温后的冷媒（热）水输送到安装在室内的风机盘管机组中，由风机盘管机组采取就地回风的方式与室内空气进行热交换实现对室内空气处理的目的。

b. 风管（道）式机组的基本工作过程是：供冷时，室外的制冷机组吸收来自室内机组的制冷剂蒸汽经压缩、冷凝后向各室内机组输送液体制冷剂。供热时，室外的制冷机组吸收来自冷凝器的制冷剂蒸汽经压缩后向各室内机组输送气体制冷剂，室内机组通过布置在天花板上的回风口将空气吸入，进行热交换后送入安装在室内各房间天花板中的风管（道）内，并通过出风口上的散流器向室内各房间输送空气。在风管（道）上设计有新风门和排风门，可以按一定比例置换空气，以保证室内空气的质量。

2. 变频空调（convertible frequency air-conditioner）：是由电脑控制的变频器和变频压缩机组成的，它运用变频控制技术（frequency control），使空调根据环境温度自动选择制冷、制热和除湿运转方式，使居室在短时间内迅速达到所需要的温度，并在低转速低能耗状态下以较小的温差波动，实现快速、节能和舒适的控温效果。

New Words

facility [fə'siliti] n. 1. 能力；2. 设备，设施

simultaneous [ˌsiməl'teinjəs] adj. 同时存在的，同时发生（或进行）的；同步的

transition [træn'ziʃən] n. 过渡；转变；变迁；变革

regulation [ˌregju'leiʃən] n. 规章；规则；章程；规章制度；法规

insulation [ˌinsə'leiʃən] n. 1. 隔离，隔绝；绝缘；隔音；2. 绝缘、隔热或隔声等的材料

sensitive ['sensitiv] adj. 易受影响的；敏感的

thermal ['θəːməl] adj. 热的，热量的，由热造成的

minimal ['miniməl] adj. 极少的，极小的

ventilation [ˌventl'eiʃən] n. 通风，通风设备

conventional [kən'venʃənl] adj. 依照传统的，传统的；习惯的

boiler ['bɔilə] n. 锅炉

chiller ['tʃilə] n. 冷冻机；冷却器；深冷器，冷却装置

dissipation [ˌdisi'peiʃn] n. （逐渐的）消失，消散

changeover ['tʃeindʒ'əuvə] n. （生产方法、装备等的）改变，（方针的）转变

induction [in'dʌkʃən] n. （电或磁的）感应

attenuation [əˌtenju'eiʃən] n. 变薄，弄细，变细；稀薄化，稀释，冲淡；减少，衰减

New Phrases

central station air-conditioning system　中央空调控制系统

transition season　过渡季节

energy-efficient building　节能建筑

at present　目前，现在

insulation standard　绝热标准

solar heat gain　太阳能获取；太阳辐射热获得

building thermal characteristic　建筑热特性

chiller plant　制冷设备

an air-to-water heat pump　气-水式热泵

fan coil system　风机盘管系统

Role Play

Discuss the advantages of central station air-conditioning system by referring to the following words：1. energy-conservation：computer-based control / automated temperature adjustment 2. environmental-friendly 3. space-saving

Exercises

I. Oral practice：*Look at the picture and make a brief account of the air conditioning according to some useful words given.*

1. If / your house / central air conditioning/ , you / probably/ a split system（分体系统）. The split system/ two primary components

/ the evaporator coil（蒸发器盘管）inside the house/ the condensing unit（冷凝装置）outside of the house/. These two components/ be connected with /refrigerant lines（制冷线）/. Furthermore/be equipped with /remote controls / various kinds / air conditioners.

Reference

If your house has central air conditioning, you probably have what is called a split system. The split system consists of two primary components：the evaporator coil inside the house and the condensing unit outside of the house. These two components are connected with refrigerant lines. And furthermore, it is often equipped with remote controls for various kinds of air conditioners.

（译文：如果你的房子装有中央空调，你就可能有个叫做分体系统的装置，该系统包括两个主要部分：装在室内的蒸发器盘管与装在室外的冷凝装置。这部分由制冷线管相连。此外还常配备有可同时适用于多种类型的空调器。）

II. Oral practice：*Making conversations about how to install PV（Photovoltaic 光电）system by using the situations offered.*

1. PV systems can be mounted on a roof or trellis（格子架）or even on the ground. They require a south-facing location with good sun exposure and no shading from trees or buildings. A device called an inverter（换流器）converts the DC（直流电）electricity produced by PV cells into the AC（交流电）electricity required by our homes. The inverter is installed in a garage or utility room（杂物间）, or in an outside cabinet.

（译文：光电系统装置可以装在屋顶上，格子架上甚至地面上。他们需要安装在阳光充足的南向的位置，没有树木和房屋的遮挡。一个称之为换流器的设备可以把光电电池产生的直流电转换成家用要求的交流电，这个换流器可安装在车库、杂物间或外面的橱柜里。）

Reference

A：Can you tell me where I should install PV system?

B：You can mount it on a roof or trellis or even on the ground.

A：It's said that they require a south-facing location with good sun exposure and no shading from trees or buildings.

B：Yes. If so, it can gather more heat from the sun.

A：And there seems to be a device called an inverter. Is that so?

B：Yeah. It's the inverter that converts the DC electricity produced by PV cells into the AC electricity required by our homes.

A：Well, where to install the inverter?

B：It is generally installed in a garage or utility room, or in an outside cabinet.

A：Thanks a lot, goodbye.

III. *Try to figure out the following manual*（操作手册）*about how to install air-condition.*

1. Locate a floor drain（安置地面排水管）near where the evaporator will be located. The shorter the hose（软管）the better. Slope the floor to the drain（使地面向排水沟倾斜）so water does not collect inside the hose.

2. Place the evaporator coil in an unfinished area（在未完工区域）such as a basement or an area with no floor finish.

3. Install a hard pipe（安装一根硬管）plastic or copper, condensate drain line with a minimum diameter of ¾". Construct the condensate drain line（冷凝水排泄）with an open vertical leg near the drain pan（在排水面板附近）.

This can be used to clean out（清除）the drain line.

IV. *Translate the following passage by referring to given words and phrases.*

The Installation of the Electrical Cable

Concerning the electrical cable installation, technicians should obtain and follow manufacturer's recommendations for storage, pulling, supporting and terminating all cables. Cables should be properly installed in each step including placement, terminating, coiling and taping of spare conductors, identification, testing, and verification of each circuit, cable, and conductor.

Since the cable reels are very heavy, it will be necessary to store them on a hard surface to prevent contact between cable insulation and earth due to the sinking of the reel. Impact damage between reels shall be prevented by aligning reels flange to flange or by using guards across flanges.

Suppose a cable was pulled into the wrong conduct or duct or cut too short to rack and train as specified, the technician should remove and replace the wrongly placed cable. To avoid that, all cable shall be carefully checked both in size and length before being pulled into conducts or ducts.

In order to ensure the cable to be bent to its required radius, the standard pulleys, rollers, sheaves, and necessary installation accessories shall be used for pulling the cable, and technicians should have radius exceeding at least 1.5 times the minimum bending radius of the cable pulled.

Technicians should take measures for protecting the cable ends during the installation. Cable ends which extend from raceway after pulling shall be protected against mechanical damage, excessive bending, sparks, and against submersion or connection to equipment.

Since the electrical installation need more technology and skill for implementation, electrical engineers and technicians should be qualified for the job, have rich experience for similar works, and possess certificates issued by the trade association.

Words and phrases for reference

terminate ['tə：mineit] vt. & vi. 1. 结束,使终结; 2. （公共汽车或火车）到达终点站

verification [ˌverəfi'keiʃən] n. 核实，查对；查清

conductor [kən'dʌktə] n. 导体

reel [ri：l] n. 卷轴；卷盘；卷筒

flange [flændʒ] n. 凸缘，轮缘

duct [dʌkt] n. 管道，导管

radius ['reidjəs] n. 半径（距离）

pulley ['puli：] n. 滑轮（组）

roller ['rəulə] n. 滚轮

sheave [ʃi：v] n. 滑轮

submersion [sʌb'mə：ʃən] n. 淹没；浸入

electrical cable　电缆
standard pulley　标准滑轮
final termination　终端电缆头
trade association　专业协会

TRANSLATION SKILLS

建 筑 合 同

在合同的第一段要写清楚双方的名称。如果是个人，要写清姓和名，中间名可能的话应写上大写首字母，其他身份信息如果需要也应注明，例如：Jr.，M.D，等等；如果是公司，为避免弄错，写名称时可以到公司注册地的相应机构去核对。

确定合同双方的别称（简称）。为便于阅读，一般要在合同的第一段为双方设定一个别称，如：将詹姆士·马丁简称为"马丁"。使用法定术语作为双方当事人的别称时，要小心。除非一方当事人在法定上就是承包人，否则不要将"承包人"作为其别称。同样，除非你想让一方当事人成为法定上的代理人，否则不要称其为"代理人"，如果坚持要用，最好明确一下代理范围并找到其他可以避免将来争执的方案。

在合同的第一段要为书写签约时间留下空格。把签约时间放在第一段，当合同签署后，你就可以很容易地找到它，而且，这样做还可以给你在其他相关文件中准确地描述这个合同提供帮助，例如：不动产买卖合同，订立于 2000 年 12 月 20 日。书写引述语。引述语是指那些放在合同主体前面的"鉴于"条款。书写此类条款的目的是为了让读者（通常指合同双方，法官，陪审团）很快地了解到合同的主要内容是什么，合同双方是谁，以及他们为什么签订合同，等等。

当然，合同主体的第一段也可以加上声明，并说明其是真实准确的，如果这样做了，合同双方将来就不会就引述语作为合同的一部分是否具有法律效力而争执。列出合同大纲，按逻辑顺序列出合同段落的标题词。

合同的段落是按一定的逻辑顺序组织起来的，当然，并不需要一下子列出所有段落的标题词，想到多少就写多少。将相关的概念在一个段落或是在连续的段落里表达。比如：劳动合同的标题词：引述语，聘用，职责，期限，赔偿。在撰写每一段时要注意内容集中，不要东拉西扯。说明合同双方同意做什么，不同意做什么就可以了。放一个便笺簿在手边，以便记下需要添加的条款。在书写合同的同时，可能随时会想到一些需要添加的条款、措词和问题，要尽快记在便笺簿上，以免忘记。

另外，最好将客户列出的要点和一些类似的合同范本也放在眼前，以便在书写过程中随时查对。除非是为了更清晰地说明问题，否则不要在合同中重复陈述某个内容。反复地陈述同一个东西很容易让人模棱两可。只有当一个概念难于理解时，你才应该用不同的方式书写。另外，如果你想通过一个例子来阐明一个难以理解的概念或规则时，一定要考虑到其所有的含义、这个例子的准确性以及它和概念的相符性。

建筑合同范例

甲方：　　　　　　　　　　　乙方：

合同编号：

日期：

签约地点：

特约定：

甲方基于下文所列各种因素，特与乙方达成了协议并一致同意：由甲方在订约日期之翌日起_____天之内为乙方建造并完成_____（涉约建筑）。涉约建筑之规模及所需的钢筋、水泥、砖块、石子和其他建筑材料之数量，均在作为合同附件的设计图和施工细则中予以说明。基于上述情况，乙方及其法定代表郑重承诺向甲方支付人民币_____元整。支付方法商定如下：

在上述工程开工之日，支付人民币_____元整

在_____年_____月_____日，支付人民币_____元整

在_____年_____月_____日，支付人民币_____元整

在_____年_____月_____日，支付人民币_____元整

在_____年_____月_____日，支付人民币_____元整

余额人民币_____元整于工程完成之日付清。

定约双方并同意由甲方或其法定代表在领取各项付款时，为证明有权领用上述各次付款（第一次付款除外，因其另有保证），必须由工程师进行评估，证实收到的所有款项均为已消耗的劳务开支及材料费用。

上述协议如未能忠实执行，则违约一方同意其应享有权利自动丧失，且在违约之日后一个月之内，向对方或其法定代表赔偿人民币_____元整，作为商定之损失赔偿费。

为示信守，各方谨于上文起首载明之日期签名、盖章。

本合同当下列人员之面交付。

甲方：　　　　　　　　　　　乙方：

CONSTRUCTION CONTRACT

Party A：　　　　　　　　　　Party B：

Contract No：

Date：

Signed at：

Witnesses that the Party A for considerations hereinafter named, contracts and agrees with the Party B that Party A will, within _____ days, next following the date hereof, build and finish a _____ for Party B. (the building hereinafter is referred to as the said building.) The said building is of the following dimensions, with reinforced concrete, brick, stones and other materials, as are described in plans and specifications annexed.

In consideration of the foregoing, Party B shall, for itself and its legal representatives, promise to pay Party A the sum of _____ RMB yuan in manner as follows:

RMB _____ at the beginning of the said work.

RMB _____ on _____ / _____ / _____ (for example: 3/21/2001)

RMB _____ on _____ / _____ / _____

RMB _____ on _____ / _____ / _____

RMB _____ on _____ / _____ / _____

And the remaining sum will be paid upon the completion of the work.

It is further agreed that in order to be entitled to the said payments (the first one excepted, which is otherwise secured), the two sides contacted agreed to by the Party A or their legal representatives to receive payment, which must be assessed by the engineer to prove the paid amount has been used up us cost of labor and materials.

Party A or its legal representatives shall, according to the architect's appraisement, have expended, in labor and material, the value of the payments already received by Party A, on the building, at the time of payment.

For failure to accomplish the faithful performance of the agreement aforesaid, the party in breach agrees to forfeit and pay to the other _____ RMB yuan as fixed and settled damages, within one month form the time of breach.

To keep the promises, the parties should set out on the date mentioned above.

Signed, sealed and delivered

Party A :   Party B:

译　文

第十二单元　设备工程

对　话

管道工程和电气工程检查

咨询工程师：你能告诉我属于土建工程的管道工程的范围吗？

承　包　方：属于我们工作范围的管道工程包括自来水供应系统，雨水排放系统，下水道排放系统和消防系统。

咨询工程师：现在我想知道有关管道工程的具体情况。首先我想知道管道工程的准备情况，比如，材料的购买情况，因为有很多种材料需要说明，购买并且存放以备工程使用。

承　包　方：是的，你说的很对。我们已经递交了所有用于管线的主要材料的具体规格，并且要经工程顾问批准，比如用于自来水供应系统的镀锌钢管，用于冲洗用水系统的硬 P. V. C 管，用于从电热水器到出水处过热水的带塑料外壳的铜管，用于消防系统的可伸展钢管，用于雨水及废水排放系统的铸铁管道等等。

咨询工程师：这些材料都要依据什么标准？

承　包　方：它们都是根据英国标准生产制造的。

咨询工程师：现在让我们说说电气工程。我想你对土建承包商和安装承包商之间关于电气工程的分界很清楚吧。

承　包　方：是的。我们的电气工程属于土建工程范围。它覆盖了建筑物外的配电系统以及建筑物内外的照明系统。

咨询工程师：你们安装工程的安装程序是怎样的？

承　包　方：详细的安装程序包括：接收，卸载，存放，从存放处移走，运送，清理，安装在（建筑物）的底座上，以及其他使所有设施成功运转所需要的必要步骤。

咨询工程师：你们组装设备吗？

承　包　方：是的。我们的安装工程包括将未经组装运输的设备完整地组装起来，拆卸并重新组装设备来进行调整以及提供安装人员和设备来检测并将设备投入使用。

咨询工程师：我认为你还应该加上设备保护这一环节。从货物卸载一直到准备开始运转期间要使设备免于任何形式的损坏这一点是非常重要的。

承　包　方：我们会做的。为了确保安装和检测的质量，我们还会在工程进行期间邀请生产商代表给予检查和指导。

课文 A　给水和排水

为了保证未来建筑物的安全使用，满足未来居民们的卫生需要，应安装下列系统：

- 冷饮水系统
- 热饮水循环系统
- 灭火系统
- 住户排水的收集与处置系统
- 雨水和融水的收集与处置系统

给水

住户给水

建筑物内部的生活用水将用于居民的卫生需要和楼内灭火。

饮用水将由外部的供水网供给到建筑物。水表装置——用来控制整个建筑物的普通水表，将安装在地下室里设置有灯和暖气的技术室中。在普通水表安装之后，还要在共用场所——楼梯平台为每个用户安装冷、热水表。这些水表的读数将记录在控制建筑物的计算机系统中。

水净化设备——安装水软化除铁过滤器以保证水质优良，维持卫生设施及供暖系统和热水系统设备的寿命，并维护居民的卫生与健康。

热水在建筑物的保温装置中加热以满足居民的需要。循环的热水系统使热水快速地流到特定的使用处。在浴室中还要安装干燥器和盘曲管。给水管道内部要安装高质量的管子和连通饮用水的连接件。

防火给水

消防栓需要安装在地下室和建筑物楼梯平台处，保证快速确定起火位置并灭火。灭火的水从外部给水网络供给。

排水系统

要在建筑物内部安装住宅排水和雨水排水系统。

住宅排水系统

住宅排水系统是为居民的清洁活动服务的。这些污水将由内部设施收集并流出进入外部住宅排水网。住宅排水管线由吸收噪声的铸铁或塑料排水管建造。这将保证系统在操作时不影响居民生活。

雨水排水系统

建筑物屋顶和平台上的雨水和冰融水要流入外部住宅排水网。来自建筑物其他系统（如暖气系统）的其他情况的干净水要排入内部雨水管道，再由这里排入外部排水管道。

由于停车场要建在地下，表面低于地表水的高度，这里的水要收集起来并用泵将其排入外部排水网。为了不让停车场的污水污染环境，在将污水排入外部排水网之前要将油性物质从污水中提取出来。建筑物外部要安装油水分离器。

课文 B 中央空调系统

在英国，为大型建筑服务的中央空调系统一般设计能力为能够保证全年的增温和制冷。在过渡性的季节同时需要增温和制冷。然而，目前正在设计之中的符合绝热标准方面建筑规范的节能建筑不易受太阳日照的影响。而且，通过对建筑热特性分析得出，在过渡性季节中冷负荷是最小的。

如果建筑热特性是通过空气通风设备的冷却效果就能够满足春秋两季制冷需要的话，传统的锅炉和冷却机的功能就可以通过气——水式热泵来完成。在冬季运行时热泵使用外部空气作为热源，当作为冷却机在夏季运行时可以散热。

由于习惯上对中央空调机改变控制的怀疑，常规的设计方法一直都以未做改变的两管和四管感应操作或风机盘管系统等为基础。在未改变的控制系统下锅炉和冷却机运转可以全年同时进行增温和制冷。大面积镶嵌玻璃的，在春秋两季日照热量过多的建筑物需要这种操作。然而，按照新规范设计的建筑物可以使光热获得量大幅度地减少，在某些情况下能够在改变操作的情况下保持稳定的空间条件。镶嵌玻璃的面积减小到整个墙面的百分之三十是影响建筑物经过春秋两季过渡性月份的主要热量影响因素。

UNIT 13

Ornamental（Decoration）Works（装饰工程）

DIALOGUE

Inspection of decoration works

E: Yesterday I have walked around the building where the finishing works are going on. Frankly speaking I am not satisfied with the works performed by your decoration working teams.

C: The finishing works cover carpentry and joinery, ironmongery, plastering, glazing, painting works and so on. I hope to know which part of the works you are not satisfied with.

E: I will show you on the exact places where the quality is not complied with the required standard. You must remember that before the commencement of any of the joinery works, you submitted three samples of each of the teak, teak ply and hardwood that is proposed for use in the office building and all timber used in the buildings should be the same in appearance and quality to the approved samples. Now these timber materials on the site are quite different from samples.

C: Let me see. These materials look of the same quality as samples we submitted.

E: The grades of timber seem of no difference, but the moisture content is much higher than the specification required. In accordance with the specification the moisture content should be no less than 10% and not more than 20%. But from our test the moisture content is higher than that.

C: We will make the test for the timber. And we will not do the assembling and installation until the material reaches the required wet condition.

E: Now let's see some aluminum windows and doors. There are several distortions on some components.

C: We will instruct the supplier to take care of the delivery otherwise the material will be rejected.

E: One other thing to be taken care is that the aluminum frame and glass should be kept away from concrete, mortar, plaster or similar materials.

C: It will be certainly done like that.

E: Concerning the quarry tiles, you should pay more attention to it.

C: Yes, we will. The concrete sub-floors are to be swept and well washed before the tiling is laid and the areas to be set out with tiles before bedding to avoid unnecessary cutting.

E: And do not forget that the tile floor must be cleaned off and protected with sawdust immediately after laying.

New Words

decoration ['dekə'reiʃən] n. 装饰，装潢

carpentry ['kɑːpəntri] n. 木工手艺；木匠业

joinery ['dʒɔinəri] n. 细木工作；细木工

ironmongery ['aiən₁mʌŋəri] n. 铁器类，铁器店，五金

plaster ['plɑːstə] vt. 抹灰；用灰泥抹（墙等） n. 灰泥

glaze [gleiz] vt. 1. 装玻璃；2. 上釉于，上光，使光滑，使光亮

commencement [kə'mensmənt] n. 开始，开端

teak [tiːk] n. 柚木

ply [plai] n. （夹板的）层片

hardwood ['hɑːd₁wud] n. 硬（木）材；硬木树；阔叶树

moisture ['mɔistʃə] n. 水分，水气，湿气

content ['kɔntent] n. 1. 所容纳之物，所含之物；2. （书等的）内容，目录3. 容量，含量

timber ['timbə] n. （用于建筑或制作物品的）树木，林木；用材林

aluminum [ə'luːmənəm] n. <美>铝

distortion [di'stɔːʃən] n. 扭曲；变形；失真，歪曲

supplier [sə'plaiə] n. 供应者；供货商；供货方

mortar ['mɔːtə] n. 砂浆，灰浆

concerning [kən'sə：niŋ] prep.（表示论及）关于，有关，就…而论，涉及

quarry ['kwɔ：ri：] n.（采）石场；露天矿场

tile [tail] n. 瓦片，瓷砖 vt. 用瓦片、瓷砖等覆盖

soak [səuk] vt. & vi. 1. 浸，泡；2. 浸透，湿透

sawdust ['sɔ：ˌdʌst] n. 锯末

New Phrases

finishing works　修整工程

painting works　油漆

be complied with　…与…相符合

teak ply　柚木层板

be different from　…与…不同

moisture content　湿度

aluminum frame　铝框架

quarry tiles　方形瓷砖

concrete sub-floors　混凝土地板

expansion joints　伸缩缝

corner fittings　角件

round edge tiles　圆边瓷砖

Role Play

Discuss with your partner about the materials used for decoration, such as glass, aluminum alloy, timber, tile, etc, and talk about their application in the decoration works.

TEXT A

Structural Glass Assembly

DESIGN/PERFORMANCE REQUIREMENTS

GENERALLY

Requirements specified in this section apply to the entire structural glass assembly, including flashings and junctions with adjacent parts of the building. Full allowance must be made for deflections and other movements.

INTEGRITY

Determine size(s) and thickness(es) of glass panes, types and locations of assembly fixings and supports and other structural requirements in accordance with BS 6262 or CP3 to ensure that the structural glass assembly will resist all wind loads, dead loads and design live loads, and accommodate all deflections and thermal movements without damage.

GENERAL MOVEMENT：

The structural glass assembly must accommodate anticipated building movement as follows Movement due to temperature variation, settlement, creep racking etc.

WEATHER RESISTANCE

- There should not be any Leakage of air through sealed glass and glass joints.

- There should not be any Leakage of water through any part of the structural glass assembly under site exposure conditions.

HEAT CONSERVATION

The average thermal transmittance (U-value) of the structural glass assembly must not be more than 2.0 W/m2K.

CONDENSATION

Condensation must not form on the internal surfaces of glass panes or units in the following conditions.

External: Summer : 52℃ maximum @ 100% RH

           Winter : 7℃ minimum @ 55% RH

Internal: Summer : 22℃ @ 55% RH

           Winter : 22℃ @ 55% RH

SOLAR AND LIGHT CONTROL

Total solar radiation transmission of glass panes or units should not be more than 50% and their total light transmission be less than 60%.

THERMAL SAFETY

Glass panes or units must resist thermal stress generated by orientation, shading, solar control and construction.

ACCURACY OF ERECTION

Allowing for manufacturing and installation tolerances, the maximum permitted deviation in glass joint width is ± 4 mm.

SECURITY

All threaded assembly fixings and assembly support fixings must be locked or pinned at the completion of structural glazing to prevent rotation due to building movement or unauthorized adjustment.

DURABILITY

Products used in the structural glass assembly must not be liable to attacked by fungi, insects or vermin. Submit to the Engineer a schedule for maintenance and for replacement of sealants and secondary components.

Notes

1. CP: Control Program 控制程序

New Words

assembly ［ə'sembli］ n. 装配，组装

flashing ［'flæʃiŋ］ n. 防水板，遮雨板

junction ［'dʒʌnkʃən］ n. 联结点，会合点

adjacent ［ə'dʒeisənt］ adj. （地区、建筑、房间等）与…毗连的；邻近的

integrity ［in'tegriti］ n. 完整，完全，完善

thickness ［'θiknis］ n. 厚；厚度

pane ［pein］ n. 窗玻璃，（一片）窗玻璃

accommodate ［ə'kɔmədeit］ vt. 1. 调节，改变…以适应（to）；2. 考虑到，顾及

deflection ［di'flekʃən］ n. （尤指击中某物后）突然转向，偏斜，偏离

leakage ［'li：kidʒ］ n. 1. 漏，漏出；2. 漏出物，渗漏物；泄漏量；漏损量

exposure ［iks'pəuʒə］ n. 1. 暴露，显露；2. 透露，泄露

transmittance ［træns'mitəns］ n. 播送，发射，传动，传送，传输，转播

condensation ［ˌkɔnden'seiʃən，-dən-］ n. 1. 冷凝，凝聚，凝结；2. 冷凝液

external ［eks'tə：nl］ adj. 1. 外面的，外部的；2. 外观的，表面的

internal ［in'tə：nəl］ adj. 内部的，里面的

orientation ［ˌɔ：rien'teiʃən］ n. 方向

tolerance ［'tɔlərəns］ n. 偏差，公差，容限

deviation ［ˌdi：vi：'eiʃən］ n. 1. 背离，偏离，违背；2. 偏差

rotation ［rəu'teiʃən］ n. 旋转；转动

fungi ［'fʌngai］ n. （fungus 的复数）真菌（如蘑菇和霉）；霉，霉菌

vermin ［'və：min］ n. 害虫

sealant ［'si：lənt］ n. 密封剂

New Phrases

structural glass　玻璃砖，建筑玻璃

wind loads　风荷载

dead loads　静载荷

design live loads　设计动荷载

thermal movements （构件因温度变化而膨胀或收缩）热移动

sealed glass　封闭（密封）玻璃

solar energy transmission　太阳能穿透率

solar radiation　太阳辐射

total light transmission　光透过率

be liable to　有…的倾向，易于…

secondary components　次要成分

Role Play

Discuss with your partner about the requirements of glass assembly mentioned in the passage , then talk about the advantages and disadvantages of glass curtain wall.

Exercises

I. Answer the following questions .

1. What will the requirements specified in this section apply to?

2. What should the requirements of size(s) and thickness (es) of glass panes, types and locations of assembly fixings be in accordance with?

3. Should there be any Leakage of air through sealed glass to glass joints?

4. Allowing for manufacturing and installation tolerances, what is the maximum permitted deviation in glass joint width?

5. Concerning the durability of the structural glass, what should the contractor submit to the Engineer?

II. Complete the sentences with the given words or expression. Change the form where necessary.

1. Are you interested in interior _____ (decorate)?

2. We will not assemble and _____ (installation) the timber until the material reaches the required wet condition

3. We decide to _____ (assemble) the structural glass tomorrow.

4. Glass panes or units must be able to _____ (transmittance) total solar energy of not more than 50% of normal incident solar radiation.

5. This project allows for manufacturing and installation _____ (tolerate).

III. Translate the following words or phrases into English.

木工_____   伸缩缝_____

细木工_____   圆边瓷砖_____

五金_____   玻璃砖_____

柚木_____   风荷载_____

密封剂_____   静载荷_____

修整工程_____   设计动荷载_____

湿度_____   热移动_____

铝框架_____   太阳能穿透率_____

瓷砖铺砌_____   太阳辐射_____

混凝土地板_____   光透过率_____

IV. Translate the following sentences into Chinese.

1. There should not be any leakage of water through any part of the structural glass assembly under site exposure conditions.

_____

_____

_____

2. All threaded assembly fixings and assembly support fixings must be locked or pinned at the completion of structural glazing to prevent rotation due to building movement or unauthorized adjustment.

_____

_____

_____

3. Products used in the structural glass assembly must not be liable to attack by fungi, insects or vermin.

_____

_____

_____

V. Direction：Make up a short conversation according to the TIPS given.

Decorative reconstituted stone （文化石） can be used as a local piece in an interior, giving the field of vision or a partition （隔墙） an individual feel.

As far as function is concerned, this material can help insulate （使…隔离） sound from other parts of the flat; this makes it an excellent material to put as a backdrop （背景） for the television or the music system. From a decorative aspect, the swirling （旋转的） pattern and natural look of the stone plays well off the electrical appliances （应用） to highlight （增强） their style.

A：What can be used as _____ ?。

B：Decorative _____, also called culture stone.

A：Can you tell me the function _____ ?

B：Sure. This material _____ .

A：Is it _____ to put as a _____ ?

B：_____ .

A：What is the purpose of the electrical appliance?

B：_____ .

VI. Direction：Make a brief account of the following useful information in your own words.

Hanging Your Own Wallpaper D. I. Y

Tools：Soft bristled brush （毛刷）; stiff bristled brush; scissors; metal ruler; a number of razor blades （刀片）

Paste：Water-soluble wallpaper paste（糊粉）is easiest. Getting the right thickness is the key to success. Mix up two separate batches（批、组）：a thinner one for the front side of the wallpaper and a thicker batch to put on the back so that it sticks firmly to the wall.

（Note：different types of wallpaper paste have different techniques for application，always check the instructions on the box.）

You can begin with

" When you want to hang your own wallpaper，you should prepare such tools as …"

Example

……soft bristled brush，stiff bristled brush，scissors，metal ruler，and a number of razor blades. Pay attention to get the right thickness，which is the key to success. If you want the wallpaper to stick firmly to the wall，you must mix up the thinner one for the front side of the wallpaper and a thicker batch to put on the back. You must always check the instructions on the box because different types of wallpaper paste have different techniques for application.

TEXT B

Painting or Clear Finish

PRELIMINARY INFORMATION / REQUIREMENTS

Requirements

The Main Contractor should：

Be responsible for the supply and installation of the painting /clear finish to meet the requirements of this specification.

Be responsible for ensuring that finishes meet the standards specified herein and have been independently inspected and certified as specified.

Health & Safety

The Main Contractor should ensure that he complies with the latest 'Code of Construction Safety Practice'（Guidelines for the Construction Industry in the Emirate of Dubai），the Health and Safety section of the Contract Documents and ensure that full consideration is given to the health and safety of operatives when manufacturing，handling and installing the works.

TYPE（S）OF PAINTING / CLEAR FINISH（PARTIALLY）

PAINT FINISHES

TYPE A：	ACRYLIC COPOLYMR WASHABLE EMULSION EGGSHELL FINISH
Surface（s）：	Internal plasterboard/smooth render/fair-faced block-work
Preparation：	Prepare coatings in accordance with decorative manufacturer's recommendations
Finishing coats：	2 full coats, eggshell emulsion paint
Color：	TBA
Location：	Apartments, general areas as per schedule.
TYPE B：	INTERNAL HIGH BUILD EPOXY FINISH
Surface（s）：	Internal render or in-situ fair-faced concrete

Preparation:	As section M60. 600
Undercoat:	1 coat epoxy filler
Mid coat:	1 coat epoxy high built 100 microns
Finishing coat:	2 coat polyurethane 100 microns
Application method:	Airless spray except undercoat
Color:	TBA
Finish:	Small unpressed
Location:	LV/HV rooms, plant rooms, stairs structures at tower roof level electrical room, ETISALAT room

PERFORMANCE REQUIREMENTS

Thermal Movement

All materials shall resist thermal movement resulting from: the maximum and minimum surface temperature differentials, maximum annual range, diurnal range, absolute highest and lowest temperature for mid-summer and surface temperature in accordance with recommendations of BS 5427.

The annual range of external air temperature is generally about 45 Degree centigrade.

The 24 hour range of external air temperature is generally about 20 degree centigrade.

The highest recorded temperature range is 50. 5 degree centigrade and the lowest recorded temperature range is 1 degree centigrade.

The selection of materials shall cater for all temporary and permanent conditions envisaged for the works.

MATERIALS

General Requirements Painting/Clear finishing materials.

All materials to be delivered in sound and sealed containers, clearly labeled with the following information on printed labels:

Type of material

Brand name

Intended use

Manufacturer's batch numbers

APPLICATION

Materials to be used must be types recommended by their respective manufacturers according to (their understanding of) the actual situation (condition).

The (main) contractor should take measures to prevent its staffs from being exposed to detrimental working environment with excessive dust, vapor and fumes, according to the current Health & Safety Executive (HSE) document EH40.

Clean off dirt, grease and oil from surfaces. If contamination of surfaces/substrates has occurred, obtain instructions before proceeding. Smooth surface irregularities. Fill joints, cracks, holes and other depressions with stoppers/fillers worked well in and finished off flush with surface. Abrade to a smooth finish.

Apply oil based stoppers/ fillers after priming. Remove dust and particles from dry abrasive preparation of surfaces. Remove residues from wet preparation of surfaces by rinsing with clean water, wiping and allowing to dry.

Notes

1. TBA：To Be Determined 有待确定
2. LV/HV rooms：Low Voltage / High Voltage rooms 低压、高压房
3. ETISALAT：阿联酋电信公司（Emirates Telecommunications Corporation 简称 ETISALAT）成立于 1976 年 8 月 30 日，政府持有其 60% 的股份。ETISALAT 是阿联酋联邦政府除石油部分外开发项目中最大的分销商，曾获得包括社会责任奖等多种奖项，并在中东地区享有较好的声誉。在《金融时报》的市场资本 500 家公司中排名第 140 位；在 Middle East 杂志的资本和利润被评为第 6 大公司；在 2008 年 12 月份福布斯（阿拉伯版）每年评选的 40 家阿拉伯品牌中，名列第 8，是入选前十名中唯一一家通信公司；并在三年中连续五年由于海外市场扩展被评为"中东最优电信公司"等。

New Words

certify ['sə：tifai] vt.（尤指书面）证明，证实
acrylic [ə'krilik] n. 1. 丙烯酸塑料，丙烯酸纤维，丙烯酸树脂；2. 丙烯酸树脂漆，丙烯酸树脂颜料；3.〈画〉丙烯画；4. 塑胶
　　　　adj. 1.〈化〉丙烯酸的；2.〈化〉丙烯酸衍生物的
copolymer [kəu'pɔlimə] n. 共聚物
emulsion [i'mʌlʃən] n.1. 乳胶，胶状液；乳剂；2. 乳胶漆（干后无光泽）；3. 感光乳剂
plasterboard ['plɑ：stəbɔ：d] n. 石膏板
render ['rendə] vt. 粉刷；给（墙壁）抹灰
　　　　　n.（抹在墙上的）底灰；底层
fair-faced adj 无瑕面的
block-work ['blɔkwə：k] n. 砌块墙；预制砌块体，大方块
coat [kəut] n. 涂料层；覆盖层 vt. 为某物涂抹，给…涂上一层；用…覆盖
epoxy [e'pɔksi] adj. 环氧的 n. 环氧树脂
　 e. g. epoxy finish 环氧面漆；epoxy primer 环氧底漆
filler ['filə] n. 填充料；掺入物；填补空白之物；腻子，填料，填充剂
　 e. g. epoxy filler 环氧腻子
micron ['maikrɔn] n. 微米（百万分之一米）
polyurethane [ˌpɔli'juəriθein] n. 聚氨酯；聚氨基甲酸酯
differential [ˌdifə'renʃəl] adj. 不同的，有分别的；基于差别的；区别性的 n. 差异
diurnal [dai'ənəl] adj. 1. 白天的；2. 每日的

envisage ［inˈvizidʒ］ vt. 想象，设想，展望；正视，面对，拟想，观察

fume ［fju：m］ n. 烟雾，气味

grease ［gri：s］ n. 1. 动物油脂；2. 油膏，油脂

contamination ［kənˌtæməˈneiʃən］ n. 1. 污染，弄脏，毒害；2. 玷污；3. 致污物

substrate ［ˈsʌbˌstreit］ n. （供绘画、印刷等的）底面，基底；基片

stoppers ［ˈstɔpə］ n. 阻塞物

flush ［flʌʃ］ vt. & vi. 冲刷，清除

abrade ［əˈbreid］ vt. 刮擦，磨损

prime ［praim］ vt. 在（金属、木材等上）打底漆

particle ［ˈpɑ：tikl］ n. 微粒，颗粒，〈物〉粒子

abrasive ［əˈbresiv］ adj. 摩擦的；研磨的

residue ［ˈreziˌdu］ n. 剩余，余渣

rinse ［rins］ vt. 1. 漂洗，冲洗；2. 用清水漂洗掉（肥皂泡等）；3.（用清水）冲掉，洗刷

New Phrases

clear finish　清漆罩面

eggshell finish　粗装饰，蛋壳状装饰

finishing coats　最后覆盖面

internal epoxy finish for high building　高层建筑内部环氧效果

in-situ　就地，在现场

undercoat　底层油漆

mid coat　中间层油漆

finishing coat　面漆，表面修饰层，饰面层

application method　涂刷方法

airless spray　无气喷涂

plant room　机械设备间，工作间

surface temperature differentials　表面温度差异

mid-summer　仲夏

degree centigrade　摄氏温度度数

cater for　投合，迎合

intended use　预期用途

manufacturer's batch numbers　生产批号

occupational exposure standards　职业暴露安全标准

Health and Safety Executive （HSE） document　职业健康与安全执行文件

a smooth finish　最后一层光漆

wet preparation　湿选法

Exercises

I. Read the following dialogue, and try to make a new one based on the given situation.

A：Interior decoration is both an art and a hobby. Nothing is more rewarding or satisfying than building up an elegant interior for our home.

B：That's right. Do you think a home has to be beautiful from the outside as well?

A：One cannot have much control over the exterior. But it should fit in with the surroundings and please the passers-by.

B：We spend most of our lifetime at home. And what kind of home do you hope to have?

A：Everyone wants a home pleasing and functional. We should aim at combining beauty and comfort with a welcoming friendliness.

B：I think a well-equipped home makes living more joyful and exciting.

A：It is the individual touch that makes a house a home. Nobody likes a home, big and well-furnished, but wrecked by a poor color scheme.

B：Buying furniture and decorating home interiors may be a very important investment for most families. I prefer to make my home applicable, economical and different.

A：A couple can furnish and decorate their home with a little imagination and by creating beautiful things out of ordinary material with a little cost. The children's bedrooms can be furnished with a few pieces of painted furniture, or refined old furniture can easily be arranged with good taste.

New Words for reference

interior [in'tiəriə] adj. 1. 内部的；2. 内地的，国内的
exterior [eks'tiəriə] adj. 外部的，外面的
functional [″fʌŋkʃənəl] adj. 1. 有用的，实用的；2. 能起作用的，产生影响的；3. 能起工作的，正常运转的
wreck [rek] vt. 毁坏［毁灭］某物
furniture ['fə：nitʃə] n. 家具，（可移动的）家具
furnish ['fə：niʃ] vt. 1. 陈设，布置；2. 提供
arrange [ə'reindʒ] vt. & vi. 安排；准备

Task：Now suppose you are decorating a house. Some wants to make the house look modern and beautiful. Others want to make it applicable and economical. Make a dialogue, giving us your reasons.

II. Read the following passage and try to answer the questions given at the beginning.

Questions：

1. How many kinds of lighting do we have in our homes? What are they?
2. High lamps look good with open tops. Why?
3. What are the appropriate materials used for lamp shades?
4. Why should the lamp for reading be able to be adjusted?
5. What kind of light is suitable to the garden?

Lighting in interior decoration

Light is one of the basic concepts of interior decoration. There are unlimited possibilities to produce many visual effects with the light.

The light fixtures should be functional as well as decorative. In our homes, usually we have two kinds of lighting-general and local.

General lighting should be designed in such a way that by turning on various lights, we can have desired effects of bright, medium or dim light for various occasions.

Too many fluorescent lights produce a monotonous effect. We should go for a mixture of direct and indirect lighting arrangement.

Style of lamps should match other decoration. Lamp shades do not look good with too much painting on them. High lamps look good with open tops so that light can be well distributed. But the lamps below the eye level of a standing person should have lids or tops to conceal the bulbs.

The appropriate materials used for lamp shades are plastics, fabrics, metals, paper and so on. Off-white shades go well with any color scheme.

An indirect lighting at the ceiling line produces general illumination. A ceiling fixture can be lowered to any desired height. In drawing-rooms, concealed lighting is more effective. But a pair of identical lamps may stand at each end of a sofa on small tables.

Kitchens should be particularly well lighted. One should have wall or ceiling light over the working places in the kitchen. Tube lightings can be fixed under the cabinets over the cooking range.

Bedroom lights should usually be local lights. Lights attached to either side of a dressing table mirror or one light-tube placed at the top of the mirror would be an excellent idea. The lamp for reading in bed should be able to be adjusted so that light shines on the book.

In the study, a desk should have a separate lamp. Some people might like to have a ceiling light as well.

The bathroom needs a light fixture beside or above the mirror.

Strong lights over the front and rear entrances are necessary. There should be one light near the number plate and one near the steps if any.

If the garden is big, some floodlights can be installed.

New Words for reference

decorative［'dekərətiv］adj.（物体或建筑）装饰性的；作装饰用的

medium［'mi：djəm］adj. 中等的，适中的

fluorescent［fluə'resnt］adj. 1. 荧光的，发荧光的；2. 颜色、材料等强烈反光的

monotonous［mə'nɔtənəs］adj. 无变化的，单调乏味的

conceal［kən'si：l］vt. 隐藏；隐瞒，遮住

fabric［'fæbrik］n. 织物，布

illumination［iˌlu：mə'neiʃən］n. 照明，光源；强度

rear［riə］adj. 后面的；后部的

floodlight［'flʌdˌlait］n. 泛光灯

TRANSLATION SKILLS

科技论文标题的写法

学术文章的标题主要有三种结构：名词性词组（包括动名词），介词词组，名词词组＋介词词组。间或也用一个疑问句作标题（多用在人文社会科学领域），但一般不用陈述句或动词词组作标题。

一、名词性词组

名词性词组由名词及其修饰语构成。名词的修饰语可以是形容词、介词短语，有时也可以是另一个名词。名词修饰名词时，往往可以缩短标题的长度。以下各标题分别由两个名词词组构成。例如：

Latent demand and the browsing shopper（名词词组＋名词词组）

Cost and productivity（名词＋名词）

二、介词词组

介词词组由介词十名词或名词词组构成。如果整个标题就是一个介词词组的话，一般这个介词是"on"，意思是"对……的研究"。例如：

From Knowledge Engineering to Knowledge Management（介词词组＋介词词组）

On the correlation between working memory capacity and performance on intelligence tests

三、名词/名词词组＋介词词组

这是标题中用得最多的结构。例如：Simulation of Controlled Financial Statements（名词＋介词词组）

The impact of internal marketing activities on external marketing outcomes（名词＋介词词组＋介词词组）

Diversity in the Future Work Force（名词＋介词词组）

Models of Sustaining Human and Natural Development（名词＋介词词组）

标题中的介词词组一般用来修饰名词或名词词组，从而限定某研究课题的范围。这

种结构与中文的"的"字结构相似，区别是中文标题中修饰语在前，中心词在后。英文正好相反，名词在前，而作为修饰语的介词短语在后。例如：

Progress on Fuel Cell and its Materials（燃料电池及其材料进展）

四、其他形式

对于值得争议的问题，偶尔可用疑问句作为论文的标题，以点明整个论文讨论的焦点。例如：

Is B2B e-commerce ready for prime time?

Can ERP Meet Your Business Needs?

有的标题由两部分组成，用冒号（：）隔开。一般来说，冒号前面一部分是研究的对象、内容或课题，比较笼统，冒号后面具体说明研究重点或研究方法。这种结构可再分为三种模式。

模式 1　研究课题：具体内容。例如：

Microelectronic Assembly and Packaging Technology：Barriers and Needs

The Computer Dictionary Project：an update

模式 2　研究课题：方法/性质。例如：

B2B E-Commerce：A Quick Introduction

The Use of Technology in Higher Education Programs：a National Survey

模式 3　研究课题：问题焦点。例如：

Caring about connections：gender and computing

译　文

第十三单元　装饰工程

对　话

装饰工作检查

咨询工程师：昨天我到正在搞装修的楼里转了转。坦率地说，我对你们装饰工程队干的活不满意。

承　包　方：装饰工程包括木工、细木工、五金、抹灰、玻璃、安装、油漆等等，我想知道你对哪部分工作不满意？

咨询工程师：请跟我去现场吧，我会带你到质量不符合标准的具体地方看一看。

承　包　方：让我们现在就去吧。

咨询工程师：到了。请看这些木料，你一定记得在细木工作开始前，你拿来三个计划用于办公大楼的柚木样本、柚木胶合板样本和硬木样本。用在办公建筑中的木料在外观和质量上都应该与已批准使用的样本一致。现在这些木材与样本有很大区别。

承　包　方：让我看看。这些材料和我们递交的看起来质量是一样的。

咨询工程师：木材的等级似乎没有区别，但是潮湿度却比规定要求的高多了。根据工程规范，潮湿度应不低 10% 且不超过 20%。但是根据我们的检测，这些木料的潮湿度要高于那个标准。

承 包 方：我们会对木材进行检测。当材料达到规定的湿度标准时我们再进行装配和安装工作。

咨询工程师：再看看铝合金门窗，有些地方变形了。

承 包 方：我们会告诉供货商送货的时候小心点，否则拒收。

咨询工程师：还有一件事情要注意的，铝合金框架和玻璃要避免粘上水泥、灰浆、灰泥等类似的东西。

承 包 方：肯定会的。

咨询工程师：至于瓷砖铺砌，那就更要小心。

承 包 方：会的，在铺砌瓷砖前，地板会彻底扫干净并冲洗，然后才开始铺砌，避免不必要的割损。

咨询工程师：铺砌好的瓷砖地面必须记得清理干净，并洒上锯末以保护瓷砖。

课文 A　建筑玻璃装配

设计/安装要求

总体要求

　　在这一部分里所说明的要求适用于整体建筑玻璃装配，包括防水板和与建筑物邻近部位的联结点。要充分留出偏离和其他移动的余地。

完整性

　　根据 BS6262 或 CP3 来确定窗玻璃的尺寸和厚度，玻璃类型以及安装位置，支固以及其他要求，确保安装的建筑玻璃能够抵御所有的风荷载，静荷载和设计动荷载，且能够通过调节，适应所有的偏离和热移动而不使玻璃受损。

一般移动

　　建筑玻璃装配必须能通过调节适应预期的温度变化，沉降，徐变等导致的建筑物移动。

抵御天气影响

　　从密封玻璃到玻璃连接处要密封。安装室玻璃也要密封防水。

热保护

　　建筑玻璃装配的平均热传导（u 值）不应大于 $2.0w/m^2 \cdot K$。

冷凝

　　下列情况下在窗玻璃或部件内部表面上下不应形成冷凝。

　　外部：夏季：最高 52℃@100% RH

　　　　　冬季：最低 7℃@55% RH

　　内部：夏季：22℃@ 55% RH

　　　　　冬季：22℃@55% RH

阳光和光控制

　　窗玻璃或其部件总的太阳能穿透率不应超过正常太阳辐射的 50% 和其透光率应不低于 60%。

温度安全

　　窗玻璃或部件必须能耐得住由于方向、阴暗、阳光控制和施工产生的温度压力。

安装准确

　　留出生产和安装的误差，玻璃连接处宽度允许的最大偏差为 ±4mm。

安装安全

在建筑玻璃安装完工的时候，所有连在一起的装配固定装置和装配支护固定装置必须锁好、划好，以防由于建筑物移动或违章校验引起的转动。

耐久

在建筑玻璃安装中使用的产品应不易受真菌，昆虫和害虫的侵扰。向咨询工程师递交一份维修、更换密封剂和次要部件的计划表。

课文 B　涂料或清漆罩面

准备工作情况/要求

要求

主承包方必须做到：

根据工程要求，负责提供和安装涂料或清漆罩面。

确保装饰工程达到此规定的标准，且按照说明进行单独检查并出具证明。

健康与安全

主承包方应保证遵守最新的"施工安全工作规范"（迪拜酋长国施工作业准则）以及合同文件中的健康与安全部分，并且保证充分考虑到在生产、处理、使用过程中工作人员的健康与安全。

涂料或清漆罩面的种类（部分）

涂料

A 型：丙烯酸树脂漆共聚物可清洗乳胶漆粗装饰

表面：内部石膏板/平滑打底层/清水墙

准备工作：按照装饰材料生产商的建议准备涂料

最后覆盖面：整体 2 层乳胶漆

颜色：TBA

位置：公寓、计划中的所有区域

B 型：内部高层建筑环氧效果

表面：内部底层或现场无瑕面混凝土

准备工作：按照 M60. 6000 部分执行

内层油漆：一层环氧腻子

中间层油漆：100 微米一层高层建筑环氧

饰面层：100 微米二层聚氨酯

涂刷方法：除内层油漆外无气喷涂

颜色：TBA

饰面：小型未压缩

位置：LV/HV 间，机械设备间，塔顶层楼梯间，电气室，ETISALAT 室

性能要求

热运动

所有材料应不受以下原因导致的热变化影响：最大与最小表面温度差，最大年温差，日温差，仲夏时的绝对最高和最低温度以及符合 BS5427 规定的表面温度。

外部空气温度的年温差一般为 45℃左右。外部 24 小时的日温差一般为 20℃左右。有记载的最高温为 50.5℃，有记载的最低温为 1℃。选择材料应考虑到工程将面临的暂时性的及永久性的情况。

材料

常规涂料/清漆材料

运送的材料要完好、密封，在标签上按照下列要求标明：

材料品种

品名

使用方法

生产批号

安置

用于制备的材料必须由其生产商推荐为现场使用或由涂层生产商推荐来为面层做准备。

主承包方要按照现行《职业与安全执行标准》中 EH40 条规定，严防工作人员在有灰尘、潮气和烟雾的环境中工作。

清除表面的灰尘、油脂和油。如果表面或底面被弄脏，要在继续实操之前采取措施。如果表面参差不齐，用效果好的阻塞物/填充物来填补接缝、裂缝、孔洞和其他凹陷处，并保证表面齐平。刮擦后上最后一层光漆。

上打底漆后使用油底阻塞物/填充物，在颗粒干燥前把表面的颗粒清除掉，用干净的水通过表面湿选法来去除余渣，擦拭然后晾干。

Part four
Inspection Acceptance of Finished Works(竣工验收)

UNIT *14*

Acceptance of Finished Works(竣工验收)

DIALOGUE

I. The Issue of Completion Certificates

C: Today we would like to submit our application for the section completion certificates for this project. The early issuing of the certificate will be very much appreciated.

E: In my opinion it is too early to issue the section completion certificate for the building.

C: I'm afraid I can not agree with you at this point. In accordance with Clause 32. 2 of Conditions of Contract: "A section completion certificate will be issued at the stage that building is completed substantially and the function of it can be used by the Employer". We should be given the section certificate since the works has been completed at 95% of the total value of the building.

E: But from our calculation you have only completed 92% of the works of the building.

C: We believe your calculation is on the basis of the payment sheet of last month. From then on, 25 days has passed, the value of the finished works of this building should be already over 95%. Here is the works statistics report and the monthly payment application we prepared for your reference.

E: (Reading the materials) That's right. After further inspection to the whole building, the certificate of the completion will be issued to you.

C: Does the retention period start from the day of issuing the Certificate?

E: Yes, of course. But you should have a through check of all the built-drawings without missing and submit them to us within 20 days. Besides this, all necessary information, such as QA/QC (quality assurance/ quality control) inspection forms, survey records, execution tracing files should be ready for submission.

C: No problem. We propose we will be paid a half of the amount of the money for the retention, which is 2.5% of the total contract value after we send you a bank guarantee of the same value and the other half be paid to us after the maintenance period is over.

E: We will study your proposal and reply to you soon.

II. The works are ready to be taken over.

(Taking over the works is an important step in the execution of the project to both the Contractor and the Owner. As often stipulated in the Contract, once the Works reach substantial completion, the Contractor can proceed to prepare for the transferring of the works by giving a notice to the Owner, and the taking-over procedure starts.)

C: We are pleased to inform you that the whole Works have, in our opinion, reached substantial completion under the Contract. No doubt you will wish to seewhether the site is satisfactory and to do some relevant tests. We look forward to receiving a Taking-over Certificate.

E: I am pleased to learn that the Works are ready for acceptance. So it's time to make a plan for taking over the works.

C: We have brought a plan with us. It includes a timetable for the taking-over procedure, as-built drawings and a list of all the parts of the Works to be inspected and tested. Here it is.

E: Thank you. Is there any work which you think is still outstanding?

C: Yes, but they are minor items, like ground surface reinstating.

E: Our out expert panel, accompanied by your technicians, will inspect the completed Works and see if they are satisfactory.

C: OK.

(*The whole acceptance procedure goes smoothly and lasts 5 days.*)

E: I'm glad to say that the whole works have been passed all the tests and our engineers are quite satisfied with the test results. However, a few minor defects have been found and there's still some outstanding work. What do you say about those items?

C: It's true that a few minor defects remain to be rectified and some items of work to be completed, but they do not affect the normal operation of the whole Works, as you can see from all the functioning tests. This means, according to the contract, that substantial completion has been achieved and that we should receive a taking-over certificate from you.

E: We can issue a taking-over certificate to you provided that you give us a written undertaking that you will finish the outstanding work and making good the defects with due expedition during the Maintenance Period.

C: No problem.

E：In that case，we can acknowledge that the works were substantially completed today.

Notes

1. 在工程达到实质性竣工（substantial completion）或基本竣工（practical completion）时，组织工程的验收对承包商来说是十分重要的一项工作，因为工程一旦移交给业主，工程的照管责任（responsibility for the care of the works）即从承包商转到业主一方，承包商并且能获得相应的权益（rights and benefits）。

2. 由于每一项工程的性质（nature of the works）与所签订的合同类型（type of contract）不尽相同，工程的移交程序也有差异，但其程序大致如下：

（1）承包商通知业主工程已经达到实质性竣工，并按业主要求提交一份移交计划（plan for taking over the works）。计划中应包括；要求业主进行检查与试验的时间表（timetable）；竣工时应提交业主的各类资料，未完成的扫尾工作（outstanding work）等。

（2）制定记录验收检查与试验结果的各类表格（recording forms）。

（3）制定记录验收报告（completion report）。

这以报告应是对工程项目的公正的评价（fair evaluation），在其中说明工程于某某日期竣工和缺陷责任期（维修期）开始日期，以及指出承包商应在缺陷责任期应完成的扫尾工作和小缺陷。

（4）颁发移交证书

在工程验收中常出现实质性竣工（substantial completion），检查（inspection），试验（test）等术语，合同中往往对这些术语的含义有所定义。实质性竣工（substantial completion）是指工程已基本竣工，可以投入运行，允许在验收时存在部分完成的扫尾工作和一些小缺陷，但不能影响工程的正常运行（normal operation）。检查是指工程及其安装到工程上的永久设备（incorporated plant），装置（device）和构筑物（structures）等的外观检查，试验是指对上述设施按一定的方法去测试。

一旦承包商收到了移交证书，承包商要催促业主按合同规定退还保留金（retention money），同时组织维修期的维修工作。

New Words

submit［səb′mit］vt. 提交，呈递
appreciate［ə′priː∫ieit］vt. 感激，感谢；为…表示感激（或感谢）
issue［′isjuː］vt. 发表，发布；vi. 发行；颁布
substantially［səb′stæn∫əli］adv. 本质上，实质上；大体上
substantial［səb′stæn∫əl］adj. 实质的，基本的，大体上的
function［′fʌŋk∫ən］n. 功能；作用；职责
calculation［ˌkælkjə′lei∫ən］n. 计算，计算（的结果）
retention［ri′ten∫ən］n. 保留，保持
execution［ˌeksi′kjuː∫ən］n. 实行，执行，实施

guarantee [ˌgærən'tiː] n. 担保，担保品，抵押品

maintenance ['meintinəns] n. 维持；维护；保养；维修

outstanding [ˌaut'stændiŋ] adj. 未解决的，未完成的

reinstate [ˌriːin'steit] vt. 1. 使恢复原职，使恢复原有权利；2. 把…放回原处

defect [di'fekt] n. 缺点，过失，瑕疵，缺陷，毛病

rectify ['rektifai] vt. 改正，矫正

New Phrases

section completion certificates   部分完工证明

payment sheet   付款清单

works statistics report   工程统计报表

monthly payment application   月度工程进度款支付申请函

retention period   保修期

QA/QC inspection form   质保/质控检测表格

execution tracing file   隐蔽工程记录

bank guarantee   银行保证书

maintenance period   保修期

minor defects   小缺陷

outstanding work   扫尾工作

taking-over certificate   移交证书

as-built drawings   竣工图纸

surface reinstating   恢复地表面

expert panel   专家组

Role Play

Talk about the taking-over process and the inspection work of client.

TEXT A

Certificate and Payment in FIDIC Conditions

Payment of Retention Money

（a）Upon the issue of the Taking-Over Certificate with respect to the whole of the works, one half of the Retention Money shall be certified by the Engineer for payment to the Contractor.

（b）Upon the expiration of the Defects Liability Period for the Works the other half of the Retention Money shall be certified by the Engineer for payment to the Contractor.

Statement at Completion

Not later than 84 days after the issue of the Taking-Over Certificate in respect of the whole of the works, the Contractor shall submit to the engineer six copies of a Statement at Completion with supporting documents showing in detail, in the form approved by the Engineer.

（a） The final value of all work done in accordance with the Contract up to the date stated in such Taking-over Certificate.

（b） Any further sums which the Contractor considers to be due, and

（c） An estimate of amounts which the contractor considers will become due to him under the Contract.

The estimated amounts shall be shown separately in such Statement at Completion.

Final Statement

Not later than 56 days after the issue of the Defects Liability Certificate, the Contractor shall submit to the Engineer for consideration six copies of a draft final statement with supporting documents showing in detail, in the form approved by the engineer.

（a） the value of all work done in accordance with the Contract, and

（b） any further sums which the contractor considers to be due to him under the Contract or otherwise.

If the Engineer disagrees with or cannot verify any part of the draft final statement, the Contractor shall submit such further information as the Engineer may reasonably require and shall submit such changes in the draft as may be agreed between them. The contractor shall then prepare and submit to the Engineer the final statement as agreed （ for the purpose of these Conditions referred to as the "Final Statement"）.

Discharge

Upon submission of the Final Statement, the Contractor shall give to the Employer, within a copy with the Engineer, a written discharge confirming that the total of the Final Statement represents full and final settlement of all monies due to the contractor arising out of or in respect of the Contract.

Final Payment Certificate

Within 28 days after receipt of the Final Statement, and the written discharge, the Engineer shall issue to the Employer （with a copy to the Contractor） a Final Payment Certificate.

Notes

1. 保留金支付 （Payment of Retention Money）

保留金 （retention money） 即通常我们所说的质量保证金，工程师在每月的支付证明中保留按合同规定比例的保留金，直至合同规定的保留金限额为止。一般合同规定保留金的比例为合同价的5%，在工程师向承包人颁发永久工程的一区段或部分的移交证书（Taking-Over Certificate） 时，该部分相应价值的保留金的一半应支付给承包人，同样，在颁发整个工程的移交证书时，工程师应把另一半保留金支付给承包商。

2. 竣工报表及支付

承包商在整个工程移交证书（Taking-Over Certificate）日后 84 天内，应向工程师提交竣工报表（Statement at Completion），其中详细列明合同规定所有工作的最终价值及变更等应进一步支付的款项。工程师根据竣工图（As-Built Drawings）对工程进行详细核算，对支付项目认真审核后，确定工程竣工报表的支付金额，上报业主批准支付。

　　想要及时收到款项，承包商应及早准备，将竣工报表报出时间尽量缩短。

　　3. 最终报表（Final Statement）与最终支付证书（Final Payment Certificate）

　　FIDIC 条件规定，在工程缺陷责任期（Defects Liability Period）满后，工程师认为承包商已尽其义务完成其施工任务，并修补工程缺陷。工程已竣工，应向承包商颁发缺陷责任证书（Defects Liability Certificate）。承包商在颁发缺陷责任证书之后 56 天之内，向工程师提交一份最终报表（Final Statement）和书面结清单（a Written Discharge），报表应说明根据合同所完成的所有工作的价值及承包商根据合同认为应支付给他的任何进一步款项，包括保留金金额。

　　工程师在接到最终报表和书面结清单后，应在 28 天之内，向承包商开具最终支付证书（Final Payment Certificate），并退还承包商在签订合同前向业主提交的履约保证书（Performance Securities）。

　　由于最终报表的特性，承包商在递交后，即已无权向业主索赔，工程的付款则最终被确定。

New Words

expiration［ˌekspiˌreiʃən］n. 满期，届期；截止，告终

liability［ˌlaiə'biliti］n. 责任，义务

due［djuː］adj. 1. 应支付［给予］的；2. 应有的，应得到的；3. 到期的

separately［'sepəritli］adv. 分离地；个别地，分别地，单独地

verify［'verifai］vt. 1. 证实，核实；2. 查对，核准

discharge［dis'tʃɑːdʒ］n. 免除，解除，去除属于负担性质的东西

confirm［kən'fəːm］vt. 证实，证明；肯定，确认

arise［ə'raiz］vi. & link-v. 呈现；出现；发生

New Phrases

with respect to　关于，（至于）谈到

Defects Liability Period　工程缺陷责任期

Statement at Completion　竣工报表

in respect of　关于

Final Statement　最终报表

Defects Liability Certificate　缺陷责任证书

a written discharge　书面结清单

Final Payment Certificate　最终支付证书

Role Play

Try to describe the following pictures according to the words and phrases given below.

The contractor had been accepted to fulfill（完成）all the execution and completion of the works and remedy all the defects and the client shows his appreciation and congratulation.

congratulation（祝贺）

Exercises

I. Answer the following questions.

1. How will the retention money be paid to the contractor?

2. When shall the contractor submit to the engineer six copies of a Statement at Completion?

3. When shall the Contractor submit to the Engineer for consideration six copies of a draft final statement?

4. Shall the contractor provide the supporting documents when submitting a draft final statement?

5. When shall the Engineer issue to the Employer（with a copy to the Contractor）a Final Payment Certificate?

II. Complete the sentences with the given words or expression. Change the form where necessary.

1. The client shall issue a _____（complete）certificates for this project.

2. The building is completed _____（substantial）and the function of it can be used by the Employer now.

3. After the client carries out further _____（inspect）to the whole building, the certificate of the completion will be issued to the contractor.

4. The contractor shall finish the outstanding work and making good the defects with due expedition during the _____（maintain）Period.

5. Upon _____（submit）of the Final Statement, the Contractor shall give to the Employer, within a copy to the Engineer, a written discharge.

III. Translate the following words or phrases into English.

部分完工证明 _____

付款申请书 _____

工程统计报表_____

月度工程进度款申请书 _____

保修期 _____

质保/ 质控检测文件 _____

银行保证书 _____

保修期 _____

扫尾工作_____

移交证书_____

竣工图纸_____

恢复地表面 _____

专家组 _____

工程缺陷责任期_____

竣工报表 _____

最终报表 _____

缺陷责任证书_____

书面结清单_____

最终支付证书 _____

IV. Translate the following sentences into Chinese.

1. We can issue a taking-over certificate to you provided that you give us a written undertaking that you will finish the outstanding work and making good the defects with due expedition during the Maintenance Period

_____

_____

_____

2. If the Engineer disagree with or cannot verify any part of the draft final statement, the Contractor shall submit such further information as the Engineer may reasonably require and shall submit such changes in the draft as may be agreed between them.

_____

_____

_____

TEXT B

The Issue of Final Completion Certificate

In accordance with the Condition of Contract, when the maintenance period for the project is over, the contractor shall submit the application for issuing the final Completion Certificate for the project. After certain procedure is fulfilled, the Final Completion Certificate will be issued by the client.

Firstly, it will be an inspection group set up jointly by the Employer, Contractor and representative of relevant Government Departments. The group will inspect all buildings in the scope of the Contract within the following 10 days and the inspection report will be issued to all relevant aspects.

Usually, some defects will be found during the inspection such as leakage on deep substructure or roof, some damages in widow-glass, some of the worn-out painting area, some dead trees of landscape and so on; the contractor will be required to repair them within a period of time.

After a short period of repairs by the contractor and after the Employer make sure that all defects have been erased through correct repairing, the final completion certificate will be issued in a formal conference.

Supposing during the maintenance period a disaster happens, such as typhoon, flood, war, earthquake and the like which makes the works damaged heavily, the contractor will repair all damages to the buildings within the scope of the Contract with his own material, manpower and machinery except the force majeure.

The force majeure means the disaster is unpredictable and unavoidable. For example, if a flood which happens less than once in one hundred years can be considered as a force majeure. Sometimes the force majeure is also caused by human's behavior such as rebelling, war, turmoil and so on. Normally the Contractor is responsible for all the damages during the maintenance period.

New Words

jointly ['dʒɔintli] adv. 共同地，联合地
representative [ˌrepri'zentətiv] n. 1. 代表；2. 代理人
relevant ['reləvənt] adj. 有关的
leakage ['liːkidʒ] n. 1. 漏，漏出；2. 漏出物，渗漏物
substructure [sʌb'strʌktʃə] n. 底部构造；基础
damage ['dæmidʒ] vt. & vi. 损害，毁坏，加害于 n. 损失，损害，损毁
disaster [di'zɑːstə] n. 灾难，灾祸
majeure [mə'dʒer] n. 压倒的力量，不可抗力
unpredictable [ˌʌnpriˌdiktəbəl] adj. 无法预言的，不可预测的
unavoidable [ˌʌnə'vɔidəbəl] adj. 不可避免的
turmoil ['təːmɔil] n. 混乱

New Phrases

final completion certificate   最后完工证明
an inspection group   验收小组
force majeure   不可抗力

Exercises

I. The following is a Certificate of Completion. Based on what you have learnt in this unit, try to figure out its content and pay especial attention to its format.

CERTIFICATE OF COMPLETION

Construction Completion Certificate No: _____

    THE UNDERSIGNED, _____ (the " contractor/ Engineer ") hereby certifies that the construction completed pursuant to Servicing Agreement No: _____ which is dated the _____ day of _____, 2 _____, between _____ (the "Owner") and _____ the Contractor / Engineer has been completed in its entirety as of the _____ day of _____, 2 _____ .

    1. The Contractor /Engineer hereby certifies that all construction completed is in compliance with the provisions of the Servicing Agreement, including but not limited to, all specifications, amendments and drawings.

    2. The Contractor /Engineer further certifies that all payments which were due and owing to any and all employees of the contractor/ engineer and to any other third parties in respect of the completion of the construction have been paid in full.

    3. The Contractor /Engineer has obtained full and final releases from all suppliers, subcontractor which provided services or material to the Contractor/Engineer in its performance of the construction contemplated in the Serving Agreement and certifies that there are no liens by any supplier or subcontractor.

    4. Any and all defects in workmanship or materials used for or in connection with the construction completed have been corrected.

    5. The total cost of the construction completed by the Contractor /Engineer is _____ ($ _____) USD /Canadian Dollars.

    DATED this _____ day of _____, 2 _____ .

                                 (**CONTRACTOR/ENGINEER**)

                                   Per: _____

                                   _____

                                   Name:

                                   Title :

                                   I have authority to bind the company.

    (extracted from http: //www. docstoc. com/docs/17325282/Certificate-of-Completion)

II. The following are some attachments needed to be fulfilled when being issued a certificate of completion. Based on what you have learnt in this unit, try to figure out the content and pay especial attention to its format.

1. *NEC Engineering and Construction Contract（NEC ECC2）*
COMPLETION CERTIFICATE

	day	*month*	*year*
Completion achieved on：			
The Completion Date is：			
The defects date is：			
The Defects on the attached schedule are to be corrected within the defects correction period which ends on：			

Works checked by the Supervisor：

. . . .
. . . .
Signature：   *Name：*   *Date：*

Certified by the Project Manager：

. . . .
. . . .
Signature：   *Name：*   *Date：*

2. *NEC Engineering and Construction Short Contract.（ECSC）*
COMPLETION CERTIFICATE

	day	*month*	*year*
Completion achieved on：			
The Completion Date is：			
The defects date is：			
The Defects on the attached schedule are to be corrected within the defects correction period which ends on：			

Certified by the Employer：

. . . .
. . . .
Signature：   *Name：*   *Date：*

III. The followings are two taking-over certificates in FIDIC conditions, and try to figure out their content and format.

1. *FIDIC Conditions of Contract for Construction (Red Book)*

TAKING OVER CERTIFICATE

It is hereby certified that the abovementioned works were in terms of clause 10 of the FIDIC Conditions of Contract for Construction completed on . . . . The work described in the attached schedule is outstanding.

. . . .

. . . .

Signature: *Name*:   *Date*:

Engineer

2. *FIDIC Conditions of Contract for Plant and Design (Yellow Book)*

TAKING OVER CERTIFICATE

It is hereby certified that the abovementioned works were in terms of clause 10 of the FIDIC Conditions of Contract for Plant and Design-Build completed on . . . . The work described in the attached schedule is outstanding.

. . . .

. . . .

Signature: *Name*:   *Date*:

Employer

IV. The following is an affidavit of the employer in a project. try to figure out the content and format of it.

CERTIFICATE OF CONSTRUCTION COMPLETION

Project: _____

OWNER'S AFFIDAVIT

I. Certify that the work under the above named project including all appurtenances thereto, has been satisfactorily completed; that all charges or bills for labor or services performed or materials furnished, and other charges against the subcontractors, have been paid in full and in accordance with the terms of the contract; that no liens have attached against the property and improvements of owner; that no notice of intention to claim liens is outstanding that no suits are pending by reason on the project under the contract; that all Worker's Compensation claims have been settled and no public liability claims are pending.

Affidavit is made for the purpose of inducing the JEA to accept said construction for ownership.

_____   _____
Owner's Signature   Please Print Name

_____   _____
Address   Date

_____
City，State & Zip
Sworn to and subscribed before me，a notary public，
This day of _____，_____

_____
Notary Public Signature

（**Notes**：affidavit［ˌæfi′devit］n. ＜律＞宣誓作证书，（经陈述者宣誓在法律上可采作证据的）书面陈述，书面证词

（extracted from http：//www. jea. com/about/pub/downloads/OwnerAffidavit. pdf）

TRANSLATION SKILLS

学术论文的英文写作简介

一、科技论文的结构

Title（标题）

Abstract（摘要）

Keywords（关键词）

Table of contents（目录）

Nomenclature（术语表）

Introduction（引言）

Method（方法）

Results（结果）

Discussion（讨论）

Conclusion（结论）

Acknowledgement（致谢）

Notes（注释）

References（参考文献）

Appendix（附录）

一篇完整规范的学术论文结构如右所示：

其中，

Title，

Abstract，Introduction，Method，

Result，Discussion，Conclusion 和 Reference

八项内容是必不可少的，其他内容则根据具体需要而定。

二、正文

学术论文的正文一般包括 Method，Result，Discussion 三个部分。这三部分主要描述研究课题的具体内容、方法，研究过程中所使用的设备、仪器、条件，并如实公布有关数据和研究结果等。Conclusion 是对全文内容或有关研究课题进行的总体性讨论。它具有严密的科学性和客观性，反映一个研究课题的价值，同时提出以后的研究方向。

为了帮助说明论据、事实，正文中经常使用各种图表。最常用的是附图（Figure）和表（Table），此外还有图解或简图（Diagram）、曲线图或流程图（Graph）、视图（View）、剖面图（Profile）、图案（Pattern）等。在文中提到时，通常的表达法为：

如图 4 所示 As（is）shown in Fig. 4；

如表 1 所示 As（is）shown in Tab. 1。

三、结论

在正文最后应有结论（Conclusions）或建议（Suggestions）。

（1）关于结论可用如下表达方式：

① The following conclusions can be drawn from …（由……可得出如下结论）

② It can be concluded that …（可以得出结论……）

③ We may conclude that…或 We come to the conclusion that…（我们得出如下结论……）

④ It is generally accepted（believed，held，acknowledged）that…（一般认为……）（用于表示肯定的结论）

⑤ We think（consider，believe，feel）that…（我们认为……）（用于表示留有商量余地的结论）

（2）关于建议可用如下表达方式。

① It is advantageous to（do）

② It should be realized（emphasized，stressed，noted，pointed out）that …

③ It is suggested（proposed，recommended，desirable）that …

④ It would be better（helpful，advisable）that…

四、结尾部分

1. 致谢

为了对曾给予支持与帮助或关心的人表示感谢，在论文之后，作者通常对有关人员致以简短的谢词，可用如下方式：

I am thankful to sb. for sth.

I am grateful to sb. for sth.

I am deeply indebted to sb. for sth.

I would like to thank sb. for sth.

Thanks are due to sb. for sth.

The author wishes to express his sincere appreciation to sb. for sth.

The author wishes to acknowledge sb.

The author wishes to express his gratitude for sth.

2. 注释

注释有两种方式，一种为脚注，即将注释放在出现的当页底部；另一种是将全文注释集中在结尾部分。两种注释位置不同，方法一样。注释内容包括：

（1）引文出处。注释方式参见"参考文献"。

（2）对引文的说明，如作者的见解、解释。

（3）文中所提到的人的身份，依次为职称或职务、单位。如：

Professor，Dean of Dept…University（教授，……大学……系主任）

Chairman，… Company，USA（美国……公司董事长）

（4）本论文是否曾发表过。

3. 参考文献

在论文的最后应将写论文所参考过的主要论著列出，目的是表示对别人成果的尊重或表示本论文的科学根据，同时也便于读者查阅。参考文献的列法如下：

如果是书籍，应依次写出作者、书名、出版社名称、出版年代、页数。如：

Dailey，C. L. and Wood，F. C.，Computation curves for compressible Fluid Problems，John Wiley & Sons，Inc. New York，1949，pp. 37-39

如果是论文，应依次写出作者、论文题目、杂志名称、卷次、期次、页数。如：

Marrish Joseph G.，Turbulence Modeling for Computational Aerodynamics，AIAA J. Vol-21，No. 7，1983，PP. 941-955

如果是会议的会刊或论文集，则应指出会议举行的时间、地点。如：

Proceedings of the Sixth International Conference on Fracture Dec. 4-10，1984，New Delhi，India

如果作者不止一人，可列出第一作者，其后加上 et al。如：Wagner，R. S. et al，…

译　文

第十四单元　竣工验收

对　话

1. 颁发竣工证明

承　包　方：今天我想提交此工程工段竣工说明书的申请，如果能早点发给我们竣工证明我们将非常感谢。

咨询工程师：依我看现在发工程的完工证明还为时尚早。

承　包　方：恐怕在这一点我不能同意你的观点。按照合同条款第32条第二项："在工程大体竣工，业主可以使用其功能阶段将颁发工程完工证明。"目前工程总额95%的工作都已完成，所以应该发完工证明了。

咨询工程师：但是根据我们的计算，你们只完成了整个工程的92%。

承　包　方：我想你这是根据上个月的付款单来计算的。从那时到现在已经过去了25天了，本工程已经完成的工作总额已经超过95%。这是工程统计数值报告和我们准备供您参考的月付款申请。

咨询工程师：没错，进一步检查这个工程后，会把竣工证明发给你们的。

承　包　方：保留期是从发竣工证明那天开始算起吗？

咨询工程师：是的，当然。但是你应该彻底地、没有任何遗漏地检查一下所有的施工图纸，然后在 20 天之内交给我们。此外，所有必要的材料，比如 QA/QC（质量保证/质量管理）检查表格，检查记录、施工跟踪文件也应该一并交上。

承　包　方：没问题。我们提议在我们给你等值的银行保证后你们给我们付一半的保留期费用，即总合同价的 2.5%。等维修期结束后再付另一半费用。

咨询工程师：我们会研究你们的提议并尽快给你们答复。

2. 准备移交工程

（在项目实施过程中，移交工程对承包方和业主都是一个重要环节。合同中通常规定，一旦工程达到实质性竣工的程度，承包方可以通知业主着手准备工程的移交工作，这时移交程序开始。）

承　包　方：我们很高兴地通知贵方，我们觉得整个工程已经达到了合同要求的实质性竣工程度。无疑贵方将希望到现场检查看看是否令你们满意，并安排相关的试验。我们希望收到贵方的移交证书。

咨询工程师：我很高兴得到工程已经准备验收的消息。所以现在是该制订移交计划的时候了。

承　包　方：我们带来了一份计划。它包括移交程序时间表，竣工图纸和以备检查试验的所有项目列表。文件都在这里。

咨询工程师：谢谢。还有什么你们觉得尚未完成的工作吗？

承　包　方：是的，但都是些小问题，像地面平整之类的工作。

咨询工程师：我们的专家组将在你们技术人员的陪同下检查这一完工工程，看看工程是否令人满意。

承　包　方：好的。

（整个验收工作顺利进行且持续 5 天。）

咨询工程师：我很高兴地通知贵方整个工程通过了所有的试验，我方的工程师对试验结果非常满意。但是也发现了几处小问题并且仍有些工程未完成。你们对这些问题有什么想法？

承　包　方：确实有几处小问题需要修补，还有些项目没有完工，但它们不影响整个工程的正常运行，这正如你们通过所有功能性试验中所看到的。根据合同这意味着已经达到实质性竣工程度，我们应当收到贵方的移交证书。

咨询工程师：如果贵方能给我方出具书面保证完成扫尾工作并且在维修阶段迅速妥善地处理缺陷之处，我们就可以向贵方颁发移交证书。

承　包　方：没问题。

咨询工程师：要是那样的话，今天我们就可以宣布工程实质性竣工。

课　文　A
FIDIC（国际咨询工程师联合会）条件下的证书和付款

保留金支付

（a）有关整个工程的移交证书一经颁发，保留金的一半将由咨询工程师证明并支付给承包方。

（b）在整个工程缺陷责任期满后，另一半保留金也将由咨询工程师证明并支付给承包方。

竣工报表

在整个工程的移交证书颁发 84 天之内，承包方应向工程师提交竣工报表，一式六份，详列相关文件以备工程师核准。

（a）根据合同整个工程到移交证书颁发之日的最终款项。

（b）承包方认为应进一步支付的任何款项。

（c）承包方认为应支付给他们的预计总额。

预计总额应该在竣工报表中单列。

最终报表

在颁发缺陷责任证书之后 56 天内，承包方应向工程师提交最终报表草案，一式六份，详列相关文件以备工程师核准。

（a）合同规定的总工程量。

（b）承包方认为根据合同或其他应进一步支付给他们的款项。

如果工程师不同意或不能核准最终报表草案的任何部分，承包方将根据工程师的合理要求递交进一步的资料，根据双方达成的一致意见，在草案中做进一步的修改。承包方然后要根据协议向工程师提交最终报表（以达到最终报表所提及的条件）。

结清

在提交最终报表时，承包方将向雇佣方提供一份书面结算清单，同时给工程师复本，说明最终报表总额款项及根据合同应支付给承包方的所有款项和最后金额。

最终支付证书

在收到最终报表和书面结算清单的 28 天之内，工程师将向业主提交最终支付证书（同时给承包方复本）。

课文 B　颁发最后完工证明

根据合同条件，当工程的维修期结束时，承包方将提交颁发最后完工证明的申请。在完成指定程序后，业主来颁发最后完工证明。

首先，要由雇佣方、承包方和相关政府部门的代表共同组成一个验收小组。小组在接下来的 10 天内检查合同范围内所有建筑物并提交所有相关方面的检查验收报告。

通常在验收过程中会发现某些问题，比如地下工程或屋顶渗漏，窗户玻璃破损，墙漆脱落，园林的树木没有成活等等；承包方需要在一定期限内对上述问题进行修复。

在由承包方迅速修理并经雇佣方确认所有缺陷都通过修理得到弥补之后，将在一个正式的会议上颁发最后完工证明。

假如在维修期间有灾难发生，如台风，洪水，战争，地震等等使建筑物严重受损，承包方需要使用自己的材料、人员和机器修理合同范围内的所有损坏部分，除了不可抗力的原因。

不可抗力指不可预期的，难以避免的灾难。例如百年不遇的洪水即为不可抗力。有时不可抗力也会人为造成，比如叛乱、战争、混乱等等。一般来说承包方要对维修期间的所有损坏负责。

Glossary（词汇表）

A

a chemical content analysis 化学成分分析

a letter of invitation to tender 招标函

a lump sum firm price 包干价合同价格

a lump sum 一次性总付款，包干价

a material tracking schedule 原材料跟踪计划

a parking lot 施工设备停放场

a rate basis contract 单价合同

a smooth finish 最后一层光漆

a social mechanics survey 土力学勘察

a trial operation 试验施工

a vertical load 垂直荷载

a written discharge 书面结清单

abbreviation [ə'bri:vi,eiʃən] n. 1. 缩写；缩写词；2. 略语；缩写词；缩写形式

abnormal [æb'nɔ:məl] adj. 反常的，异常的

abrade [ə'breid] vt. 刮擦，磨损

abrasive [ə'bresiv] adj. 摩擦的；研磨的

absorb [əbsɔ:b] vt. . 吸收（液体、气体等）；吸收（热、光、能等）

access road 入口通道

accessory [æk'sesəri] n. 附件，配件，附属物

accommodate (sb.) for the night 留（某人）住一夜

accommodate [ə'kɔmədeit] vt. 给方便，帮助，供给… 住宿，容纳

accommodation [ə'kɔmə'deiʃən] n. n. 膳宿，预订铺位，适应性调节，调和，

accompany [ə'kʌmpəni] vt. 1. 陪伴，陪同；2. 伴随…同时发生

accountability [ə,kauntə'biliti] n. 1. 有责任，有义务，可说明性；2. 应作解释

acoustic [ə'ku:stik] adj. 1. 声音的，听觉的；2. 原声的；自然声的

acrylic [ə'krilik] n. 1. 丙烯酸塑料，丙烯酸纤维，丙烯酸树脂；2. 丙烯酸树脂漆，
丙烯酸树脂颜料；3. <画>丙烯画；4. 塑胶
adj. 1. <化>丙烯酸的；2. <化>丙烯酸衍生物的

adequate ['ædikwit] adj. 1. 充分的，足够的；2. 适当的，胜任的

adjacent [ə'dʒeisənt] adj. （地区、建筑、房间等）与…毗连的；邻近的

adjoin [ə'dʒɔin] vt. & vi. 邻近，毗连

adjoining property 邻产

adjust [ə'dʒʌst] vt. & vi. （改变…以）适应；调整；校正

aggregate ['ægrigit] n. 骨料，集料（可成混凝土或修路等用的）

agreement [ə'gri:mənt] n. 协定，协议，契约

airless spray 无气喷涂

alteration [,ɔ:ltə'reiʃən] n. 1. 改动，更改，改变；2. 变化；改变

alternate［ɔːlˈtəːnit］adj. 1. 轮流的，交替的；2. 间隔的；3. 代替的

                 vt. & vi. 其他读音：［ˈɔːltəːneit］（使）交替，（使）轮换

alternative［ɔːlˈtəːnətiv］adj. 两者（或两者以上）择一的，二择其一的，可从数个中

                 任择其一的；（两种选择中）非此即彼的

                 n. 可供选择的事物；可供选择的机会；替换物，替代品

aluminum［əˈluːmənəm］n.. ＜美＞铝

aluminum foil 铝箔

aluminum frame 铝框架

an air-to-water heat pump 气-水式热泵

an inspection group 验收小组

anchor［ˈæŋkə］n. 1. 锚；2. 给人安全感的物（或人）

             vt. & vi.（把…）系住，（使）固定

anchor shoring and frame 锚固件和框架

ancillary［ˈænsəˌleri］adj. 1. 辅助的；补充的；2. 附属的；附加的

annexed［ˈæneksid］adj. 附加的，附属的

announcement［əˈnaunsmənt］n. 通告，布告，通知；预告

APP：abbr. Application 应用；已被批准的；已被承认的；良好的；有效的

apparatus［ˌæpəˈreitəs］n.（pl. -es）（通常指有专门用途的成套）仪表，器械，仪器，

             装置，设备

appendices［əˈpendiˌsiːz］n. 附录，附属品

applicable［ˈæplikəbl］adj. 适当的；合适的

application method 涂刷方法

appreciate［əˈpriːʃieit］vt. 感激，感谢；为…表示感激（或感谢）

approval［əˈpruːvəl］n. 核定；批准；赞成；认可；通过，证明

approve［əˈpruːv］vt. 赞成，赞许；批准，审定，通过 验收

approve of … 赞成，赞同

arc［ɑːk］vi. 作弧形运动；2. 形成电弧

arc welding 电弧焊接头

architect［ˈɑːkitekt］n. 建筑师

architectural［ˌɑːkiˈtektʃərəl］adj. 建筑学的

architecture［ˈɑːkitektʃə］n. 1. 建筑学，建筑术；2. 建筑风格，建筑式样，建筑设计

arise［əˈraiz］vi. & link-v. 呈现；出现；发生

artificial stone 人造石材

as a consequence of…作为……结果

as-built drawings 竣工图纸

asphalt［ˈæsˌfɔːlt］n. 1. 沥青；柏油；2.（铺路等用的）沥青混合料

asphalt felt 沥青油毡

assemble［əˈsembl］vt. 装配，组合，组装

assembly［əˈsembli］n. 装配，组装

assess［əˈses］vt. 1. 估价，估计；2. 评定，核定，评估

assessment［əˈsesmənt］n. 评估，评定，评价

assurance［əˈʃuərəns］n. 保证，担保，确信

at least 至少

at present 目前，现在

At regular interval 定期

at the cost of 以…为代价

at the room temperature 常温下

attachment [ə'tætʃmənt] n. 1. 附着，附属；2. 附属物，附件

attenuation [ə,tenju'eiʃən] n. 变薄，弄细，变细；稀薄化，稀释，冲淡；减少，衰减

audit ['ɔ:dit] n. 审计，审查，查账

authorize ['ɔ:θəraiz] vt. 授权，批准；委托

Auto-Batching plant 自动搅拌机

axial ['æksiəl, -sjəl] adj. 轴的，轴向的，轴流式的

   axial force 轴向力

   axial load 轴压；轴向载重

   axial strain 轴向应变

   axial stress 轴向应力

   axial tensile strength 轴向抗拉强度

B

backfill ['bækfil] vt. 回填（挖掘的洞穴）

ballast ['bæləst] n. 道砟材料

bank guarantee 银行保证书

bar [bɑ:r] n. 长条，棒，栏杆（常用作护栏）

basement floors 地下室层

batching plant 混凝土搅拌厂

be capable of 有…的能力

be compatible with sth 与…不矛盾，与…一致，与…相容

be complied with 与…相符合

be composed of 由…组成

be different from 与…不同

be economical of one's time 节省时间

be liable for... 对…应负责任的

be liable to 有… 的倾向，易于…

be qualified to 具有…的资质

be responsible for 对…负责

be short of 缺乏…

be similar to 与…相似

beam [bi:m] n. 梁，横梁

bear [bɛə] vt. & vi. 承担，负担（过去式：bore；过去分词：borne/born）

bearing pressure 支撑压力

Bentonite ['bentə,nait] n. 美〉斑脱土（火山灰分解成的一种粘土）

Bill of Quantities 工程量清单

bind［baind］vt. & vi.（使）结合，（使）联合在一起

bitumen［bi'tu: mən］n. 沥青，柏油

bitumen mortar 沥青砂浆层

bitumen paste material 沥青粘合材料

block-work［'blɔkwə: k］n. 砌块墙；预制砌块体，大方块

BMU 氨基树脂皮革鞣剂

Board cast-in-place piles 钻孔灌注桩

boiler［'bɔilə］n. 锅炉

bolt［bəult］n. 螺栓

bond［bɔnd］n. 1. 联系，关系；2. 连接，接合，结合

bore［bɔ: ］vt. & vi. 挖，掘，钻，开凿（洞、井、隧道等）

borehole［'bɔ: həul］n. 钻孔

boring rig 钻车，钻探架，钻探设备

bottom formwork 底部模板

bound connection 绑扎连接

building thermal characteristic 建筑热特性

building［'bildiŋ］n. 建筑物，房屋

build-up［'bildʌp］adj. 组合的

built-up membrane roofing 组合薄膜屋面

C

calculation［ˌkælkjə'leiʃən］n. 计算，计算（的结果）；2. 推断；预测，估计

cantilever［'kæntili: və］n. 悬臂

cantilevered slab 悬臂板

carbon content 含碳量

carbon steel bar 碳素钢筋

carpenter［'kɑ: pintə］n. 木工，木匠

carpentry［'kɑ: pəntri］n. 木工手艺；木匠业

carry out . 实行，执行；实现，完成

cast［kæst］vt. & vi. 浇铸（过去式 & 过去分词：cast）

cast iron pipes 铸铁管道

cast-in-situ 现浇；就地浇筑；原地铸造

cast-iron or plastic drainage pipes 铸铁或塑料排水管

cater for 投合，迎合

cement greeting 抹灰层

cement grouting mortar 灌浆水泥砂浆

cement mortar 水泥砂浆层

cement paste 水泥浆

cementitious［ˌsimen'tiʃiəs］adj. 似水泥的，有黏性的

cementitious material 胶凝材料

central station air-conditioning system 中央空调控制系统

certificate of Guarantee 保单，保证书

certified [ˈsəːtifaid] adj. 1. 被鉴定的；2. 被证明的；有保证的

certify [ˈsəːtifai] vt. （尤指书面）证明，证实

changeover [ˈtʃeindʒˈəuvə] n. （生产方法、装备等的）改变，（方针的）转变

channel [ˈtʃænəl] n. 沟渠，海峡，通道

Chartered Civil engineer 注册土木工程师

Chartered Structural engineer 注册结构工程师

chemical additives 化学外加剂

chemical components 化学组成成分

chief engineer 主任工程师，总工程师，总技师

chief executive 总经理

chiller [ˈtʃilə] n. 冷冻机；冷却器；深冷器，冷却装置

chiller plant 制冷设备

China Labor Law 中国劳动法

Chinese Construction Ministry 中国建设部

chipping [ˈtʃipiŋ] n. 碎屑，破片

circulative [ˈsəːkjuleitiv] adj. 循环的，促进循环的，流通的

circulative system of hot drinking-water 热饮水循环系统

civil [ˈsivl] adj. 1. 公民的，平民的；民用的；2. 民事的，民法的

Civil Engineer 土木工程师

Civil Engineering 土木工程

civil works contractor 土建承包商

civilian [siˈviljən] n. 市民，平民，老百姓（与军人相对而言）e. g. civilian use 民用

civilian use 民用

cladding works 骨架外墙工程；面板工程

claim [kleim] n. （根据保险政策、赔偿法等）要求的付款；索款、索赔

clarify [ˈklærifai] vt. 澄清；说明，阐明

clear finish 清漆罩面

client [ˈklaiənt] n. 业主

coat [kəut] n. 涂料层；覆盖层 vt. 为某物涂抹，给…涂上一层；用…覆盖

coil pipe 盘管；盘曲管

cold bending degree 冷弯曲度

cold bending test 冷弯试验

cold rolled and twisted bar 冷轧扭钢筋

cold working 冷加工

cold-drawn low carbon steel wire 冷拔低碳钢丝

cold-stretched steel bar 冷拉钢筋

collar [ˈkɔlə] n. 圈；衣领，领子

column [ˈkɔləm] n. 柱，圆柱

come into use 开始被使用

commencement [kəˈmensmənt] n. 开始，开端

commendation [ˈkɔmənˌdeiʃən] n. 奖，奖品；表扬；嘉奖状

comment ［'kɔment］n. 1. 评论，意见，解释，批评 vt. & vi. 评论；谈论

common water-meter 普通水表

compact ［kəm'pækt］vt. & vi. 压紧，（使）坚实，把…紧压在一起（或压实）

compaction ［kəm'pækʃən］n. 压实；夯实

compatible ［kəm'pætəbl］adj. 可以并存的，相容的，协调的

complaint ［kəm'pleint］n. 1. 抱怨，诉苦，埋怨，不满；2. 投诉

completion ［kəm'pli: ʃ(ə)n］n. 完成，实现

compliance ［kəm'plaiəns］n. 服从，听从，顺从；依照

compliance with 遵守

comply ［kəm'plai］vi. 遵从，依从，服从

comply with 依从，服从，遵从

compound ［'kɔmpaund］n. 复合物，化合物，混合物，围场，围地（场内有建筑物）

compressible ［kəm'presəbl］adj. 可压缩的，可压榨的

compressible soil 软土

compressive ［kəm'presiv］adj. 有压缩力的；压缩的

compressive strength 抗压强度

concentric ［kən'sentrik］adj. 同一中心的，同轴的

concerning ［kən'sə: niŋ］prep.（表示论及）关于，有关，就…而论，涉及

concrete ［'kɔnkri: t］adj. 固结成的,混凝土制的,水泥的。; n. 1. 混凝土;2. 具体物;具体情况;具体概念;vt. 1. 铺以混凝土,以混凝土浇注;2. 使凝固,使固结;使融洽;vi. 1. 凝固,固结,变坚固;2. 使用混凝土

concrete block 混凝土块

concrete -in-situ 现浇混凝土

concrete mixer 水泥搅拌车，混凝土搅拌车

Concrete Mixing Procedure 混凝土搅拌工序

concrete mixture rate 混凝土配合比

concrete panel 混凝土面板

concrete pump 混凝土泵

concrete screed 混凝土找平层

concrete strength 混凝土的强度

concrete sub-floors 混凝土土地板

concrete surface 混凝土表面

condensation ［ˌkɔnden'seiʃən, -dən-］n. 1. 冷凝，凝聚，凝结；2. 冷凝液

Conditions of Contract 合同条件

confidential. ［ˌkɔnfi'denʃəl］adj. 秘密的，机密的

confine ［kən'fain］vt.. 限制；局限于

confined areas 密闭空间

confirm ［kən'fə: m］vt. 证实，证明；肯定，确认

conform to… 符合，遵照

conformity ［kən'fɔ: miti］n. 依照，遵从；符合，一致

consequence ［'kɔnsikwəns］n. 结果，后果

construct ［kən'strʌkt］vt. 1. 修建，建立，建筑，建造；2. 构成，组成

construction ［kənˈstrʌkʃən］n. 1. 建造，建设；建筑业；2. 建造物，建筑物

construction accidents and reporting 施工事故和报告

construction joint 施工缝

construction machine schedule 施工机械计划表

construction material 建材

Construction Method Statement（CMS）施工方案

construction project 建设项目

construction schedule. 施工进度计划表

construction site 工地

construction technology 施工工艺

construe ［kənˈstruː］vt. 1. 理解；领会；2. 翻译；作句法分析

consult ［kənˈsʌlt］vt. & vi. 商议，商量 vt. 请教，咨询

consultant ［kənˈsʌltənt］n. 顾问

contaminate ［kənˈtæmineit］vt. 把…弄脏，污染

contamination ［kənˌtæməˈneiʃən］n. 1. 污染；弄脏；毒害；2. 玷污；3. 致污物

content ［ˈkɔntent］n. 1. 所容纳之物，所含之物；2.（书等的）内容，目录；
　　　　　　　　3. 容量，含量；4.（书、讲话、节目等的）主题；主要内容

continuous ［kənˈtinjuəs］adj. 连续的，没有中断的

continuous foundation 连续基础

Contract Conditions 合同条款

Contract Price 合同价格

contractor ［ˈkɔnˌtræktə］n.（建筑、监造中的）承包人；承包单位，承包商

convenient ［kənˈviːnjənt］adj. 方便的，便利的，合适的

conventional ［kənˈvenʃənl］adj. 依照传统的，传统的；习惯的

co-ordination n. 合作

copolymer ［kəuˈpɔlimə］n. 共聚物

copper ［ˈkɔpə］n. 1. 铜；2. 铜币

cordon ［ˈkɔːdn］vt. 封锁；用警戒线围住

core wall 隔水墙；岩心墙

corner fittings 角件

corrosion ［kəˈrəuʒən］n. 1. 腐蚀；受腐蚀的部位；2. 腐蚀生成物如绣等；衰败

covenant ［ˈkʌvənənt］n.（有法律约束的）协议，盟约，公约；承诺，合同
　　　　　　　　covenant with 与… 立约

crack ［kræk］vt. & vi.（使…）开裂，破裂 n. 裂缝，缝隙

craftsman ［ˈkræftsmən］工匠

crane safety 起重机安全

crane ［krein］n. 吊车，起重机，升降架，升降设备

crescent ［ˈkresnt］n. 新月，月牙 adj. 新月形的，逐渐增加的

critical ［ˈkritikəl］adj. 决定性的，关键性的，危急的

crushing system 破碎机

cubic compressive strength 立方体抗压强度

culminate ［ˈkʌlmineit］vi. 达到极点，达到最高潮；【天】到子午线，到中天［最高度］；

告终，完结（in）

cure［kjuə］vt. 治愈，治好（人或动物）；养护（混凝土）

curing［'kjuəriŋ］n. 养护

curing（cure）concrete 养护混凝土

D

dam［dæm］大坝

damage［'dæmidʒ］vt. & vi. 1. 损害，毁坏，加害于 n. 1. 损失，损害，损毁

damp［dæmp］adj. 潮湿的，不完全干燥的

dampness［'dæmpnis］n. 湿气，潮湿

dead loads 静载荷

decoration［ˌdekə'reiʃən］n. 装饰，装潢

deem［di:m］vt. 认为，相信 vi. 想

defect［di'fekt］n. 缺点，过失，瑕疵，缺陷，毛病

Defects Liability Certificate 缺陷责任证书

Defects Liability Period 工程缺陷责任期

deflection［di'flekʃən］n.（尤指击中某物后）突然转向，偏斜，偏离

deform［di'fɔ:m］vt. 使变形

deformed steel bar 变形钢筋

degree centigrade 摄氏温度度数

deliver［di'livə］vt. & vi. 递送，交付

demanding［di'mændiŋ］adj. 1 工作要求高的；需要高技能（或耐性等）的；费力的；
　　　　　　　　　　　　　2. 要求极严的；苛求的；难满足的

demarcation［ˌdi:mɑ:'keiʃən］n.（＝demarkation）边界，分界，设界限

design drawing 设计图

design live loads 设计动荷载

design strength 设计强度

design［di'zain］v&n 设计

designation［ˌdezig'neiʃən］n. 1. 名字，称号；2. 选派，指定，委任

desirous［di'zaiərəs］adj. 渴望…的；想得到…的；希望…的

deviation［ˌdi:vi:'eiʃən］n. 1. 背离，偏离，违背；2. 偏差

diameter［dai'æmitə］n. 直径

differential［ˌdifə'renʃəl］adj. 不同的，有分别的；基于差别的；区别性的 n. 差异

differential settlement 不均匀沉降

dimension［di'menʃən］n. 尺寸，度量；2. 方面，部分

disaster［di'zɑ:stə］n. 灾难，灾祸

discharge［dis'tʃɑ:dʒ］n. 免除，解除，去除属于负担性质的东西
　　　　　　　　　　　vt. & vi. 放出；流出

disinfestations［ˌdisinˌfes'teiʃən］n. 灭（昆）虫法

dismantle［dis'mæntl］vt. 拆开，拆卸

dismantle a car 拆掉汽车上的零件

disposition [ˌdispəˈziʃən] n. 安排；布置；排列

dissipation [ˌdisiˈpeiʃn] n. （逐渐的）消失，消散

distinguish [disˈtiŋgwiʃ]（区别）

distortion [diˈstɔːʃən] n. 扭曲；变形；失真，歪曲

diurnal [daiˈanəl] adj. 1. 白天的；2. 每日的

dozer [ˈdəuzə] n 推土机

drain [drein] vt. & vi. 1. （使）流干，排空，放光；（使）逐渐流走 n. 排水沟，排水管

drainage [ˈdreinidʒ] n. 1. 排水，放水；2. 排水系统，下水道；3. 废水，污水，污物

drainage and irrigation work 排灌工程

draw off 1. 排出，抽出（某物），拉走（某人）；2. （使）撤离，（使）后退；3. 使转移掉

draw off point 出水处

drilling fluid 钻探泥浆

drinking water facilities 饮用水设施

drinking water 饮用水

dryer [ˈdraiə] n. 1. 干燥机，干燥器，烘缸；2. 干燥剂，催干剂，速干剂

Dubai Municipality 迪拜市政府

ductile [ˈdʌktəl] adj. 可延展的，有韧性的

ductile iron pipe 可伸展铁管

due [djuː] adj. 1. 应支付［给予］的；2. 应有的，应得到的；3. 到期的；4. 适当的，正当的，n. 1. 应有的权利；应得到的东西；2. 应缴款
adv. 1. 正向；正对着 prep. 1. 该由…所得；应向…支付；2. 应得；被欠

duplex apartment 复式套间

duplicate [ˈdjuːplikeit] vt. 使加倍；使成双 n. 复制品，抄件
adj. 完全一样的，复制的，成双的，成对的

durability [ˌdjurəˈbllItI] n. 耐久性；耐用性

duration [djuəˈreiʃən] n. 持续；持久；持续时间；延续性；期限［间］；存在时间

duty-free 免税的

E

easement [ˈiːzmənt] n. 在他人土地上的通行权，地役权

eave n. 屋檐

economical [iːkəˈnʌmikəl] adj. 节俭的，节省的，经济的；经济学的

efficiency [iˈfiæənsi] n. 1. 效率；效能；功效；2. 提高功效的方法

eggshell finish 粗装饰，蛋壳状装饰

elaborate [iˈlæbərət] -rated, -rating 详细阐述

electric water heater 电热水器

electrical cables 电缆线

electrical safety 电气安全

electrical works 电气工程

electroslag [iˈlektrəuslæg] adj. 电渣焊接法的；电渣冶炼法的

electroslag pressure welding 电渣压力焊接头

eliminate［i'limineit］vt. 1. 消除；2. 排除；3. 淘汰

emirate［e'miərit］n. 酋长国

employer［im'plɔiə］n. 业主

emulsion［i'mʌlʃən］n. 1. 乳胶，胶状液；乳剂；2. 乳胶漆（干后无光泽）；3. 感光乳剂

enclose［in'kləuz］vt. 把…装入信封，附入

encrustation［inˌkrʌs'teiʃən］n. 结壳，用覆盖物，镶嵌，硬壳

energy-efficient building 节能建筑

engineered Formwork Systems 工程模板系统

engineering［ˌendʒi'niəriŋ］n. 工程

environmental［inˌvaiərən'mentl］adj. 环境（产生）的；周［包］围的

environmental/sanitary engineering 环境或环卫工程

envisage［in'vizidʒ］vt. 想像，设想，展望；正视，面对，拟想，观察

epoxy［e'pɔksi］adj. 环氧的 n. 环氧树脂

equivalent［i'kwivələnt］adj. 1. 相等的，相当的；2.（数量、度量、价值、力量、意义、重要性等）均等的；同等重要的，等量的；等价的，等值的

erect［i'rekt］vt. 使竖立，使直立，树立，建立

erection［'irekʃən］n. 建立；建造；竖立；安装

erection contractor 安装承包商

erection drawing 安装图

excavation［ˌekskə'veiʃən］n. 发掘；挖掘；开凿

excavator［'ekskəveitə］n. 开凿者；发掘者；挖掘机；挖土机；挖沟机；电铲

execute［'eksikju:t］vt. 履行，执行，贯彻，实行，实施；完成

execution［ˌeksi'kju:ʃən］n. 实行，执行，实施

execution tracing file 隐蔽工程记录

expansion joints 伸缩缝

expedite［'ekspiˌdait］vt. 1. 加快进展；2. 迅速完成

expense［iks'pens］n. 1. 消耗，花费；2. 花费的钱，费用，开支，花费

expert panel 专家组

expiration［ˌekspi'reiʃθn］n. 满期，届期；截止，告终

exploitation［ˌeksplɔi'teiʃən］n. . 开发；开采；开拓

exposure［iks'pəuʒə］n. 1. 暴露，显露；2. 透露，泄露

extension rate 延伸率

external［eks'tə:nl］adj. 1. 外面的，外部的；2. 外观的，表面的
External Landscape Area 外部观景台

extinguish［iks'tiŋgwiʃ］vt. 使熄灭，扑灭

extruded polystyrene insulation 挤塑聚苯乙烯绝缘

F

fabricate［'fæbrikeit］vt. 1. 建造；2. 制造，装配，组装

facility［fə'siliti］n. 设备，设施

factory mark 厂标

fair-faced adj 无瑕面的

Fall arrest equipment 防止坠落设施

falsework ['fɔːlswɜːk] n. 脚手架，工作架，临时支架

falsification [ˌfɔlsəfə'keʃən] n. 弄虚作假；歪曲

fan coil system 风机盘管系统

felt [felt] n. 毛毡；毡制品；油毛毡

filler ['filə] n. 填充料；掺入物；填补空白之物；腻子，填料，填充剂

filter layer 过滤层，渗透层

final completion certificate 最后完工证明

Final Payment Certificate 最终支付证书

Final Statement 最终报表

fine and coarse aggregate 粗细骨料

finished slab 最终饰面

finishing coat 面漆，表面修饰层，饰面层

finishing coats 最后覆盖面

finishing spiral reinforcement 精轧螺旋钢筋

finishing works 修整工程

fire fighting equipment 消防设施

fire fighting works 消防

fire protection and prevention 防火

fire service system 消防系统

fire tap 消防栓

fire-extinguishing system 灭火系统；消防系统

first aid and emergency aid procedure 急救和紧急措施

first aid 急救

first layer 底层

flash butt welding 闪光对焊接头

flashing ['flæʃiŋ] n. 防水板，遮雨板

flood light 泛光灯

fluid 浆体、泥浆体

flush [flʌʃ] vt. & vi. 冲刷，清除

flush water supply system 冲洗用水系统

foam [fəum] n. 1. 泡沫；泡沫材料；2. 泡沫橡胶；海绵橡胶；3. 泡沫剂（用于洗涤、剃须、灭火等）

foam bitumen 泡沫沥青

foam concrete 泡沫混凝土

footbridge ['futbridʒ] 行人天桥

for Construction Use 施工专用

for the purpose of … 为了…的目标

force majeure 不可抗力

foreman ['fɔːmən] n. 领班，工头

forge [fɔːdʒ] vt. 锻造

form of Tender 标书格式

form removal 拆除模板

formwork ['fɔːmwəːk] n. 模板，样板；模板成形；模板工程

foundation [faun'deiʃən] n. 地基，地脚；底座

fragment ['frægmənt] n. 碎片；片段

fresh water supply 自来水供应

Front -of-house 前场

fulfill [ful'fil] vt. 1. 履行（诺言等）；完成（任务等）；实现；2. 执行（命令等）；服从

fume [fjuːm] n. 烟雾，气味

function ['fʌŋkʃən] n. 功能；作用；职责

fungi ['fʌŋgai] n. （fungus 的复数）真菌（如蘑菇和霉）；霉，霉菌

G

galvanize ['gælvəˌnaiz] vt. 用锌镀（铁）

galvanized steel pipe 镀锌钢管

gauge [geidʒ] n. 厚度，直径

general description 概述

generalize ['dʒenərəlaiz] vt. & vi. 概括，归纳，推论

generating equipment 发电机

geotextile filter layer 土工织物过滤层

geotextile n. 土工织物

glaze [gleiz] vt. 1. 装玻璃；2. 上釉于，上光，使光滑，使光亮

glue [gluː] vt. 用胶水将物体粘合，粘牢，粘贴

Government Medical Officer of Health. 政府医疗卫生官员

grader ['greidə] n. 平地［土，路］机，推土［筑路］机

gravel ['grævəl] n. 沙砾，砾石，石子

grease [griːs] n. 1. 动物油脂；2. 油膏，油脂

Ground Floor 底层，一楼（美 = first floor）

grout [graut] vt. 用薄泥浆填塞

guarantee [ˌgærən'tiː] n. 担保，担保品，抵押品

H

hand over 移交，交出

handhold ['hændˌhəuld] n. 扶手，把手点

handrail ['hændreil] n. 栏杆，扶手

harden ['haːdn] vt. & vi. （使）变硬；（使）坚固；（使）硬化

hardwood ['haːdˌwud] n. 硬（木）材；硬木树；阔叶树

harness ['haːnis] n. （防止坠落或摔倒的）背带，保护带

haul [hɔːl] vt. 运送

hazard ['hæzəd] n. 1. 危险；公害；2. 危害物 3. 危险的根源

Health and Safety Executive（HSE）document 职业健康与安全执行文件

heat（batch）number 炉号

herringbone［'heriŋbəun］n. 鲱鱼鱼骨，交叉缝式，人字形

hessian［'hesiən］n. 粗麻布；黄麻粗布

hessian cloth 粗麻布

high-tensile bar 高强度钢条

high-tensile steel bar 高强度钢筋

honeycomb［'hʌnikəum］n. 蜂窝，蜂巢

horizontal structure 水平结构；横向结构

hot rolled ribbed steel bar（HRB）热轧钢筋

hot rolled 热轧

hydrate［'hai‚dreit］vt. & vi.（使）水合

hydraulic engineering 水利工程

hydraulic jack【化】液压千斤顶；水力千斤顶

hydraulic 英［hai'drɔːlik］adj. 1. 液力的，液压的，水力学的；2. 水、油等（通过水管等）液压的，水力的，

hygiene［'haidʒiːn］n. 卫生学，保健学

hygienic［hai'dʒiːnik］adj. 1. 卫生的，保健的；2. 清洁的；3. 卫生学的

I

ignore［ig'nɔː］vt. 1. 不顾，不理，忽视；2. 对…不予理会

imply［im'plai］vt. 1. 暗示，暗指2.（思想、行为等）必然包含，使有必要 vt. & vi. 说明；表明

in a reasonable proportion 按适当比例配合

in accordance with 依据，与…一致

in advance 预先，事先

in conformity 与…相符合

in parallel with 与…平行

in respect of 关于

inadequate［in'ædikwit］adj. 不充足的，不适当的

inclusive［in'kluːsiv］adj. 包括…的，包括一切的

incorporate［in'kɔːpəreit］vt. 1. 包含，加上，吸收；2. 把…合并，使并入

indent［'indent］vt. 切割…使呈锯齿状

indented steel wire 刻痕钢丝

independent foundation 柱下独立基础

indestructible［‚indi'strʌktəbl］adj. 不能破坏的，不可毁灭的

indicative［in'dikətiv］adj. 表明；标示；显示；暗示

induction［in'dʌkʃən］n.（电或磁的）感应

inform［in'fɔːm］vt. 告诉，通知

ingrain［in'grein］vt. 使根深蒂固

ingredient［in'griːdjənt］n. 1.（混合物的）组成部分；2.（构成）要素，因素 adj. 1. 构成

组成部分的

initial［i'niʃəl］adj. 1. 最初的；开始的；第一的；2. 原始的；初期的

insert［in'sə：t］vt. 插入，嵌入

in-situ 就地，在现场

inspection［in'spekʃən］n. 1. 检查，视察；2. 检验；审视；3. 检阅

instability［ˌinstə'biliti：］n. 不稳定，不稳固

install［in'stɔ：l］vt. 1. 安装；2. 安顿，安置

installation［ˌinstə'leiʃən］n. 安装，设置，装置

insulating concrete forms（ICF）绝缘混凝土模板（ICF）

insulation［insə'leiʃən］n. 1. 隔离，隔绝；绝缘；隔音；2. 绝缘、隔热或隔音等的材料

insulation layer 绝缘层

insulation standard 绝热标准

integrity［in'tegriti］n. 完整，完全，完善

intended use 预期用途

intent［in'tent］n. 意图，意向，目的

interface［'intəfeis］n. 接口，界面，分界面

intermediate rail 中间栏杆

internal［in'tə：nəl］adj. 内部的，里面的

Internal high build epoxy finish 内部高层建筑环氧效果

inverted［in'və：tid］adj. 反向的，倒转的

ironmongery［'aiənˌmʌŋɡəri］n. 铁器类，铁器店，五金

issue［'isju：］vt. 1. 发表，发布；2. 分配，发给

J

jobsite safety policy 现场安全策略

joinery［'dʒɔinəri］n. 细木工作；细木工

joint［dʒɔint］n. 接头，接合处，接点

jointly［'dʒɔintli］adv. 共同地，联合地

joints of formwork 模板连接处

junction［'dʒʌnkʃən］n. 联结点，会合点，枢纽

K

key dates of completion 完工关键日期

L

labor chart 劳务配备表

laitance［'leitəns］n. 1. 水泥乳，浮浆皮（混凝土表面的乳白色浆）

lap［læp］vt. 使形成部分重叠；部分叠盖 vi. 折叠 3. 部分重叠；

lap joint 搭接接头

large prefabricated formwork 大型预制模板

lateral ['lætərəl] adj. 侧面的，从旁边的，至侧面的

lay out v. 摆开，展示，布置，安排，投资

leakage ['li:kidʒ] n. 1. 漏，漏出；2. 漏出物，渗漏物

Letter of Agreement 协议书

letter of intent 意向书

level the ground 平整场地

levy ['levi] vt. 征收（捐税，罚款等）；

liability [ˌlaiə'biliti] n. 责任，义务

license ['laisəns] vt. 1. 批准，许可，颁发执照 n. 执照

lifespan ['laifˌspæn] n. 1.（人或动物的）寿命，预期生命期限；2. 存在期；使用期；有效期

light concrete slabs 轻混凝土板

lighting system 照明系统

limestone ['laimˌstəun] n. 石灰岩

line management 直接管理

low heating conductive material 低导热性材料

lubricant ['lu:brikənt] n. 润滑剂〔油〕 adj. 润滑的

M

main residential drop-off 主住宅楼落客点

maintain [menˈtein] vt. 保持；维持；供养；扶养；维修，保养（机器、道路等）；坚持，维护；主张，拥护

maintenance ['meintinəns] n. 维持；维护；保养；维修

maintenance period 保修期

majeure [məˈdʒer] n. 压倒的力量，不可抗力

man camp 生活营地

manufacturer ['mænjuˌfæktʃərə] n. 1. 制造商，制造厂，制造者，生产商

manufacturer's batch numbers 生产批号

mason ['mesən] n. 石匠，砖瓦匠

mechanical connection 机械连接

mechanical floor 设备层

mechanical property 机械性能

mechanics [miˈkæniks] n. 力学；机械学

membrane [miˈmentəu] n. 薄膜

meters of cold and hot water 冷、热水表

Method Description 施工方案

micron ['maikrɔn] n. 微米（百万分之一米）

mid coat 中间层油漆

mid-summer 仲夏

military ['militəri] adj. 军人的；军用的；军事的

military engineering 军事工程

mineral ['minərəl] n. 矿物；矿石；

mineral admixtures 矿物掺合料

minimal ['miniməl] adj. 极少的，极小的

minimize ['minimaiz] vt.. 把…减至最低数量［程度］

minor defects 小缺陷

mission ['miʃən] n. 使命，任务，天职

mixing concrete 搅拌混凝土

Mobile Scaffold Tower 可移动的脚手架

mobilize ['məubilaiz] vt. & vi. 动员起来，调动

modification [ˌmɔdifi'keiʃən] n. 变更，修正；e. g. data modification 数据修改

modified bituminous membrane polymer reinforced 聚合物改性沥青薄膜

modified bituminous membrane 改性沥青薄膜

modified reinforced bituminous membrane 改性沥青薄膜

modify ['mɔdifai] vt. & vi. 修改，更改 vt. 1. 修饰；2. 调整；稍作修改；使更适合

Modular steel frame formwork for a foundation 模块化的基础钢模框架

moisture ['mɔistʃə] n. 水分，水气，湿气

moisture content 湿度

moisture-resistant 防潮

monthly payment application 月度工程进度款申请书

mortar ['mɔ:tə] n. 砂浆，灰浆

mould [məuld] n. 铸模，模型

mount [maunt] vt. 1. 准备；安排；组织开展；2. 安置

multiply ['mʌltiplai] vi&vi 乘

multi-storey buildings 高层建筑

multi-storey residential building 高层居民楼

Multi-story residential building 高层住宅楼

municipality [mjuˌnisi'pæliti] n. 市政当局，自治市，自治区，自治市或区的政府当局

N

National Standard 国家标准

negligence ['neglidʒəns] n. 疏忽，玩忽，失职，失误，过失

negotiation [niˈgəuʃi:ˌeiʃən] n. 协商，谈判，磋商

negotiation stage 谈判阶段

nominated ['nɔmineitid] adj. 被提名的；被任命的

non-shrink mortar 无收缩砂浆

not later than …不得迟于…

O

obligation [ˌɔbli'geiʃən] n. 义务；责任；职责

obtain [əb'tein] vt. 获得，得到

occupation [ɒkju'peiʃən] n. 工作；职业

occupational exposure standards 职业暴露安全标准

oil separator 油水分离器

omission [əu'miʃən] n. 1. 省略，删节；遗漏；2. 略去或漏掉的事（或人）

on a turn-key basis 以交钥匙方式

on behalf of 代表…

on site 现场

operational strategy 运行策略

order ['ɔːdə] n. 1. 次序；顺序；2. 订购，订货；订单

ordinary low alloy steel bar 普通低合金钢筋

organization chart 组织机构表

orientation [ˌɔːrien'teiʃən] n. 方向

originally [ə'ridʒənəli] ad. 起初，原来

outdoor terrace seating. 露天看台

outdoor terrace 室外平台

outstanding [ˌaut'stændiŋ] adj. 未解决的，未完成的

outstanding work 扫尾工作

overbridge ['əuvəbridʒ] n. （跨越铁路或公路的）天桥；旱桥

P

pad [pæd] vt. 给…装衬垫，加垫子；n. 垫，护垫

painting works 油漆

pane [pein] n. 窗玻璃，（一片）窗玻璃

panel ['pænl] n. 1. 专门小组；2. 面；板；3. 控制板，仪表盘 4. （门、墙等上面的）嵌板，镶板，方格板块

parallel ['pærəlel] adj. 1. （指至少两条线）平行的；2. 类似的；相对应的；3. 并行的

particle ['pɑːtikl] n. 微粒，颗粒，〈物〉粒子

particleboard ['pɑːtikəlˌbɔːd, -ˌbəurd] n. 芯板材；碎木板，刨花板

payment sheet 付款申请书

pedestrian [pe'destriən] adj. 步行的；行人的，人行的；n. 行人，步行者，人行道

pedestrian ramp 人行道斜坡（坡道）

penalize ['piːnəlaiz] vt. 对…予以惩罚

penetrate [penitreit] vt. & vi. 渗透

penetration [ˌpeni'treiʃən] n. 1. 穿透；穿透能力；穿透深度；2. 渗透；侵入

penetration of the piles 桩的贯入

performance appraisals 奖励

Performance Specification 性能说明书，设计任务说明书

perimeter [pə'rimitə] n. 1. 周边；周围；边缘；2. 周长

periodically [piəri'ɔdikli] adv. 1. 周期性地；2. 定期地

permanent ['pəːmənənt] adj. 1. 永久（性）的，固定的；2. 稳定的；恒定的

permanent assets【会计】固定资产

Permanent casing 永久性套筒

permanent Insulated Formwork. 永久绝缘模板

permanent structures 永久性建筑结构

permanent works 永久性工程

permanently［′pəmənəntli］adv. 永久地；长期不变地

permit［pə(:)′mit］vt.（permitted；permitting）允许；许可；准许；容许

Permit-to-work 工作许可证

personal safety equipment 个人安全设备

pertinent［′pə:tinənt］adj. 有关的；中肯的；恰当的；相宜的

physical character 物理特性

pile［pail］n. 桩；桩柱

pile length 桩长

piling machine 打桩机

pipe［paip］n. 管子，管道 vt. 1. 以管输送；2. 传送，传输

pipe sleeve 管套

piping works 管道工程

place an order 订货

placement［′pleismənt］n. 1. 安置；2.（对物件的）安置，放置

plain concrete without reinforcement 不加钢筋的素混凝

plain steel bar 光面钢筋

plant room 机械设备间，工作间

plaster［′plɑ:stə］vt. 抹灰；用灰泥抹（墙等）n. 灰泥

plasterboard［′plɑ:stəbɔ:d］n. 石膏板

plastic covered copper tube 带塑料外壳的铜管

plastic deformation 塑性变形

plasticity［plæ′stisəti］n. 可塑性

plasticity［plæ′stisəti］n. 1. 粘性；成形性，柔软性；2. 可塑性 塑性

plasticize［′plæstisaiz］v. 使成可塑体

Plate compactors 压路机

Plenum floor 夹层

plinth［plinθ］n. <建>（柱的）底座；基座

ply［plaI］n.（夹板的）层片

plywood formwork 胶合模板

podium［′pəudi:əm］n. 平台

　　　　　　　　　n.（pl. -dia［-die］)【建】作基础用的矮墙

polymer［′pɔləmə］n. 1. <化>聚合物（体）adj. 聚合的

polythene［′pɔlə‚θi:n］n. <化>聚乙烯；聚乙烯化合物

polythene sheet 塑料薄膜

polyurethane［‚pɔli′juəriθein］n. 聚氨酯；聚氨基甲酸酯

Portland cement 波特兰水泥

possess［pə′zes］vt. 1. 具有；2. 占据；3. 有，拥有

possession [pəˈzeʃən] n. 拥有；占有；[pl.] 所有物；财产，财富；所有权

pouring concrete 混凝土的浇筑

pouring operation 浇筑作业

power supply system 配电系统

precast [ˌpriːˈkɑːst] adj. 预浇铸的，预制的

precast concrete beam 预制混凝土梁

precast concrete panel roof 预制混凝土板屋顶

precast concrete pile 预制混凝土桩

precast piles 预制桩

precast reinforced concrete panel roof 预制钢筋混凝土板屋顶

precaution [priˈkɔːʃən] n. 预防措施；预防；防备

precaution [priˈkɔːʃən] n. 预防，警惕，谨慎，小心；预防措施［方法］

prefabricaiton n. 预先制造【化】预加工

prefabricate [priːˈfæbriˌkeit] vt. 预制 n. 预制

prefabricated [ˈpriːˈfæbrikeitid] adj. （建筑物、船等）预制构件的

prefabricated fiber-reinforced plastic forms 预制强化纤维塑料模板

premise [ˈpremis] n. 1. 前提，假定；2. ［复数］房屋；房屋连地基；生产经营场所

pressure welding 气压焊接头

prestress [ˈpriːˈstres] vt. 给…预加应力

prestressing wire 预应力钢丝

prime [praim] vt. 在（金属、木材等上）打底漆

prior [praiə] adj. 1. 优先的；在前的；较早的；2. 占先的；较重要的；3. 在前面的

prior to . 在…之前

priority [praiˈɔriti] n. 1. 优先权，重点；2. 优先考虑的事；3. （车辆的）优先通行权

procure [prəuˈkjuə] vt. . （努力）取得，（设法）获得，得到

project manager n. 项目管理人［经理］

promotion [prəˈməuʃən] n. 1. 提升，晋级；2. 宣传；推销；3. 推广；促进

property [ˈprɔpəti] n. 1. 财产；资产；所有物；2. 房地产，不动产

protrusion [prəˈtruːʒən] n. 伸出，突出

purlin [ˈpəːlin] n. 檩桁条

Q

QA/QC inspection form 质保/ 质控检测文件

Quality and Safety Programs 质量和安全措施

Quality assurance 质保手册

Quality Assurance and Quality Control system 质量保证与质量控制系统

Quality Assurance Program 质保文件

quality assurance system. 质量保证体系

Quality Certificates 产品合格证

quality control station 质检站

quality defect 质量缺陷

quarry［ˈkwɔːri］n.（采）石场；露天矿场

quarry tiles 瓷砖铺砌

quench［kwentʃ］vt. 1.（用水）扑灭（火焰等）；熄灭；2. 将（热物体）放入水中急速冷却

quenching and tempering heat treatment 淬火和回火的调质热处理

quotation［kwəuˈteiʃən］n.【商】行情，时价；报价，估价；行市表；估价单，报价单

R

raft［rɑːft］n. 木筏

raft foundation 筏式基础；筏式地基；板式基础

rainwater and waste water drainage system 雨水及废水排放

rainwater drainage 雨水排放

raw material 原材料

ready-mixed concrete 商品混凝土/预拌混凝土

reasonable［ˈriːznəbl］adj. 合情合理的，有道理的

reassemble［ˌriːəˈsembəl］vt. 重新组装

rebar bending schedule 下料表

rebar cross-section 钢截面面积

rebar testing 钢筋试验

rebar［riˈbɑː］n. 钢筋；螺纹钢筋

rectify［ˈrektifai］vt. 1. 改正，矫正

refer to 提及；涉及，谈到，提到；关系到

refractoriness［riˈfræktəriːnis］n. 耐火性；耐热度；耐熔度；耐熔性

regulation［ˌregjuˈleiʃən］n. 1. 管理，控制；2. 规章；规则；章程；规章制度；法规

regulation［ˌregjuˈleiʃən］n. 规章；规则；章程；规章制度；法规

reinforce［ˌriːiinˈfɔːs］vt. 加固；使更结实

Reinforced and prestressed concrete 钢筋混凝土

reinforced concrete 钢筋混凝土

reinforcement［ˌriːinˈfɔːsmənt］n. 巩固，加强，强化

reinforcement works 钢筋工程

reinforcing steel 钢筋

reinstate［ˌriːinˈsteit］vt. 1. 使恢复原职；使恢复原有权利；2. 把…放回原处

rejection［riˈdʒekʃən］n. 拒绝；退回

relevant［ˈreləvənt］adj. 有关的

remained heat treatment ribbed steel bar（RRB）余热处理钢筋

remained heat treatment 余热处理

remedy［ˈremidi］n. 处理方法；改进措施；补偿 vt. 改正；纠正；改进

remind［riˈmaind］vt. 1. 使想起；2. 提醒

removal［riˈmuːvəl］n. 移［调］动，迁移

render［ˈrendə］vt.. 粉刷；给（墙壁）抹灰 n.（抹在墙上的）底灰；底层

replacement［riˈpleismənt］n. 代替，替换，更换

represent [ˌrepriˈzent] 1. 表现，描绘；2. 代表，象征，表示

representative [ˌrepriˈzentətiv] n. 1. 代表；2. 代理人

resident [ˈrezidənt] adj. 定居的；常驻的；（在某地）居住的

residential [ˌreziˈdenʃəl] adj. 1. 住宅的，适于作住宅的；2. 与居住有关的

residential building 住宅楼

residue [ˈreziˌdu] n. 剩余，余渣

respectively [risˈpektivli] adv. 1. 分别；各自；顺序为；依次为

respirator [ˈrespəˌreitə] n. 1. 口罩，防毒面具；2.（人工）呼吸机

respiratory [ˈrespərəˌtɔːri:] adj. 呼吸的，呼吸用的

respiratory protection 呼吸防护

responsibility [riˌspɔnsəˈbiliti] n. 1. 责任；2. 责任感，可信赖性；3. 职责

resume [riˈzju: m] vt. & vi. 重新开始；重新获得；（中断后）又继续

retarder [riˈtɑː də] n. 阻滞剂，缓凝剂，减速器

retention [riˈtenʃən] n. 保留，保持

retention period 保修期

re-usable plastic formwork 可重复使用的塑料模板

revise [riˈvaiz] vt. 1. 修订，修改；2. 改变，修改（意见或计划）

rib [rib] n. 1. 肋骨，骨架;2.（船或屋顶等的)肋拱,肋材 ;3.（织物的)凸条花纹,罗纹

rinse [rins] vt. 1. 漂洗，冲洗；2. 用清水漂洗掉（肥皂泡等）；3.（用清水）冲掉，洗刷

rock quarry 采石厂

roll [rəul] vt. & vi. 1.（使）打滚，（使）转动，滚动；2. 卷，把…卷成筒状 vt. 碾平

rotation [rəuˈteiʃən] n. 旋转；转动

roughen [ˈrʌfən] vt. & vi.（使）变得粗糙；（使）变得不平

round edge tiles 圆边瓷砖

rust [rʌst] n. 铁锈 vt. & vi.（使）生锈

S

Safety Officer 安全主任

safety organization 安全工作人事结构

safety regulations 安全制度

salary adjustments 薪酬调整

saline [ˈseiˌli: n] adj. 1. 含盐的，咸的；2. 盐的 n. 1. 盐湖，盐泉；2. 盐溶液

sample [ˈsɑː mpl] n. 样品，标本，样本；vt. 抽样调查；抽样检验；取样；采样

sanitary [ˈsæniˌteri:] adj. 1. 清洁的，卫生的，保健的；2. 环境卫生的；公共卫生的

sanitary facilities 卫生设施

sanitary engineering [ˌendʒiˈniəriŋ] 卫生工程

saturate [ˈsætʃəreit] vt. 1. 浸湿，浸透；2. 使…大量吸收或充满某物

sawdust [ˈsɔː ˌdʌst] n. 锯末

scaffold [ˈskæfəld] n.【建】脚手架，鹰架；交手（临时搭的）展览台；看台

scaffolder 脚手架工

schedule [ˈʃedju: əl] vt. 排定，安排 n. 时间表，日程安排表

Scope of Works 工程范围

screw threaded steel pipe joint 螺纹套管钢筋接头

screw thread 螺纹

seal［si:l］vt. 1. 盖章于；盖戳；在…上加盖检验封印；2. 密封

sealant［'si:lənt］n. 密封剂

sealed glass 封闭（密封）玻璃

secondary components 次要成分

section completion certificates 部分完工证明

senior executive 高级管理人员

sensitive［'sensitiv］adj. 易受影响的；敏感的

separately［'sepəritli］adv. 分离地；个别地，分别地，单独地

setting out 放样；定线；划定地界

settlement［'setlmənt］n. 沉降

sewer［'su:ə］n. 污水管，下水道

sewer systems 污水处理系统

sewer water drainage 下水道排放

sheer［ʃiə］adj. 1. 陡峭的；垂直的；2. 极薄的，轻的，透明的

sheer tests 剪力试验

shock absorber 减震器

shoring［'ʃɔ:riŋ］n. 利用支柱的支撑，支柱

shortage［'ʃɔ:tidʒ］n. 不足；缺少；缺少量；不足额

signage［'sainidʒ］n. 指示牌；标志牌

signature［'signitʃə］n. 1. 签名，签字；2. 署名；签署

simultaneous［ˌsiməl'teinjəs］adj. 1. 同时存在的，同时发生（或进行）的；同步的

site engineer 现场工程师

site preparation 现场准备

skirting［'skə:tiŋ］n. 裙料，壁脚板

slab［slæb］n. 板

slab floor 楼板

slacken［'slækən］vt. & vi. 1.（使）松弛；2.（使某物）放慢，迟缓；3. 松懈下来；变迟缓

sleeve［sli:v］n. 1. 衣服袖子；2. 套管，套筒

sleeve cold-pressure joint 套筒冷压接头

slip formwork 滑模

slump test 坍落度试验

soak［səuk］vt. & vi. 1. 浸，泡；2. 浸透，湿透

softening point 软化点

soil consolidation. 土壤固结

soil samples 土样

soil-sampling equipment 取土样的设备

solar energy transmission 太阳能穿透率

solar heat gain 太阳能获取；太阳辐射热获得

solar radiation 太阳辐射

span ［spæn］ n. 跨度

specialize in 专攻于

specific ［spiˈsifik］ adj. 1. 明确的，确切的，详尽的；2. 具体的，特有的，特定的

specificaiton ［ˌspesifiˈkeiʃən］ n. 详细说明，分类［pl.］清单，明细单；计划书，具体要求；［pl.］规范，规格，技术说明

specify ［ˈspesifai］ vt. 1. 指定；2. 具体说明；把…写入说明书；详细列举

specimen ［ˈspesimən］ n. 1. 范例，典范，实例；2. 样品，标本

spiral ［ˈspaiərəl］ adj. 螺旋形的

sponsor ［ˈspɔnsə］ vt. . 赞助，资助 n. 赞助者，赞助商，资助者

sporadic ［spəˈrædik］ adj. 不定时发生的；偶发性的；零星的。

spot check 抽查

spray ［sprei］ vt. & vi. 喷；喷洒；向…喷洒

squash courts 壁球室

Stainless steel wire mesh 不锈钢金属网

stamp ［stæmp］ vt. 1. 在…上盖章；盖上…的戳记；2. 在…上压印图案（或标记等）

standard yield strength 标准屈服强度

Statement at Completion 竣工报表

static tensile test 静力拉伸试验

stay-in-place structural formwork systems 永久性结构模板系统

steel bars for concrete reinforcement 钢筋钢

steel grade 钢号

steel heat treatment 热处理钢筋

steel manufacturer 钢材生产厂家

steel mill 钢铁厂

steel reinforcement bar 钢筋

stoppers ［ˈstɔpə］ n. . 阻塞物

storage ［ˈstɔːridʒ］ n. 1. 贮存，贮藏；2. 储藏处，仓库

storage tank 贮存罐

storey ［ˈstɔːri］ n. 楼层

straighten ［ˈstreitn］ vt. & vi. 1.（使）变直；把…弄直；2.（使）变直

strand ［strænd］ n.（线、绳、金属线、毛发等的）股，缕

stranded steel wire 钢铰线

stratum ［ˈstretəm］ n. 1. 岩层；2. 地层

strength variation test 应力变化测试

strength ［ˈstreŋθ］ n. 力量，强度

stress-strain curve 应力—应变曲线

stretch ［stretʃ］ vt. & vi. 伸展；拉紧；2. 延伸

stretching equipment for prestressing reinforcement 预应力钢筋张拉设备

structural engineering 结构工程

structural glass 玻璃砖，建筑玻璃

structural steel 结构钢

subcontractor ［ˌsʌbkənˈtræktə］ n. 转包商，次承包者，分包商

subdivision［ˈsʌbdiˌviʒən］n. 细［再］分；细分分成的部分

sublet［ˈsʌbˈlet］vt. 转租；转包给；分包给

submit［səbˈmit］vt. 提交，呈递

substantial［səbˈstænʃəl］adj. 实质的，基本的，大体上的

substantially［səbˈstænʃəli］adv. 本质上，实质上；大体上

substitution［ˌsʌbstiˈtuːʃən］n. 1. 代替；代用；替换；2. 代替物；代用品；替换物

substrate［ˈsʌbˌstreit］n.（供绘画、印刷等的）底面，基底；基片

substructure［sʌbˈstrʌktʃə］n. 底部构造；基础

sufficient［səˈfiʃənt］adj. 1. 足够的；充足的；2.【逻辑学】（条件）必然的

sufficiently［səˈfiʃəntli］adv. 足够地，充分地

superstructure［ˈsjuːpəˌstrʌktʃə］n.【建】上部结构；上层构造，

supervision［ˌsjuːpəˈviʒən］n. 监督，管理

supplier［səˈplaiə］n. 供应者；供货商；供货方

supply［səˈplai］n. 供给，供应，补给

surface preparation 表面处理

surface reinstating 恢复地表面

surface temperature differentials 表面温度差异

suspension［səˈspenʃən］n. 悬浮液

synthetic fiber lanyard 合成纤维的系索

system of cold drinking-water 冷饮水系统

system of collection and disposition of domestic drains 住户排水的收集与处置系统

system of collection and disposition of rain and thaw water
雨水雪水的收集与处置系统

T

take possession of 占有，拥有

taking-over certificate 移交证书

tanker［ˈtæŋkə］n. 运送大量液体或气体的轮船［卡车］；油轮；罐车；油槽车

task risk assessment 工作风险分析

teak［tiːk］n. 柚木

teak ply 柚木层板

Technical Specifications. 技术规范

technician［tekˈniʃən］n. 技术人员

temper［ˈtempə］vt. 1. 使缓和；使温和 ；2. 使（金属）回火

temporary［ˈtempərəri］adj. 暂时的，临时的；一时的

Temporary casing 临时护筒

tenant amenities 租赁设施，租赁场所

tender［ˈtendə］n. 投标，清偿，偿付

tender document 标书

tender opening 开标

Tender Use 投标专用

tenderer ['tendərə] n. 投标人

tensile ['tensəl] adj. 1. 拉力的，张力的，抗张的；2. 可伸展的；可拉长的；可延展的

tensile strength 抗拉强度

tension test 拉伸试验

test blocks of concrete 混凝土试块

test report 试验报告

thaw [θɔ:] vi. 1. （冰、雪及冷冻食物）溶化，溶解 n. 融化，解冻

the award of a contract 授标

The Bill of Quantities 工程量清单

The drawing 图纸

the initial setting time of concrete 混凝土的初凝时间

the specification 规格；规范

the total settlement 总沉陷量

the transportation of concrete 混凝土的运输

the triaxial tests 三轴试验

therein [ðeər'in] adv. 1. 在那里，在那方面，在那时，在其中；2. （用于强调某事是由某种情况引起的）那就是，此即，缘此

thermal ['θə:məl] adj. 热的，热量的，由热造成的

thermal movements （构件因温度变化而膨胀或收缩）热移动

thickness ['θiknis] n. 厚；厚度

tile [tail] n. . 瓦片，瓷砖 vt. 用瓦片、瓷砖等覆盖

timber ['timbə] n. （用于建筑或制作物品的）树木，林木；用材林

Timber formwork for a concrete 灌注混凝土的木制（质）模板

time-consuming 费时

toe board 踢脚板

toilet facilities 盥洗设施

tolerance ['tɔlərəns] n. 1. 宽容，容忍，忍受；2. 偏差，公差，容限

total light transmission 光透过率

toughness ['tʌfnis] n. 韧性，坚韧，刚性，健壮性

tower roof 塔顶

toxic substances 有毒物质

traceability label 可追溯性标签

track [træk] n. 轨道

traditional timber formwork. 传统的木制板模

transit ['trænsit] n. 搬运；载运；运输

transition [træn'ziʃən] n. 过渡；转变；变迁；变革

transition season 过渡季节

transmit [trænz'mit] vt. 传播；播送；传递

transmittance [træns'mitəns] n. 播送，发射，传动，传送，传输，转播

transport [træns'pɔ:t] vt. （用交通工具）运输，运送，输送

trench [trentʃ] n. 深沟，地沟

triaxial [trai'æksiəl] adj. 三轴的，三维的，空间的

turmoil［ˈtə:mɔil］n. 混乱

twist［twist］vt. & vi. 扭，搓，缠绕

U

unavoidable［ˌʌnəˈvɔidəbəl］adj. 不可避免的

undercoat 内层油漆

underground works 地下工程

uniform［ˈju:nifɔ:m］adj. 全都相同的，一律的，一致的，统一的

unique［ju:ˈni:k］adj. 唯一的；无与伦比的；独特的

unplasticized P. V. C. pipe 硬 P. V. C 管

unpredictable［ˌnpriˈdiktəbəl］adj. 1. 无法预言的，不可预测的

unqualified mix 不合格的拌和料

upward-arched 起拱

urban planning and design 城市规划

V

Vacuum Prestressing 真空预压

valid［ˈvælid］adj. 1. 有效的；2. 有法律效力的；3. 系统认可的；4. 奏效的，生效的

vehicular［viˈhikjulə（r）］adj. 车辆的

vehicular access 车路；车辆通道

ventilation［ˌventlˈeiʃən］n. 通风，通风设备

verify［ˈverifai］vt. 证实，核实；2. 查对；核准

vermin［ˈvɜ:mIn］n. 害虫

vertical［ˈvə:tikəl］adj. 垂直的，竖的

vertical structure 纵向结构；垂直结构

vertical tolerance 垂直度误差

vibratory roller compactors 振动压路机

void［vɔid］n. 空隙，孔隙

volume［ˈvɔlju:m］n. 1. 卷，册，书卷；2. 体积；容积，容量

W

water / cement ratio 水灰比

water［ˈwɔ:tə］vt. 浇水

water content 含水量

water curing of concrete 混凝土水养护

water leakage 漏水

water purification 水的净化

water softening deironing filter 水软化除铁过滤器

water supply 供水

water tanker 运水车

Water Tank 水箱，水槽

water-improvement equipment 水净化设备

water-metering unit 水表装置

waterproof ['wɔːtəpruːf] adj. 不透水的，防水的 vt. 使防水；使不透水 n. 防水衣物

weight [weit] n. 重量

weld [weld] vt. & vi. 焊接；熔接；锻接

welded connection 焊接连接

welding performance 焊接性能

wet preparation 湿选法

win the tender 中标

wind loads 风荷载

with regard to 关于

with respect to 关于，谈到

withdraw [wið'drɔː] vt. (-drew [['druː]]；withdrawn [[-'drɔːn]]）取回；收回；领回；撤回；缩回；移开；拉开；取消；撤消；撤退

witness ['witnis] n. 1. 目击者；证人 vt. 亲眼看见，目击；2. 作证，证明

work shift 工作班

working procedure 施工程序

working section 施工队

workmanship ['wɜːkmən,ʃip] n. . 技艺，工艺，手艺

works statistics report 工程统计报表

workshop ['wɔːkʃɔp] n. 工场，车间，工厂

Y

yield [jiːld] vt. （受压）活动，变形，弯曲，折断

yield strength 屈服强度

yielded point 屈服点